There is no question that physical infrastructure impacts on the quality of human life. Every new road or bridge that connects a remote barangay to the town proper opens new opportunities for a hundreds to sell and buy goods and interact with other communities; every schoolroom built brings literacy and a chance to improve the lives of thousands of Filipino children; every health center put up or potable water source developed makes numerous lives healthier; and every seaport or airport constructed or improved connects communities around it to the rest of the world. Public investment in physical infrastructure is an imperative.

"Night Owl" documents the making of the physical infrastructure projects that the Duterte administration completed in six years under its Build, Build, Build program. But beyond this, it expounds on the vision of an administration determined to take bold steps to close the country's infrastructure gap and the key persons who pushed hard to realize this ambitious program. This book reveals the strong political will of President Rodrigo Duterte and his people to uplift the quality of our countrymen's lives. "Night Owl" is as much an undisputable record of what President Duterte and his team have achieved to upgrade our country's physical infrastructure as it is a well-documented tribute to the sacrifices of the men and women of this administration — both the early birds and the night owls — who toiled day and night to deliver on their commitments.

For the next set of technocrats who want to know what must come with political will to accomplish such a tremendous undertaking; the doubters who won't believe unless presented with figures and photos; the armchair travelers who wish to experience our provinces vicariously; and the families and friends of the people who took part in constructing these school buildings, evacuation and health centers, roads, bridges, flood control projects, seaports, and airports, this book is a good read.

— GLORIA MACAPAGAL-ARROYO
14th President of the Philippines

Build, Build, Build is one of the best legacies of the administration of President Rodrigo Duterte that carve a profound niche in our nation's history.

The roads, bridges, school buildings, health centers, irrigation systems, airports, seaports, and other projects under this centerpiece program helped propel our country's economic development and infrastructure modernization.

"Night Owl," authored by Anna Mae Lamentillo, not only records the infrastructure achievement of the Duterte administration, but also provides readers with anecdotes and insights on such challenging but laudable enormous undertaking.

This book is a good read.

— JOSE DE VENECIA JR.
Former five-time Speaker of the House of Representatives

The pursuit to give Filipinos a more comfortable life is an obstacle-laden path that leaders of our country ought to tread. "Night Owl" encapsulates the Duterte Administration's arduous yet highly productive journey to elevate our citizen's way of life through its massive infrastructure program.

Build, Build, Build increased mobility and connectivity, especially in rural and far-flung areas, and helped drive investments to the countryside. The roads, bridges, and other infrastructure projects that have been accomplished in the span of five years provided our citizens improved access to basic needs and services, and growth opportunities.

Through this book, readers will appreciate the crucial role of infrastructure development not only in a nation's economic growth and overall development, but also in the welfare and quality of life of its people.

— IVAN JOHN E. UY
Secretary, Department of Information and Communications Technology

Build, Build, Build will go down in Philippine history as one of the greatest legacies of any administration. We have practically leapfrogged to the Golden Age of Infrastructure, accomplishing in one presidential term the infrastructure gap that has hounded several administrations past.

In "Night Owl," Anna Mae Lamentillo narrates the painstaking process to transition from blueprints to actual roads and bridges. This includes the Department of Public Works and Highways' efforts to institute reforms, address decades-old challenges, and utilize technology for efficient and effective progress monitoring.

She dissects every facet of the program—from the kilometers of roads, number of bridges, flood control projects, classrooms, evacuation centers accomplished in each region, to the number of jobs created and its impact on growth, including the country's progress in becoming a trillion-dollar economy.

While acknowledging the vision and the strong political will of President Rodrigo Duterte and the passion and commitment of his Build, Build, Build team to accomplish the task at hand, "Night Owl" is also generous in recognizing the 6.5 million Filipino workers whose blood, sweat, and tears have actually made this program a monumental achievement not only of the administration, but also of the Filipino nation.

Hats off to Ms. Lamentillo for diligently recording the statistics and stories behind these projects to dispel rumors and combat disinformation. She expertly weaves such information and her personal knowledge and experience as Build, Build, Build committee chair into a narrative that will inspire more leaders to be ambitious for our country and give nothing less than what the Filipino people deserves.

— CYNTHIA A. VILLAR
Senator

B uild, Build, Build has brought Filipinos not only hope for a better future, but also concrete opportunities for growth of our communities, especially those in the countryside.

Also worth noting are projects that are in line with our advocacy on disaster resilience and sustainability. The flood risk management projects in our rivers, the Leyte Tide Embankment Project, the Metro Manila Priority Bridges Seismic Improvement Project, and many others make our communities safer from natural hazards such as flooding, landslides, Yolanda-like supertyphoons and storm surges, and the Big One. Roads that have been built with bike lanes and sidewalks address our call to promote sustainable mobility options.

"Night Owl" by Anna Mae Lamentillo provides us statistics and the stories of these projects, the men and women behind them, the struggles that had to be overcome, and the early triumphs brought about by Build, Build, Build.

Congratulations on this worthy read!

— LOREN LEGARDA
Senate President Pro Tempore

A s if looking through the author's eyes, the reader will be able to witness the step-by-step progress of the Build, Build, Build program of the Duterte administration.

The book featured the humble beginnings of the program, the hurdles it encountered, and its current accomplishments. It also introduced the people behind the program and of course, the most important contributor, the Filipino people. The program's goal to connect Luzon, Visayas, and Mindanao through land has slowly become a reality. Within five years, the program produced kilometers of roads and thousands of bridges. It was also able to complete flood control projects, airport projects, and seaport projects. Going beyond transportation, evacuation centers and classrooms were also built. The Build, Build, Build project did not only focus on the connections between the areas of the country. The project also considered how these infrastructures contribute to the holistic development of the country.

The "Night Owl" gives the reader a front-row view on the progress of the Build, Build, Build program through the past years. The program might not reach its full actualization for a few more years, but it indeed laid a foundation for a better future of the country.

— BRIAN POE LLAMANZARES
Philanthropist, Entrepreneur, Public Servant

"Night Owl" is not just a chronicle of the Build, Build, Build Program of the administration of President Rodrigo Duterte. It is also the story of the passion, hard work, and perseverance of the women and men of the Department of Public Works and Highways (DPWH) who overcame the bureaucratic and political challenges of achieving the dream of providing our people a better quality of life through world class infrastructure.

Anna Mae Lamentillo displays her credentials as a development communicator by expertly weaving stories of obstacles and triumphs of this administration's ambitious attempt to usher in the country's "Golden Age of Infrstructure".

I particularly enjoyed reading the chapter on "Diplomacy" where Ms. Lamentillo explained the connection between statecraft and infrastructure development. I have always thought that one of the more underrated achievements of this administration is with regard to diplomacy. This book clearly demonstrates how President Duterte used foreign relations to pursue the interest of the Filipino people.

This book is a must read for people who want to go beyond the partisan social media altercations and fake news that surround the flagship program of the Duterte administration. It is a must read for people who wants to understand how to pursue a worthy vision even in the midst of political noises. I congratulate Ms. Lamentillo for writing this book, which confirms what People Asia has already proclaimed: that she is indeed a woman of style and substance.

— **MANNY VILLAR**
Former Senate President

The book "Night Owl" provides a deeper insight into the government, under President Duterte's initiative, to rehabilitate and re-establish Philippines as a powerhouse of innovation and ingenuity. The research is impeccable and the delivery of the narrative allows the reader a journey into the beginnings of a very promising venture the Build, Build, Build initiative has delivered. Without a doubt, a necessary read.

The book covers, with meticulous detail, significant projects which shows the milestones of what this administration had reached and inspires us, collectively, to maintain the momentum built.

It is a hard-evidenced and moving manifesto of the promising future the Philippines is promised.

— **SAMANTHA LOUISE VARGAS ALFONSO**
Cagayan Second District Representative

"Night Owl" is a remarkable journal of the government's Build, Build, Build Program from the account of someone who is personally and passionately involved in its implementation. It tells us why Build, Build, Build is a legacy of the Filipino people. It is the work of the government, the citizens who contribute to the public coffers, and the millions of Filipino workers who have completed the roads, bridges, school buildings, flood mitigation structures, evacuation centers, airports, and seaports in all the country's region.

I am not surprised that Anna Mae is devoted to Build, Build, Build. She saw herself how these projects opened opportunities, especially for those who live in the countryside; how more Filipinos now dream and aspire for a better future. These ideals resonated with Anna Mae, who learned much from her education as an alumna of the College of Development Communication, UP Los Baños, and the UP College of Law.

"Night Owl" is a journal of our nation's growth in terms of infrastructure development in the last five years. It narrates how this ambitious program – despite the criticisms and cynicism – delivered and paved the way for Filipinos to dream bigger. Hopefully, these stories will inspire more leaders to be equally generous in their ambition for our nation.

Congratulations, Anna Mae, for recording history through "Night Owl"!

— **DANILO L. CONCEPCION**
President, University of the Philippines

Anna Mae Lamentillo's book, "Night Owl," provides a bird's eye view of the government's Build, Build, Build program. It's her finishing touches, her additional contribution to her work as the project's chairperson while she was with the DPWH. Inside the pages of "Night Owl," one can read about and see the developments that have helped move the country forward, even during the most challenging years brought by the Covid-19 pandemic.

— **EMILIO YAP III**
President and Vice Chairman, Manila Bulletin Publishing Corporation

Build, Build, Build Committee Chair Anna Mae Yu Lamentillo's book, "Night Owl," takes users on a 342-page journey across five years termed as the "Philippines' Golden Age of Infrastructure." It is a valiant attempt at chronicling where the Philippines has been, where it is, and where it is headed— specifically, in terms of the grand vision of connecting 7,641 disparate islands across Luzon, Visayas, and Mindanao via land.

— **ROSE TOLENTINO**
CEO, Alike Media

The government's Build, Build, Build program provides Filipinos an optimistic view of the future. These infrastructure projects propel growth in communities and provide better, safer, and faster market access to local producers. It has also created a Philippine macroeconomic environment that is encouraging for the business sector, particularly the consumer and retail industry.

Congratulations to Anna Mae Lamentillo for chronicling these Build, Build, Build accomplishments through "Night Owl"!

— ROBINA GOKONGWEI-PE
President and CEO, Robinsons Retail Holdings Inc.

"Night Owl" by Anna Mae Lamentillo provides a front row seat to the Duterte Administration's Build, Build, Build program. It's a must read for leaders who seek the formula to effect lasting positive change.

Some of the takeaways from this book: The only way to realize a vision is to have the political will to make the necessary reforms, no matter how drastic they are. Our ambitions should match our actions. We cannot take baby steps if we want to bring the Philippines to greater heights.

— KEVIN TAN
CEO and Vice-Chairman, Alliance Global, Inc.

Anna Mae Yu Lamentillo's Night Owl is a detailed look at where the Philippines is going, as well as where it has been. In 342 pages, it is many books at once. It is part a historical account of Philippine infrastructure over the past 50 years and further back. It is part a progress report on the ongoing Build, Build, Build program of the Duterte administration. It is part a road map on the vision to connect our 7,641 disparate islands across Luzon, Visayas, and Mindanao via land travel. Part travelogue and part memoir, it is also part a blueprint for the future of every Filipino, if not even part a prospectus for emerging generations of nation builders, investors, and partners.

— AA PATAWARAN
Lifestyle Editor, Manila Bulletin

In her book, the former chairman of the Build, Build, Build program breaks down where ₱3.4 trillion in government funds went in the last five years — and why it was worth every single penny for the Filipino people.

— JOSE PAOLO DELA CRUZ
Managing Editor, Stargate People Asia

BUILD, BUILD, BUILD

NIGHT
OWL

BY
ANNA MAE YU LAMENTILLO, J.D.

EDITED BY
AA PATAWARAN

NIGHT OWL

Edited by
AA Patawaran

Cover Illustration by
Jethro Razo

Graphics by
Isabella Concepcion

Book Layout and Design by
Christian John Santos

Photography by
DPWH, Ken Jover, Hans Melvin Ang, and Dmitri Valencia

Book Project Manager
Joncristian Gerrald Cheng Tan

Published by
Manila Bulletin Publishing Corporation
P.O. Box 769 Manila Bulletin Publishing
Muralla corner Recoletos Streets
Intramuros, Manila, 1006
Philippines
www.mb.com.ph
Telephone Nos: + 632 527 8121

Second Edition, 2022
Printed in the Philippines

If you are reading this, and you're part of the
Build, Build, Build team—without you,
we wouldn't have been able to build
29,264 kilometers of roads, 5,950 bridges,
11,340 flood control projects,
222 evacuation centers, 150,149 classrooms,
214 airport projects, and 451 seaport projects.
The Philippines is in a much better place
because of your skills, work, and sacrifices.

BU

TABLE OF CONTENTS

ILD

BU

ILD

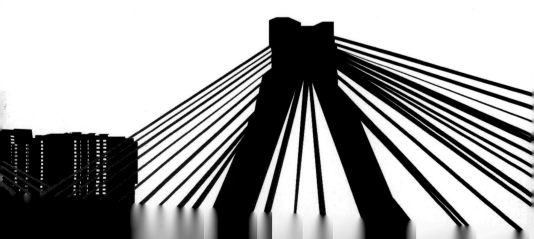

MALACAÑAN PALACE
MANILA

FOREWORD

This book that features the **Build, Build, Build** program of the government illustrates our strong commitment to put in place much-needed public infrastructure that will allow our people to lead more productive, prosperous and comfortable lives.

Through the construction of roads, bridges, flood control projects and classrooms, among others, we have succeeded in establishing physical hallmarks of progress that help sustain the development of our country.

May you continue to assist the administration in effectively disseminating information about the gains that we have made for the improved welfare of our people.

I also hope that you will remain steadfast in showcasing and communicating the achievements and milestones that we have made. Together, let us revitalize our society, especially as we recover from the COVID-19 pandemic.

Mabuhay kayong lahat.

RODRIGO ROA DUTERTE

THE PRESIDENT OF THE PHILIPPINES

Office of the Executive Secretary

FOREWORD

The impact of public investment in infrastructure is clear – every peso the government spends boosts the productivity of private capital and labor. Investing in infrastructure transforms economies through sustainable long-term growth, and reduces poverty by changing the lives of previously disadvantaged communities. In a country such as the Philippines, robust infrastructure development is, in fact, long overdue. The lack of reliable infrastructure has been holding back the Philippines from achieving its full potential.

In this light, the Duterte Administration allotted the highest budget allocation for infrastructure in Philippine history. This is intended to propel the country towards becoming an advanced economy.

We have been inspired by a clear vision of Filipinos living comfortably through the gains brought about by Build, Build, Build. Every kilometer of road, rail and bridge built has been bringing Filipinos of different ethnicities, languages and religions closer to each other.

Through this book Night Owl, author and columnist Anna Mae Yu Lamentillo provides an insider's view on the administration's Build Build Build program and how it rallied to connect 81 provinces, 146 cities and 1,489 municipalities. Together, we have built a total of 29,264 km of roads, 5,950 bridges, 11,340 flood control projects, 222 evacuation centers, 89 *Tatag ng Imprastraktura Para sa Kapayapaan at Seguridad* (TIKAS) projects, 150,149 classrooms, and 653 COVID-19 facilities.

Build, Build, Build has allowed us to aspire for a better future for this generation and the next. Behind the goal to connect every province in the Philippines is our desire to alleviate the decades-long suffering of Filipinos who yearn for an improved and expanded infrastructure.

My hope is that the last five years would truly be remembered as the Philippines' Golden Age of Infrastructure and that the pandemic that started last year, rather than overshadowing this feat, will highlight even more the grandeur of this accomplishment. I am thankful to the author for her emphasis all throughout this book that Build Build Build is a movement, not just of its leaders but of the 6.5 million Filipinos who worked together to catapult the Philippines towards becoming a first world country. That is exactly how the Duterte Administration wants it to be remembered.

SALVADOR C. MEDIALDEA

FOREWORD

Infrastructure is the backbone of a strong economy. We cannot deny that Philippines' ability to realize its full potential lies on its current and future infrastructure — one that will stand the test of time and withstand forthcoming economic, social, and environmental changes.

Movement of people, goods, and services needs to be supported by reliable infrastructure that will enable efficiency between supply chains and markets, students and schools, employment and communities.

In the past five years, Build, Build, Build provided jobs to over 6 million workers whose labor and skill paved the way to the completion of 29,264 km of roads, 5,950 bridges, 214 airport projects, and 451 seaport projects.

What started as a vision is now a movement crucial in nation building. Every hour spent by Filipino workers has led to roads and bridges that has paved the way for mothers and fathers to come home earlier to their children, for farmers and fishers to get better access to markets and for students to reach their schools more safely

As a country often struck by natural disasters, Filipinos rely on infrastructure networks for its defense. Outdated infrastructure has made us vulnerable to tsunamis, storm surges and flooding. We have to rebuild the systems on which our society thrives upon — update our piping system which are long overdue for expansion and complete the missing link that would bring Filipinos of different backgrounds together.

Build, Build, Build started a revolution that would catapult Philippines to a trillion-dollar economy and reinvigorate areas affected by conflict, crisis, and underdevelopment.

Even when plans proved to be difficult and impossible, Filipino workers forged ahead to create infrastructure that would spur growth and opportunity so that the next generation would not have to choose between safety and livelihood.

Build by Night Owl is a personal narrative of a millennial who joined the biggest work force in Philippine history and took on the challenge of bringing communities closer to healthcare, education and livelihood.

MARK A. VILLAR

PREFACE

To the 6.5 Million Build, Build, Build Team

Build, Build, Build has been the target of fake news, trolls, and critics. They have tried to redefine it far from its scope — and in their "proud, most credible voice" — report it as truth. Are they confused or just simply cunning?

Many will try to discredit the accomplishments of 6.5 million construction workers. They will say that what we have completed is not enough, that there could have been many things that we could have done still, or that we never really worked at all.

Allow me to say — if you are reading this, and you're part of the Build, Build, Build team - without you, we wouldn't have been able to build 29,264 kilometers of roads, 5,950 bridges, 11,340 flood control projects, 222 evacuation centers, 150,149 classrooms, 214 airport projects, and 451 seaport projects. Philippines is in a much better place because of your skill, work, and sacrifices.

If it weren't for your help in building Pigalo Bridge, farmers in Isabela who wanted to take their agricultural products to Manila or Tuguegarao, would still have to take the 76-kilometer detour via the Alicia-Angadanan-San Guillermo-Naguilian Road. Now, farmers are able to reach the same market within a 10-minute time frame.

If it weren't for your sacrifices in constructing the Central Luzon Link Freeway, travel time from Nueva Ecija and Tarlac would still be 70 minutes. Now, the two provinces are connected within 20 minutes.

If it weren't for your courage to complete the Marawi Transcentral Road, residents of war-torn Marawi would still have difficulty accessing basic services and goods. You have paved the way for peace.

If it weren't for your skill, it would have been impossible to build the Cebu-Cordova Link Bridge, the Philippines' longest bridgeway. You have shown Filipinos nationwide that the dream of connecting Luzon, Visayas, and Mindanao via land travel is within our reach with the right vision and action plan.

If it weren't for your hard work, we would have not finished the construction of the Skyway Stage 3, the NLEX Harbor Link, the C5 Southlink, the Kalayaan Bridge, and the Radial Road 10, among others. You are the reason why we are closer to achieving the EDSA Decongestion Program — a masterplan aimed at decongesting a 90-year-old circumferential highway. You are the reason why Filipinos spend less time on the road, and more time with their families.

Let the last five years be remembered as a collective movement of the Filipino people who wanted change and acted on it. We may have set our sights too high — but our country and the men who stood behind it — deserve nothing less.

Filipinos have built many cities, expressways, subways, railways, and airports elsewhere in the world as OFWs. The pandemic gave us the best talent pool one could ever ask for. Build, Build, Build gave OFWs an opportunity to serve their country if they wanted to. Although we couldn't match the salaries they received abroad, many stayed to ensure that Filipinos would get to use infrastructure that they only saw in photos before.

We are on the right track. The Philippines can be a trillion-dollar economy. President Rodrigo Duterte already laid the grounds to make this possible. It will be up to us to make it happen.

Right man on the job

About five years ago, on our first day of office — Build, Build, Build Czar Mark Villar and I were talking — "What can we do to make the Philippines a better place?"

His answer was simple —roads to the most rural areas so that children can go to school without risking their lives, bridges to connect farmers and fishermen to their markets and infrastructure that would open up opportunities in the countryside and allow Filipinos to dream and aspire for a better future.

What is Build, Build, Build? It is a revolution of Filipinos who want the next generation to see a better Philippines.

Skyway Stage 3

Subic Freeport Expressway

CHAPTER ONE

BUILD
BUILD
BUILD

The Philippines will be a trillion dollar club member

The economy of the Philippines is the world's 28th largest economy by GDP (Purchasing Power Parity) according to the 2018 estimate of the International Monetary Fund. Under the administration of President Rodrigo Duterte, the Philippines recorded a GDP (PPP) of ₱956 billion in 2018. If the Philippines is able to maintain its projected GDP Growth of 6.5 percent in the next decade, then the tiger cub economy might well be part of the trillion dollar club, which currently includes the United States, China, India, Japan, Germany, Russia, Indonesia, Brazil, the United Kingdom, France, Mexico, Italy, Turkey, Korea, Spain, Saudi Arabia, and Canada.

In a report titled "Philippines Tiger Economy Still Set for Dynamic Growth," IHS Markit Asia-Pacific chief economist Rajiv Biswas predicts that in 2022, the country will reach the upper middle-income status as robust economic growth trickles down to household incomes. It noted that the Philippine economy is poised to double by 2026 en route to a GDP of $1 trillion by 2032. The trickling-down effect seems to have started already. According to the Philippine Statistics Authority (PSA), poverty incidence among Filipinos has decreased by 6.6 percentage points, from 27.6 percent during the first half of 2015

Skyway Stage 3

to 21 percent during the first half of 2018. In a report of the National Economic and Development Authority (NEDA), it noted that the average income has accelerated from 15.3 percent to 21.2 percent.

According to NEDA Undersecretary Adoracion Navarro, the growth in per capita income of the bottom 30 percent of households picked up significantly to 29.2 percent in the 2015-2018 period from only 20.6 percent in the 2012-2015 period. This implies an increase in real incomes of the poor, which has helped in reducing poverty among Filipino families and individuals.

Highest credit rating

The World Economic Forum also noted the Philippines as among economies that show potential on Intergenerational Equity and Sustainability. In April 2021, the country also received its highest credit rating from international debt watcher S&P Global Ratings. S&P upgraded the Philippines' long-term sovereign credit rating from "BBB" to "BBB+" — two notches above investment grade rating — with a "stable" outlook.

While IMF had previously cautioned about the rising inflation in 2018 as a possible roadblock, this problem seems to no longer be an issue today. In fact, Asian Development Bank predicted inflation to decline at 3.8 percent in 2019 and 3.5 percent in 2020. It also forecast per capita GDP Growth to rise at 4.8 percent in 2019 and 2020.

Scaling up public investment

In its economic assessment published in 2018, IMF highlighted the need to scale up public investment in the Philippines if it were to sustain long-term growth and reduce poverty. It said that public investment, if well managed and targeted, could help boost overall productivity, stimulate private

Governor Miranda Bridge Inauguration

investment, and reduce poverty by creating jobs. According to the IMF Investment and Capital Stock Dataset, the Philippines was only spending 3.9 percent of its GDP on public investment in 2015. This is far lower when compared to neighboring countries like China (13.5%), Malaysia (9.2%), Vietnam (6.9%), Thailand (6.2%), and India (5.9%).

Build, Build, Build

The "Build, Build, Build" program is the Duterte administration's medium-term goal to increase infrastructure spending from 5.4 percent of the country's Gross Domestic Product (GDP) in 2017, to 7.3 percent by the end of 2022. This is higher than the 2.4 percent average recorded by the past six administrations in the last five decades — and the highest budget allocation for infrastructure in Philippine history.

Since then, 6.5 millions jobs have been created to build 29,264 kilometers of roads, 5950 bridges, 11,340 flood control projects, 214 airport projects, and 451 commercial and social seaports.

Mega Bridge Project

One of the landmark projects of Build, Build, Build is the Mega Bridge Program, a masterplan which lays the foundation for a series of short and long-span bridges linking island provinces to eventually connect Mindanao and Visayas to Luzon via land travel.

According to DPWH Secretary Villar, the first project under the master plan, the Panguil Bay Bridge, a 3.7-kilometer bridge connecting Tangub City in Misamis Occidental and Tubod in Lanao del Norte, already started in November 2018. Once completed in

Skyway Stage 3 Inspection

2023, travel time between Tangub and Tubod will be reduced from 2.5 hours to only 10 minutes. It will also shorten travel time between Ozamiz City in Misamis Occidental and Mukas, Kolambugan, in Lanao del Norte from 2.5 hours (using RORO operations) to only 20 minutes.

Detailed engineering designs of the Guicam Bridge in Zamboanga Sibugay and three bridges in Tawi-Tawi (Nalil-Sikkiat Bridge, Tongsinah-Paniongan Bridge, and Malassa-Lupa Pula Bridge) are also included in the Improving Growth Corridors in Mindanao Road Sector Project (IGCMRSP) under the Asian Development Bank.

Six bridges are now undergoing feasibility studies: (1) the Bohol – Leyte Link Bridge, a 22-kilometer bridge, which will shorten travel time from Bohol and Leyte provinces from three hours to only 40 minutes, (2) the Negros – Cebu Link Bridge, a 5.5-kilometer bridge that will reduce travel time from Negros and Cebu from 40 minutes to ten minutes, (3) the Cebu-Bohol Link Bridge, a 24.5-kilometer bridge that will reduce travel time from two hours and ten minutes to only 30 minutes, (4) the Luzon (Sorsogon)-Samar Link Bridge, an 18.2-kilometer bridge connecting the island of Samar in Eastern Visayas to the main island of Luzon (Allen-Matnog), (5) the Samal Island- Davao City Connector Bridge, a 2.85-kilometer bridge connecting Samal Circumferential Road to Davao City, and (6) the Bataan-Cavite Interlink Bridge, a 31-kilometer inter-island bridge connecting Mariveles in Bataan to Corregidor to Naic in Cavite.

Tarlac Pangasinan La Union Expressway

Why do I support Build, Build, Build?

Before I entered government, I was a humanitarian worker who traveled to all 18 regions of the country. I worked with both the United Nations Development Program and the Food and Agriculture Organization of the United Nations. On November 8, 2013, Supertyphoon Yolanda first made landfall in the municipality of Guiuan in Eastern Samar. The terrain was difficult. Delivery of goods proved to be challenging. Cadavers lined up on the streets. Trees and debris blocked the roads. The smell of death and decay lasted for months.

At that time, I wished the Philippines had better roads, that it would be easier for anyone who wanted to send help, to reach areas that needed medicines, food, and water. Bulldozers arrived from Cebu, Manila, and Davao via boat because a number of equipment in the region were lost or destroyed. What was left was not enough to reach far-flung areas that were completely isolated. In several towns, it took weeks before help came.

Several years after Typhoon Yolanda struck the Philippines, international development organizations remained to help in the recovery and rehabilitation process.

In my mind, it was difficult to talk about sustainable development when students had to risk their lives just to go to school, when farmers and fishers had to take whatever the middlemen were willing to give because transportation of their produce proved too difficult.

A number of municipalities could only be accessed through boats. Whenever it rained, families would have to make a decision whether to risk their lives or lose their income.

It was at this point that I realized that if we were to achieve real and inclusive economic growth, then a good infrastructure network was necessary. I would have never thought that in a matter of years I would join President Rodrigo Duterte's Build, Build, Build team.

Talk to the People

Five years later, I am more convinced that Build, Build, Build should be institutionalized.

For instance, the coastal municipalities of Northern Samar and Eastern Samar that at one point could not go to Catarman without having to pass through the island town of Laoang can now do so via the Samar Pacific Coastal Road Project. This makes a big difference to farmers who at one point had no other way but to transport their produce via small boats.

What is Build, Build, Build?

At one point in its history, the Philippines was the second richest country in Asia. We were only a little behind Japan and way ahead of China. At its peak, our rail transportation spanned 1,100 kilometers. In 2016, we only had about 77 kilometers.

The decline of our transportation network was mainly attributed to the government's chronic underspending on infrastructure, which only averaged 2.4 percent of our country's GDP for the past half century. This is minimal compared to the rest of the Association of Southeast Asian Nations (ASEAN) 5, which recorded at least five percent.

To effectively usher in the Golden Age of Infrastructure, the Duterte Administration created Build, Build, Build, a medium-term development strategy, which aimed to mobilize the largest work force in Philippine history to implement an infrastructure plan consistent with the Master Plan on ASEAN Connectivity.

Taking a whole of government approach, an inter-agency committee composed of six national agencies—the Department of Public Works and Highways, the Department of Transportation, the Bases Conversion and Development Authority, the Department of Finance, the Department of Budget and Management, and the National Economic and Development Authority—was formed.

Cost of doing nothing

The cost of indifference to our infrastructure decline is not minimal.

For instance, in NCR alone, the Philippines lost ₱2.4 billion a day in 2012 due to

Metro Cebu Expressway

traffic congestion. This has gone up to ₱3.5 billion after six years, according to a study conducted by the Japan International Cooperation Agency.

Now, road usage in Metro Manila is at about 13.4 million trips per day and could go as high as 16.1 million in 17 years. Economic losses could also rise to ₱5.4 billion in 2035 in the absence of any infrastructure intervention.

Access to the most inaccessible

The past five years has not been easy but I will always look at it fondly. It is immensely satisfying to be a part of something bigger than yourself.

Our critics were correct — it would have been impossible for us to implement Build, Build, Build alone. We knew it from the start. If not for the help of the 6.5 million Filipinos who willingly took part of the shared vision of creating a more comfortable life for all, big ticket projects would remain in the pipeline.

In 2016, critics said Build, Build, Build would not be able to deliver, that the plan to connect the northernmost part of Metro Manila to the southernmost part within 30 minutes was exaggerated. As I write this book, we have already opened Skyway Stage 3 and effectively reduced travel time from NLEX to SLEX to only 30 minutes. By 2022, EDSA will be back to its original capacity of 288,000 vehicles with the completion of BGC-Ortigas Link Bridge, Estrella-Pantaleon Bridge, NLEX Harbor Link, NLEX Connector, Binondo-Intramuros Project, and Laguna Lake Highway, among others.

In 2017, critics said Build, Build, Build was biased toward Metro Manila. This is far from reality. For instance, Northern Mindanao, Davao, Soccsksargen, and Caraga saw the realization of the Mindanao Road Development Network, a 2,567-kilometer intermodal logistics network, which aims to address constraints caused by high cost of transport and inadequate logistics infrastructure.

In 2018, critics said the Mega Bridge Program had not moved or that it had been shelved. Now, the main bridge of the Cebu-Cordova Link Bridge is almost complete. Moreover, Panguil Bay Bridge is now at 27.568 percent.

In 2019, critics said Build, Build, Build was a dismal failure. They did not see the completion of the Boracay Circumferential Road, the Camalig Bypass in Albay, the Tarlac-Pangasinan-La Union Expressway, the Lingayen Bypass in Pangasinan, the Aganan Bridge in Iloilo, and the Central Luzon Link Expressway as a success that must be celebrated.

In 2020, critics said "Hindi nakakain ang imprastraktura." They failed to remember the Kankanaey, Bago, and Ibaloi groups in Barangay Mapita who will have access to markets and basic social services once the Daang Katutubo is complete. They forgot to mention the farmers in Isabela who had to take a 74-kilometer detour before the Pigalo bridge was reconstructed.

In 2021, critics said "PPP (Public-private partnerships), hindi BBB." It is not one or the other. All infrastructure projects under the Build, Build, Build program are financed by three implementation modalities: national government financing, PPPs, or official development assistance (ODA). In other words, all PPP projects financed, constructed, and completed from 2016 to 2022 are included in the Build, Build, Build program.

Who takes the credit?

Five years later, with the completion of 29,264 kilometers of roads, 5,950 bridges, 11,340 flood control projects, 222 evacuation centers, 150,149 classrooms, 214 airport projects, and 451 seaport projects, the predominant discourse has been, "Who takes the credit?" The answer is obvious—the 6.5 million workers who worked and are still working to make the vision a reality.

But if we are to be honest, the more important question is "How do we institutionalize Build, Build, Build as a policy?"

BGC Ortigas Link Bridge

What has Build, Build, Build achieved so far?
29,264 kilometers of roads, 5,950 bridges, 214 airport, and 451 seaport projects

I began writing this piece on Build, Build, Build while on my way back to Manila from Tarlac after inaugurating the first 18-kilometer segment of Central Luzon Link Freeway with President Rodrigo Duterte, Department of Public Works and Highways Secretary Mark Villar, Senator Bong Go, and Tarlac Governor Susan Yap.

The Central Luzon Link Freeway, which connects Tarlac and Nueva Ecija within 20 minutes, is part of the Luzon Spine Expressway Network, a masterplan aimed at reducing travel time from the northernmost part of Luzon, Ilocos, to the southernmost part, Bicol, by over 50 percent via the construction of a 101-kilometer high standard highway network.

The event ended at about 8 o' clock in the evening and we reached home a little before midnight. The following day, the call time was 5 a.m. Sec. Mark and I were going to Cebu to attend the inauguration of the 129-kilometer Metro Cebu bike lane network and inspect Philippines' longest bridgeway — the 8.5-kilometer Cebu-Cordova Link Bridge.

This was our normal routine for the past five years. While it was not easy to sustain, we wanted to leave office knowing we gave it everything that we got. To us, Build, Build, Build is an opportunity to leave the Philippines in a much better state than before. It was a chance to catapult our tiger cub economy to the trillion dollar club. Fate allowed us to venture into the gigantic task of making the lives of Filipino people more comfortable in 81 provinces.

The President's instructions were clear from the onset: Finish as many Build, Build, Build projects as possible in the soonest possible time. Whoever gets the credit is none of our business.

Five years since President Rodrigo Duterte assumed position, DPWH, under Secretary Villar, has completed a total of 29,264 kilometers of roads, 5,950 bridges, 11,340 flood control projects, 222 evacuation centers, 89 Tatag ng Imprastraktura Para sa Kapayapaan at Seguridad (TIKAS) projects, and 150,149 classrooms. Also, 653 COVID-19 facilities have been built under the Build, Build, Build program.

Moreover, the Department of Transportation (DOTr), under Secretary Art Tugade, has completed 214 airport projects, 451 commercial and social/tourism seaport projects, and the country's first land port — the Paranaque Integrated Terminal Exchange (PITX).

Of the 29,264 kilometers of roads completed, 2,025 kilometers are farm-to-market roads, 94.99 kilometers are farm-to-mill roads,

1376.26 kilometers are missing links, 1,470.51 kilometers are bypasses or diversion roads, 149.65 kilometers lead to airports, 293.19 kilometers lead to seaports, 703.54 kilometers lead to economic zones, and 2,436.40 kilometers lead to declared tourism destinations. A total of 3,122.73 kilometers were maintained, 4,686 kilometers widened, and 3,591.96 kilometers rehabilitated and upgraded.

29,264
KILOMETERS
OF ROADS COMPLETED

These include the NLEX Harbor Link Segment 10, the Cavite-Laguna Expressway, the Tarlac-Pangasinan-La Union Expressway, the Laguna Lake Highway, the Candon City Bypass Road in Ilocos Sur, the Slaughter House Road in Davao City, the Pulilan-Baliuag Diversion Road in Bulacan, the Calapan-Roxas Road in Oriental Mindoro, the Mandaue Causeway Road in Cebu, the Dipolog-Oroquieta Road in Misamis Occidental, the Dumaguete North Road in Negros Oriental, and the Taytay-El Nido Road in Palawan.

Inspection of C5 Southlink

5,950 BRIDGES COMPLETED

Of the 5,950 bridges, 1,366 were widened, 355 constructed, 1,805 retrofitted, 1,389 rehabilitated, and 297 replaced. About 738 local bridges were also built.

These include the Lucban Bridge in Cagayan, the Marcos Bridge in Marikina, the Sicapo Bridge in Ilocos Norte, the Anduyan Bridge in La Union, the Tallang Bridge along Cagayan, the Bolo-Bolo Bridge in Misamis Oriental, the Caguray Bridge in Occidental Mindoro, the Tinongdan Bridge, the Pasac-Culcul in Pampanga, the Aganan Bridge in Iloilo, the Maddiangat Bridge in Nueva Vizcaya, and the Pigalo Bridge in Isabela.

11,340 FLOOD CONTROL PROJECTS

A total of 11,340 flood mitigation structures have been completed since June 2016 to expand protected flood-prone areas across the country.

These include the Mandaluyong Main Drainage Project, the pumping stations at Barangays Wawang Polo and Coloong, the Flood Risk Management Project for Cagayan River, the Flood Risk Management Project for Tagoloan River, the Leyte Tide Embankment Project, and the Pasig-Marikina River Flood Control Project.

150, 149 CLASSROOMS CONSTRUCTED

To address the need for physical facilities required for elementary and secondary schools nationwide, Villar noted that a total of 150,149 classrooms were constructed, while 17,647 classrooms are in various stages of implementation.

These include the National High School in Alaminos, Pangasinan, the Alejandra Navarro National High School in Davao City, and the Bagong Pag-Asa Elementary School.

In the aviation and airports sector, the DOTr and its attached agencies have completed 214 airport projects under the Duterte administration, with 100 more ongoing.

Completed projects include the Bohol-Panglao International Airport, the Mactan-Cebu International Airport, the Sangley Airport in Cavite, the Lal-Lo International Airport, the Tacloban Airport, the Puerto Princesa International Airport, and the Ormoc Airport.

214 AIRPORTS PROJECTS COMPLETED

Domestic airports also underwent improvements. These include the gateways in Camiguin, Virac, and Tuguegarao.

Meanwhile, ongoing airport projects include the Bicol International Airport, which was delayed for 11 years and is now more than halfway complete, as well as the second passenger terminal building of the Clark International Airport, the Davao International Airport, the Bukidnon Airport, Surigao Airport, and the Kalibo Airport.

Across the archipelago, seaports are being upgraded and rehabilitated to better serve the public. Currently, the DOTr has completed 451 commercial and social/tourism seaport projects, while 101 are ongoing.

Notable port projects include the construction of the country's biggest Passenger Terminal Building at the Port of Cagayan de Oro, and the rehabilitation of Opol Port in Misamis Oriental, Sasa Port in Davao, Butuan Port in Agusan Del Norte, Tubigon Port in Bohol, Limasawa Port in Southern Leyte, and Makar Wharf in General Santos.

The country's first barge terminal, the Cavite Gateway Terminal, which aims to reduce truck traffic on major roads and offer a cost-effective access to goods between Manila and Cavite through the waterways, has been built.

451 COMMERCIAL AND SOCIAL SEAPORTS COMPLETED

On maritime safety, as of June 2021, we now have 564 out of 600 lighthouses operational nationwide.

Railways

For railways, DOTR has six projects with ongoing construction and one undergoing rehabilitation.

In 2019, after 40 years and six administrations, the Metro Manila Subway, our country's first underground railway system, finally started with site-clearing works at the Valenzuela Depot. Two out of the 25 massive tunnel boring machines are already in the Philippines for the start of the underground works within 2021. This will reduce travel time between Quezon City and NAIA from one hour and 10 minutes to just 35 minutes.

The much-delayed MRT-7, whose Concession Agreement was signed in 2008 but had nearly zero movement until 2016, is now 60.93 percent complete. This will reduce travel time between Quezon City and Bulacan from two to three hours to just 35 minutes.

Approved by the NEDA Board in 2007 and stalled since 2009, the Common Station is now undergoing 24/7 construction, and is now 50.95 percent complete. The Common

Cavite Laguna Expressway

station, which will connect MRT-3, MRT-7, LRT-1, and the Metro Manila Subway, will have the capacity to accommodate 500,000 passengers per day.

The LRT-1 Cavite Extension, delayed for 19 years, finally started full-blast construction this year. This will reduce travel time between Baclaran and Bacoor from one hour and 10 minutes down to 25 minutes.

The LRT-2 East Extension project is now completed and open to the public. The LRT-2 East Extension reduces travel time between Manila and Antipolo from two to three hours to just 40 minutes.

The MRT-3, battered from years of poor and erratic maintenance, is now undergoing comprehensive rehabilitation with Sumitomo-Mitsubishi Heavy Industries of Japan.

The Manila to Clark Railway, planned way back in 1993, is now undergoing full-blast construction with PNR Clark Phase 1's first train set scheduled for delivery within the fourth quarter of 2021. This will reduce travel time between Tutuban and Malolos from one hour and 30 minutes to just 35 minutes.

PNR Clark Phase 2, PNR Calamba, PNR Bicol, Subic-Clark Railway, and the Mindanao Railway are all in the pipeline, now under various stages of procurement and pre-construction works.

Final Inspection of the Tarlac Pangasinan La Union Expressway

Cebu Cordova Link Expressway

Five years later: 5,950 bridges

Accoording to the World Risk Report, inadequate and inefficient infrastructure and weak logistic networks significantly increase the risk for an extreme natural hazard to backslide into a disaster. The Philippines lies along the Pacific Typhoon Belt and is within the Pacific Ring of Fire. The geographic location of the country exposes it to natural hazards. In fact, in the 2017 World Risk Report, the Philippines ranked third among 171 countries in terms of risk associated to natural events and exposure to natural disasters.

Bridges in particular have been proven to be highly vulnerable. Since July 2016, DPWH has completed a total of 5,950 bridges, 1,389 of which were rehabilitated, 1,366 widened, 355 newly constructed, 297 replaced, and 1,805 retrofitted. Also built were 738 local bridges.

These include the replacement of the 365-meter Lisap Bridge along Calapan South Road Bongabong, Oriental Mindoro, connecting Barangay Lisap and Barangay Hagan, which was completed in February 2018, and the widening of the 650-meter Governor Miranda Bridge II, which serves as the main access of motorists from Davao City to other parts of the Davao Region.

The widening of the 140-meter Davao River Bridge (Ma-a Bridge) along the Davao City Diversion Road was also completed in April 2018. Travel time has improved between Barangay Ulas and Barangay Buhangin by 62.5 percent from 80 minutes to 30 minutes, benefitting 31,576 motorists per day.

BGC Ortigas Link Bridge

Moreover, the 8.5-kilometer Cebu-Cordova Link Expressway (CCLEX) linking Cebu City and Cordova is already at 83.84 percent. When completed, it will be the longest bridge structure in the Philippines.

Metro Manila Logistics Network

In addition to the 30 existing bridges crossing the Pasig and Marikina Rivers and the Manggahan Floodway, which cater to about 1.30 million vehicles daily, 11 new bridges will be constructed in the area to provide alternative linkages between major thoroughfares and increase the number of usable roadways that would decongest traffic on Epifanio de los Santos Avenue (EDSA) and other major roads in Metro Manila.

We have completed the feasibility of six bridges under the Metro Manila Logistics Network, including the North and South Harbor Bridge, the Palanca Villegas Bridge, the East West Bank Bridge 2, the Marcos Highway - St. Mary Avenue Bridge, Homeowner's Drive - A Bonifacio Bridge, and Kabayani St - Matandang Balara Bridge.

The BGC-Ortigas Link Bridge, more popularly known as the Kalayaan Bridge, is now complete. The four-lane bridge across Pasig River linking Lawton Avenue in Makati City, Sta. Monica Street in Pasig City, and Bonifacio Global City in Taguig, effectively reduced travel time by at least 80 percent — from one hour to only 12 minutes.

The Estrella-Pantaleon Bridge, which connects Estrella Street in Makati and Barangka Drive in Mandaluyong, is also complete and is able to accommodate about 50,000 vehicles daily.

Governor Miranda Bridge

The Binondo-Intramuros Bridge, which is now at 72 percent, will link Intramuros from Solana Street and Riverside Drive and connect to Binondo at the San Fernando Bridge.

DPWH is also implementing the Metro Manila Priority Bridges Seismic Improvement Project, which involves the retrofitting and reinforcement of the Guadalupe Bridge and Lambingan Bridge. Started in 2019, it is targeted to be completed by 2021. This will ensure the safety of about 365,000 motorists who use the Guadalupe Bridge and about 30,257 motorists who pass through the Lambingan Bridge every day.

Inspection of BGC Ortigas Link Bridge

Sofa in the drainage

Out of the 171 countries assessed in the 2016 World Risk Report, the Philippines ranked third most exposed to natural hazards. According to PAGASA, the Philippines is visited by at least 20 tropical cyclones every year. Last August 2018, heavy rains brought about by tropical storm Karding led to the evacuation of at least 50,000 individuals after Marikina River's water level peaked at 20.6 meters (as compared to 23 meters during Ondoy). During the clean-up operations that followed, I was surprised to see all sorts of garbage, from sofa to refrigerators, inside our drainage canals — sediments that impede the natural flow of water.

In the World Bank's flood risk assessment study for the entire Metro Manila and Surrounding Basin Area, flooding was mainly attributed to three factors: (1) the huge volume of water discharge coming from the headwaters in the Sierra Madre mountains flowing downstream, (2) drainage capacity constraints in core area of Metro Manila, and (3) a heavily silted Laguna Lake.

The masterplan composed of 11 structural mitigation measures with an estimated cost of around ₱351 billion proposes to reduce the peak discharge of inflow equivalent to 3,600 m/s under a 100-year return period by about 75 percent by building a dam in the upstream portion of Upper Marikina River and constructing flood control structures along the priority critical sections of Pasig-Marikina River.

In May 2018, DPWH completed Phase III of the Pasig-Marikina River Channel Improvement Project (PMRCIP), which spans from the Lower Marikina River Improvement (Napindan Channel to the downstream of Manggahan Floodway) to Delpan Bridge. Revetments, parapet walls, dike embankment, sluice structures, and bridge foundation protection were constructed and installed along priority critical sections of the Pasig-Marikina River.

Flood Risk Management Project for Tagoloan River

The civil works for Phase IV are currently ongoing and address the downstream of Manggahan Floodway to Marikina Bridge. This would also include the construction of the Marikina Control Gate Structure and will further decrease flood inundation by 7.5 percent.

Apart from this, DPWH Secretary Mark Villar has adopted the Integrated Water Resources Management Program, which will complete and update the flood control and drainage master plans and feasibility studies of 18 major river basins (drainage area of more than 1,400 square kilometers), 421 principal river basins, and other critical river basins.

Phase 1 of the Metro Manila Flood Management Project, which involves the modernization of drainage areas, reduction of solid waste in waterways, and participatory housing and resettlement, among others, has also started.

The Flood Risk Management Project for Cagayan, Tagoloan, and Imus Rivers, which expects to address the serious bank erosion in Cagayan, construct river dikes and drainage channel along Tagoloan River, and build two off-site retarding basins along Imus and Bacoor Rivers, have been completed.

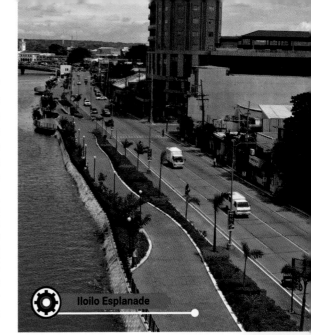

Iloilo Esplanade

Cagayan River Flood Control Project

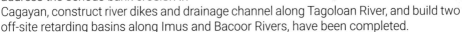

The Flood Risk Management Project in Cagayan de Oro (CDO) River is now protecting 290 hectares and about 18,000 structures in CDO. Based on a 25-year flood return period, the number of people affected by flooding in the area will also be reduced from about 281,000 to only 31,000.

Since its completion in 2020, the Integrated Disaster Risk Reduction and Climate Change Adaptation Measures in the Low-Lying Areas of Pampanga Bay reduces flood depth from 1.4-2.9 meters to 0.6-1.4 meters and will shorten flood duration from 66 days to 17 days.

Other projects include the Cavite Industrial Area Flood Management Project, which mitigates the flood damage caused by the overflow of the San Juan River and the poor drainage system of the Maalimango Creek; and the Leyte Tide Embankment Project, a 31.28-kilometer flood control project, which will protect 27.30 square kilometers of coastal communities and 30,800 houses/buildings from the destructive effects of storm surges.

Connecting Luzon, Visayas, Mindanao via land travel

When I was still in elementary, my father, Manuel Lamentillo, would tell me about the San Juanico Bridge, a 2.16-kilometer bridge connecting the island provinces of Samar and Leyte. Whenever we would go home to Iloilo, I'd often wonder why we had to take boats or airplanes to travel to Negros Occidental. There were not many bridges at that time. The Candaba viaduct, a five-kilometer bridge connecting the provinces of Pampanga and Bulacan, is the longest bridge in the Philippines and it was built in 1976, over four decades ago.

This will no longer be the case with the Duterte Administration's Mega Bridge Project, a series of short and long-span bridges linking island provinces to eventually connect Luzon, Visayas, and Mindanao via land travel.

According to Department of Public Works and Highways Secretary Mark Villar, the first project under the masterplan — the Panguil Bay Bridge, a 3.7-kilometer bridge connecting Tangub City in Misamis Occidental and Tubod in Lanao del Norte — will start construction within the year. Once completed in 2021, travel time between Tangub and Tubod will be reduced from 2.5 hours to only 10 minutes. It will also shorten travel time between Ozamiz City in Misamis Occidental and Mukas, Kolambugan in Lanao Del Norte from 2.5 hours (using RORO operations) to only 20 minutes.

The Detailed Engineering Design of the Guicam Bridge in Zamboanga Sibugay, and three bridges in Tawi-Tawi — Nalil-Sikkiat Bridge, Tongsinah-Paniongan Bridge, and Malassa- Lupa Pula Bridge — are also included in the Improving Growth Corridors in Mindanao Road Sector Project (IGCMRSP). Civil works have already started.

The preparation of the Feasibility Study and Detailed Design of these game-changing high-impact projects, such as the 22-kilometer Bohol-Leyte Bridge, the 5.5-kilometer Negros-Cebu Bridge, the 24.5-kilometer Cebu-Bohol Bridge, the 18.2-kilometer Luzon (Sorsogon)-Samar Bridge, the 4.4-kilometer Davao-Samal Bridge, and the 28-kilometer Bataan-Cavite Inter-Link Bridge, are already being undertaken under the Infrastructure Preparation and Innovation Facility (IPIF) funded by ADB.

The Bohol-Leyte Link Bridge is a 22-kilometer bridge linking Bohol and Leyte provinces, which is expected to reduce travel time from three hours (using RORO) to only 40 minutes.

The Negros-Cebu Link Bridge is a 5.5-kilometer bridge linking Negros and Cebu, which is expected to reduce travel time from 40 minutes (using RORO) to only 10 minutes.

The Cebu - Bohol Link Bridge is a 24.5-kilometer bridge linking Cebu and Bohol, which is expected to reduce travel time from two hours and 10 minutes (using RORO) to only 30 minutes.

The Luzon (Sorsogon) - Samar Link Bridge is a 18.2-kilometer bridge connecting

Cebu Cordova Link Expressway

the Island of Samar in Eastern Visayas to the main island of Luzon (Allen-Matnog). Travel time will be reduced from three hours and 20 minutes (using RORO) to only 40 minutes.

The Davao-Samal Link Bridge is a one-kilometer bridge linking Island Garden City of Samal and Davao City. Travel time will be reduced from 26 to 30 minutes (using RORO) to only 2-5 minutes.

The Bataan - Cavite Interlink Bridge is a 28-kilometer bridge connecting Mariveles in Bataan to Corregidor to Naic in Cavite. Travel time will be reduced from six hours to 45 minutes.

Also, the pre-feasibility study and the feasibility study for the Panay-Guimaras-Negros (PGN) Island Bridge Project have already been completed under China financing.

Since President Duterte assumed office in June 2016, DPWH has completed 5,950 bridges, 738 of which are local.

Bataan Cavite Interlink Bridge

Final Inspection of Cebu Cordova Link Expressway

Panguil Bay Bridge

Daang Katutubo

CHAPTER TWO

PROFILE

WHO IS
RODRIGO
DUTERTE?

Typhoon Nina, internationally known Nock-ten, entered the Philippine Area of Responsibility (PAR) on December 23. It intensified as a typhoon on December 24 and made landfall over Catanduanes province on the evening of December 25. At about three p.m., on Christmas Day, I received a message asking me to report back to central office and prepare a report on the damages sustained by the provinces affected by Typhoon Nina. We were informed that the President wanted it on his desk the following day, including actions already taken by the department. As soon as it was safe for our ground personnel, Sec. Mark Villar ordered the dispatch of our prepositioned equipment and to proceed with the clearing of debris so as to facilitate rescue operation and give way for the distribution of relief goods. By December 27, we were already on the ground with Mayor Duterte— first in Catanduanes, and then in Camarines Sur. He skipped the gift-giving ceremonies and called it "corny" and "overdramatic." But behind the doors, away from the camera, he met his men and asked them to deliver. For DPWH, we only had 48 hours to ensure that roads were passable and cleared.

This was my first time to join the President's delegation and I soon regretted the fact that we didn't bring any food. It was very different from what I originally expected it to be. In fact, at about 5 p.m., two pieces of Skyflakes brought by Sec. Briones was being passed throughout the plane.

The following Christmas, Typhoon Urduja struck the province of Biliran. Again, Mayor Duterte was the first one to arrive. He saw the damage of Caray-Caray Bridge and instructed Sec. Mark to ensure that the bridge was passable in a span of one month. When I saw the damage, I thought the timeline was impossible. But in the end, the project was done on schedule. If there is one thing that Mayor Duterte has always taught us — it is important to get things done, now and fast.

Political Underdog

In the 2016 presidential elections, Rodrigo Duterte was a political underdog. His rise to power was almost unforeseeable to the Philippine kingmakers who were betting on more popular candidates. Prior to his victory, the Philippines had never had a President from Mindanao. It took the country 117 years to elect one. Clearly, the mayor of Davao City was a statistical outlier who dared to defy the odds.

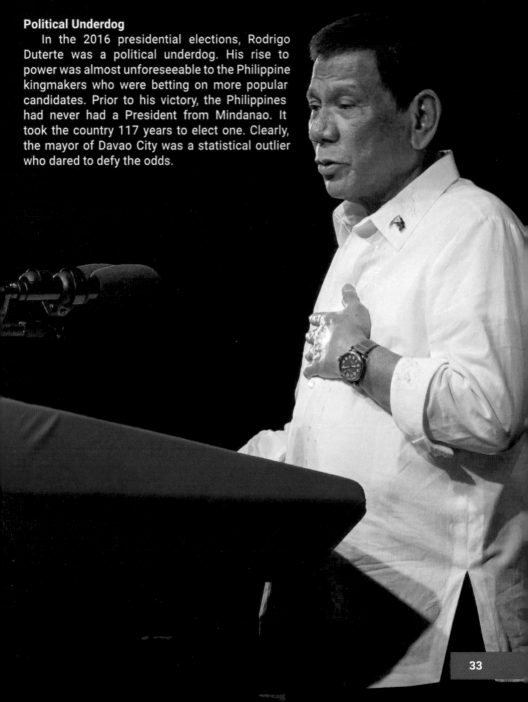

Ruling a country like the Philippines poses a very unique (and tough) challenge — what message do you send across a country of over 7,640 islands speaking more than 111 languages?

President Duterte was clear from the onset about what he wanted to achieve — a much safer Philippines for the next generation, one that accords the same opportunities to all Filipinos, regardless of their religion, ethnicity, or gender.

He dreams of a Philippines that would allow any kid to aspire to be President, whether they live in Sultan Kudarat, Northern Samar, Masbate, Davao, Makati, or Ifugao. He wants to open the door of opportunity to the next generation and, if this was not possible, build the door for them.

In August 2017, President Duterte signed RA 10931 or the Universal Access to Quality Tertiary Education Act, which provided underprivileged Filipino students the opportunity to pursue college degrees through free tuition and exemption of other fees in State Universities and Colleges (SUCs). It also provided for Tertiary Education Subsidy, which sponsors the enrollment of disadvantaged students in private institutions in locations where there are no available SUCs.

President Duterte has never forgotten who he is fighting for and always opted to defend those who cannot defend themselves. It is important to him that Filipino children who want to go to school can do so safely without fear of death or terror.

To him, the Marawi siege was personal. It was important to liberate the people of Marawi from militants linked to both ISIS and Abu Sayyaf in the soonest possible time. He was on the ground, in the battle zone, and armed with rifle when Philippine troops recaptured the Islamic center, the main mosque where the gunmen had taken cover with their hostages.

He went to the main battle area against the advice of his own men and proceeded to communities heavily damaged in the fighting.

If there is one thing I have observed, I have never seen him scared — not in the face of militants, or powerful men or even death. It is important to him that Filipinos who feel powerless can rely on him for protection.

Build, Build, Build

President Duterte was never stingy on dreams. He wanted to build an infrastructure network in every region in the country that would propel Philippines to becoming a trillion dollar economy. It was never about his legacy. He never cared about credit.

What mattered to him the most was that infrastructure projects were completed in the soonest possible time so that the farmers in Isabela would not have to take a 74-kilometer detour whenever it rained, so that the people of Lanao del Norte could reach Misamis Occidental

President Duterte visits Marawi City

in seven minutes (instead of 3.5 hours), and so that residents of Metro Manila would no longer have to endure a three-hour drive from Quezon City to Muntinlupa.

When the President knew that some of the slippages in the delivery of infrastructure projects were attributed to the delay in the release of permits, he pushed for the enactment of RA 11032 or the Ease of Doing Business and Efficient Government Service Delivery Act of 2018.

The reforms instituted during his time propelled the Philippines to jump 29 notches in The World Bank - Doing Business Report, from 124th in 2019 to 95th in 2020.

It is impossible for any President to solve all his country's woes in six years. But Mayor Duterte knew that in every meter of road, bridge, and rail we built, we opened opportunities to thousands of Filipinos who at one point didn't have access to hospitals, schools, and work.

Since 2016, more than five years since President Rodrigo Duterte assumed office, a total of 29,264 kilometers of roads, 5,950 bridges, 11,340 flood control projects, 214 airport projects, 451 commercial and social-tourism seaport projects, 222 evacuation centers, 89 TIKAS projects, 150,149 classrooms, and 653 COVID-19 facilities have been completed.

Candon City Bypass Inauguration

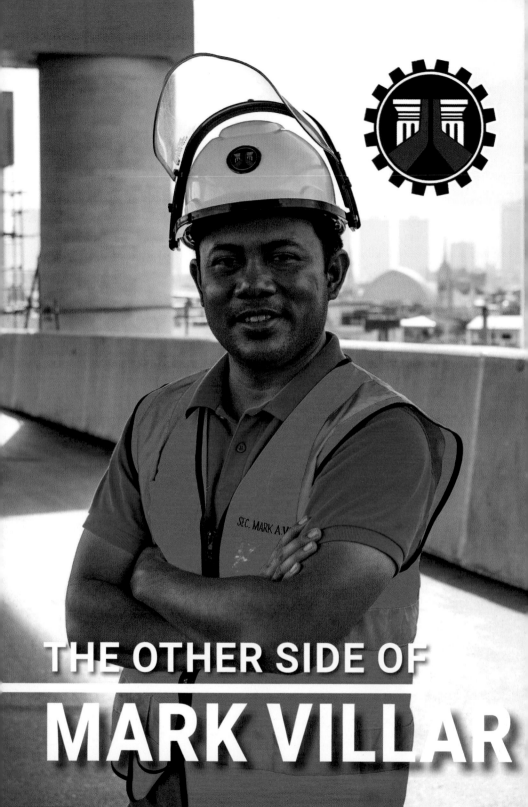

THE OTHER SIDE OF
MARK VILLAR

When Secretary Mark Villar was first appointed in 2016, a lot were critical. But after working with him for several years, I had no doubt, he would deliver. He has shown leadership in the most critical times — even when his own life is in danger.

When we were in Marawi to inspect ground zero a few days after Isnilon Hapilon and Omar Maute were killed, we had to shorten our aerial inspection because a bomb detonated. We saw smoke in one of the buildings a few meters from where our chopper was. It was my first time to see war up close. Secretary Mark was calm and prompt. He asked our pilot to fly higher so that we were not at a shooting distance. Even in the most precarious situation, he would show leadership.

This man was willing to work 18 hours a day to build infrastructure that would allow Filipinos to dream of a better future. From the onset, Sec. Mark wanted to end his stint as czar of Build, Build, Build knowing that he gave it everything he got.

His first meeting would usually be at 7 a.m. Some days, he wouldn't even have the time to dry his hair or have breakfast. But I'd often notice that before leaving the house, he'd go to the room of Emma Therese, his two-year-old daughter, first.

He tells me the country's huge infrastructure deficit is not only causing the country ₱2.4 billion a day, it has also made life even shorter.

People who work with Sec. Mark would know he works more than 14 hours a day. He would schedule his last meeting very late at night, and when DPWH has to open a new road or highway in a high traffic transport area, he'd insist to schedule it as early as 12:01 a.m. His instruction is clear: Opening and construction of new roads should cause as minimal traffic as possible.

Cebu Cordova Link Expressway Inspection

When he started institutionalizing reforms in DPWH, there were many challenges, from ghost projects, and delays, to right-of-way issues, and death threats. But we knew that if we were to make genuine change in the way government infrastructure was built, then reforms were a prerequisite.

On the first six months of his stint, Sec. Mark adopted drone and satellite technology for monitoring of DPWH projects and eliminated ghost projects via a geotagging system. Excel sheets, which had been used in the department for decades, became obsolete. Now, monitoring is fully automated under the Infra Track app.

"Finish the project or swim in Maysilo flood"

One of the first challenges we faced was the delay in the implementation of the Maysilo Mandaluyong Flood Control Project. The flooding problem was so bad that every time it rained, pedicabs were replaced by makeshift boats.

NLEX Connector Inspection

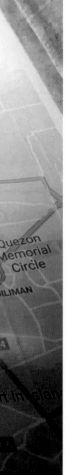

When Sec. Mark gave the contractor the ultimatum to finish the project on or before September 30, or swim in the Maysilo flood, we knew he meant business.

A 24/7 catch up program was immediately prepared with weekly deliverables. Inspections were detailed and unannounced. At times, even we were surprised. There would be days when we'd receive a text late at night to gather the team and meet him at 11:30 p.m. So when the Maysilo drainage project was completed on time, we all felt relieved and hopeful.

The Maysilo prototype was the basis for Department Order 193, which provided guidelines on contracts with negative slippages. Now, as soon as the project records a delay of five percent, the contractor will automatically be given a warning and required to submit a catch up plan that allows for a 24/7 construction schedule.

Despite all the challenges, I've rarely seen him complain about work. When he does, it would only be because he no longer sees Undersecretary Em Aglipay - Villar and Emma.

Love against all odds

When Sec. Mark first asked Usec. Em to go on a date, she declined. She thought he was superficial and would not be able to handle the rashes, the hair loss, and the frequent visits to the hospital. She was not interested in dating around and was comfortable being single. She knew lupus, an autoimmune disease, was difficult to accept and live with. At one point, she was experiencing excruciating joint pains that she needed someone to feed her.

It took Sec. Mark one year to convince Usec. Em to go out for lunch. The first date went well, better than they both expected. But after several dates, Usec. Em wanted him to see her without the wig and makeup. At that time, she was bald and had butterfly rashes on her face. He didn't run away like she expected him to do. Instead, Sec. Mark laughed and told her she didn't have to wear the wig or the makeup when they were together. He would often joke Usec., "Pati asawa ko, nakuha ko sa Sipag at Tiyaga".

Inauguration of Mella Hotel

ART TUGADE

MAN OF ACTION

One of my earliest recollections of Department of Transportation Secretary Art Tugade was during the inspection of the LRT-2 East Extension Project. The event was scheduled to start at 7 a.m. Secretary Art arrived at 5:30 a.m. Five years after the launch of Build, Build, Build, this work ethic is even more evident and Secretary Art has revolutionized the way transportation is done in the Philippines.

In a socio-economic context, Secretary Art believes that public transportation is an important component of the economy, and a significant enabler of development. He believes that when transport systems are reliable, safe, and efficient, they provide social and economic benefits that create multiplier effects, such as better accessibility to workplaces, homes, schools, tourist destinations, and more opportunities. Moreover, during times of crisis, transport development remains a key enabler of total economic recovery.

Low-Hanging Fruits

Since July 2016, the DOTr, under Sec. Tugade's leadership, has worked on finding solutions to difficult issues that seem impossible to address.

Who can ever forget the infamous "Laglag-Bala" racket at the Ninoy Aquino International Airport? Before, air passengers would travel with tapes covering their bags, fearing they might fall for the racket. Now, "Laglag-Bala" is a thing of the past, as stringent procedures have been set in baggage handling. From being tagged as one of the world's "worst airports," the NAIA is now recognized as one of the "world's most improved."

Before, the MRT-3 was often plagued with train derailment, unloading incidents, long lines, and constant service interruptions. Today, with its ongoing massive rehabilitation, trains are running smoothly on brand new rails, at a record speed of 60 kilometers per hour, and with faster turnaround time. New air-conditioning units have been installed on trains, and all elevators and escalators are now fully operational.

Before, a driver's license was a piece of paper. Driver's license backlogs also topped at three million.

Now, driver's license applicants can get their license cards with a five-year validity, which can be extended to ten years, provided that a driver has a clean record.

Before, vehicles—from cars to motorcycles – would ply the roads with no license plates. Now, the country is not just producing plates locally via the LTO Plate Making Facility, but also addressing the millions of backlog that has accumulated since 2014. To date, 3.9 million pairs of motor vehicle plates and 3.6 million motorcycle plates have been produced.

Neglected seaports and airports devastated by calamities are now getting a much-needed facelift with our non-stop rehabilitation works and development projects.

Building Transport Infrastructure

The DOTr has also been relentless in pushing for the completion of various transport infrastructure projects across the country, under the Build, Build, Build Program of the Duterte Administration.

Aviation and Airports

In the aviation sector, the DOTr has completed 214 airport projects, while working on more than 100.

Completed projects include:

- The Clark International Airport's new Passenger Terminal Building, which should become operational within 2021.
- The Bohol - Panglao International Airport, which was inaugurated on November 27, 2018. Feasibility study for the Bohol-Panglao International Airport started way back in year 2000.
- The Mactan-Cebu International Airport was also inaugurated on June 7, 2018.
- The Sangley Airport in Cavite was inaugurated on February 15, 2020.
- The Dumaguete Airport was inaugurated on March 11, 2021.
- The Communications, Navigation, Surveillance / Air Traffic Management. Inaugurated on January 16, 2018, the CNS/ATM increased the number of the country's air traffic radars from merely three in 2016 to 13. This enables air traffic authorities to monitor 100 percent of the Philippine airspace.

Other airport projects inaugurated since July 2016 include those located in Calbayog in Samar, Kalibo in Aklan, Ormoc, Tuguegarao, San Vicente Airport in Palawan, Butuan Airport, Siquijor Airport, Catarman Airport Rehabilitation Project, and many more.

Before the end of President Duterte's term in 2022, the DOTr will inaugurate the New Bicol International Airport, an airport that has a capacity of two million per year. Prior to this administration, the Bicol Airport was delayed for 11 years and went through three groundbreaking ceremonies. The General Santos International Airport will also be inaugurated in September 2021.

Railways Sector

In the railways sector, the DOTr has completed the LRT-2 East Extension Project in July 2021. This project got its NEDA approval way back in 2012.

Before 2021 ends, two more projects are for completion and for partial operations.

One is the Common Station, a project originally approved by the NEDA ICC in 2006. It is targeted for completion in December 2021. Second is the MRT-3 Rehabilitation project, which is also slated for completion in December 2021.

Meanwhile, several ongoing massive railway projects are due for trial runs before the end of President Duterte's term. These include:

- The MRT-7 Project. Slated for Trial runs for Stations 4 to 8 in April 2022. The Unsolicited Proposal for the MRT-7 was first submitted to the then DOTC in 2001, while the Concession Agreement was signed in 2008.

- The Metro Manila Subway. Trial runs will be conducted from East Valenzuela to the Philippine Railway Institute in April 2022. Two of its 25 massive tunnel boring machines are already in the Philippines. Concept for the Metro Manila Subway started in 1973. That was 50 years and six administrations ago.
- The Philippine Railways Institute, the country's first railways research and training center, will have its partial operations in June 2022.
- Construction works are likewise in full swing for the LRT-1 Cavite Extension. NEDA ICC Approval was received two decades ago and the Right-of-Way Acquisition started in 2007.
- PNR Clark Phase 1 of the massive North-South Commuter Railway or NSCR will reduce travel time between Tutuban and Malolos from one hour and 30 minutes to just 35 minutes.
- PNR Clark Phase 2, the second leg of the NSCR, will reduce travel time from Malolos to Clark from one hour and 30 minutes to just 35 minutes.
- PNR Calamba will cut travel time from Solis, Manila to Calamba, Laguna from three hours to just one hour.
- Works are also ongoing to revive the much-awaited PNR Bicol, which will connect Manila to Sorsogon and the Port of Batangas.
- Over in the South, the Mindanao Railway is expected to have partial operations of its Tagum-Carmen segment in October 2022.

Road Transport and Infrastructure

Amid the COVID-19 pandemic, the DOTr, along with the DPWH, has completed the establishment of almost 500 kilometers of Bike Lanes in Metro Manila, Metro Cebu, and Metro Davao. Secretary Tugade also spearheaded the establishment of dedicated median lanes for public utility buses on EDSA. With the EDSA Busway, commuter travel time via bus from Monumento to PITX has been reduced from three to four hours to just 50 minutes.

In 2018, the DOTr was also able to start the operation of the Paranaque Integrated Terminal Exchange (PITX). It has a maximum capacity of 100,000 passengers daily.

Maritime Transport

In the maritime sector, the DOTr and the Philippine Ports Authority have completed 451 seaport projects, and are working on 101 more.

Included in the list of completed seaport projects are the Port of Cagayan de Oro, the country's biggest port passenger terminal building to date; the Ports of Tagbilaran and Maribojoc in Bohol; the Ports of Borac, San Fernando, and Bataraza in Palawan; the Port of Dumaguete; Salomague in Ilocos Sur; Babak Port in Davao Del Norte; the Port of Claveria in Cagayan; the Pangasinan Riverlanding Project; and the General Santos Port.

Ongoing projects are also scheduled to be completed before the Duterte administration ends. These include the Calapan Port in Mindoro, which can accommodate 3,500 passengers at any given time, and the Zamboanga Port, which can accommodate 4,000 passengers at any given time.

The Port of Lucena in Quezon and the Port of Abra De Ilog in Occidental Mindoro are also ready for inauguration, while the Coron Port Expansion Project is scheduled for inauguration in December 2021. The Currimao Port in Ilocos Norte will be inaugurated in November 2021.

The Philippine Coast Guard is now stronger in terms of workforce. From only 7,000 in 2016, the PCG is now almost 21,000-strong. In July, the PCG has also launched one of its two 94-meter multi-role response vessel, the largest of its fleet, which will further boost the agency's maritime security and safety capabilities.

DOTr COVID-19 Efforts

As part of the whole-of-government approach to put an end to the raging COVID-19 pandemic, the DOTr has also been doing its part in extending the necessary assistance to the transportation sector.

For the first time in history, the Service Contracting Program, where drivers are paid on a per kilometer run basis, with or without passengers, was established and implemented.

DOTr also provided Free Ride service for medical frontliners and essential workers. As of September 5, 2021, this program has recorded a total of 31.6 million ridership nationwide.

Secretary Tugade also approved the waiving of rental payments for airport food, retail, and lounge concessionaires at the NAIA and CAAP-operated regional airports for the entire 2021.

As the strict quarantine classifications are enforced in Metro Manila, the DOTr also offers free train rides to vaccinated APORs at the MRT-3, LRT-2, and PNR lines.

Through the Hatid Tulong program, the DOTr also gave assistance to individuals returning to their home provinces. As of September 5, 2021, a total of 1,121,739 Returning Overseas Filipinos have been transported via air, maritime, and road transport.

Several Crew Change Hubs were also activated in different parts of the country to protect and uphold the welfare of our Filipino seafarers amid the pandemic.

The DOTr Maritime sector has likewise converted two of its quarantine facilities into isolation facilities—the Eva

Macapagal Super Terminal in Pier 15, Manila and the Port of Capinpin in Bataan; while another Quarantine Facility was established by the Coast Guard in its base in Taguig City.

Financial Contribution to Government Coffers

In 2020, the DOTr remitted a total of ₱19.27 billion in dividends from its attached GOCCs to support government spending measures amid the COVID-19 crisis. In the last five years, the DOTr and its attached GOCCs have remitted a record-breaking ₱50 billion+ to the National Treasury. Among its top-performing agencies are the PPA, Civil Aviation Authority of the Philippines (CAAP), and the Manila International Airport Authority (MIAA.)

Culture, Values, and Ways of Doing Things

Secretary Art Tugade has also been strictly advocating for transparency, and an uncompromising culture against corruption and red tape in the DOTr.

Live streams of procurement processes are posted on the DOTr's Facebook account, from pre-procurement to opening of bids.

As part of its anti-corruption drive, the DOTr has dismissed 203 personnel, and suspended 42, due to corruption-related cases since July 2016.

In the last four years, the DOTr has been recognized as one of the top-performing agencies in the Freedom of Information Awards, which gives recognition to agencies that exhibit utmost transparency to the public.

Further, the DOTr and its attached agencies have shifted to digitization, which includes the implementation of online application or renewal of licenses; use of Automated Fare Collection System (AFCS) for PUVs; cashless toll collection; use of contact-tracing application at ports, airports, and rail lines, among others.

These accomplishments in the transportation sector have created a much broader spectrum of opportunities for the country's development.

Sec. Art believes that the development of public transportation covers a wide segment of our day-to-day lives that benefit not just transport stakeholders, such as drivers and commuters. Developing our country's transport system also translates to better opportunities in every industry from education and tourism to trade, logistics, and business.

For Secretary Art, addressing transportation infrastructure bottlenecks and gaps, and investing in mobility and connectivity across the archipelago, will translate to an improved quality of life for the Filipino people.

If there is one thing I know, Secretary Art is definitely a man of action. Under his leadership, transformation has been initiated and implemented, and efforts to revolutionize our country's transport system have fully gained momentum.

EXECUTIVE SECRETARY
SALVADOR MEDIALDEA

BIG TASK FOR THE LITTLE PRESIDENT

n political circles, the Executive Secretary is often referred to as the "Little President," but the task is not little as could be attested by ES Salvador Medialdea himself, who was already thinking of retirement when he was given the daunting task by President Rodrigo Duterte.

Secretary Medialdea dedicated much of his professional life to private law practice, first at ACCRA and PECABAR law offices before establishing his own law firm. He had short stints in the government—as Administrator of the Livelihood Corporation (LIVECOR) in 1998, and as Presidential Assistant for Political Affairs in 2000—but he preferred private practice.

However, when he was handpicked by the President to be Executive Secretary, he could not say no to the man whom he holds in high regard and whom he considers as one of his mentors.

Secretary Medialdea looked up to his father, Leo D. Medialdea, who was also a lawyer and later on an Associate Justice of the Supreme Court. Thus, when he was appointed in government, his father's example served as his guiding principle in public service. He recalls his father's words that he took to heart: "So long as you can soundly sleep with what you are doing, you are in the right direction."

As ES, Secretary Medialdea assists the President in managing the vast government bureaucracy so that it would be aligned with the President's vision of a better Philippines for Filipinos. He crafts critical issuances to implement the President's programs, such as Build, Build, Build, a program he greatly believes in as it will enable the efficient flow of goods and movement of people, which are needed for progress.

BGC - Ortigas Center Link Project Inauguration

In fact, if the Little President was President, he would also prioritize infrastructure, stressing that it makes the most impact in the lives of people. He says, "The presence or absence of good infrastructure shape a country's destiny. Good infrastructure nurtures progress and growth."

He shares that the work of an ES is not easy, but the President's work energy and commitment to the people are so contagious that they inspire the Secretary to always deliver his best.

His dream is that "the next generations of Filipinos, when they look back at this period of our history, will find us faithful stewards of the offices entrusted to us during this difficult time."

While his work can be daunting, the Secretary still finds time to do things that he loves. He enjoys riding motorbikes, playing golf, and playing musical instruments such as the piano and guitar. He also loves to travel domestically to appreciate the beauty of the Philippines.

But when asked about his fondest memory of President Duterte, Secretary Medialdea goes decades back to the time when, while waiting for his client's case to be called at a trial court in Davao City, he randomly sat on a chair just outside the courtroom. He saw a man walking toward him and a girl shouted telling him he was sitting on the Fiscal's chair. The man said to him, "No problem, Attorney. You can use my seat." That man he met was then Fiscal Rodrigo Duterte, and that brief encounter would later change his life.

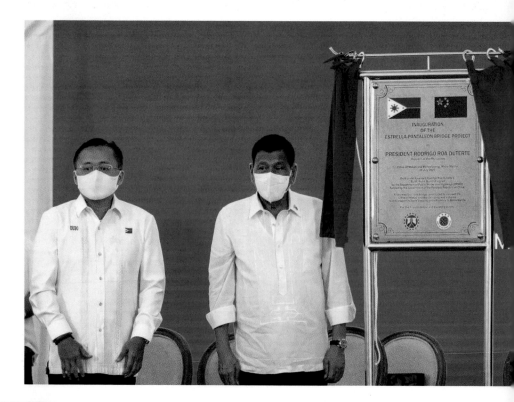

Skyway Stage 3 Inauguration

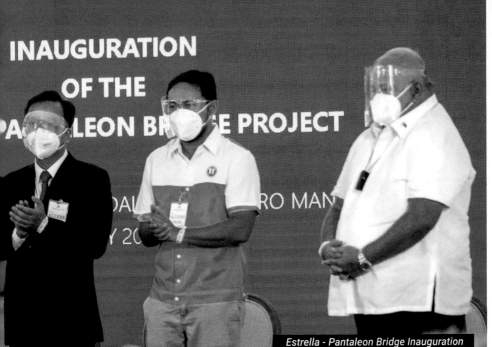

Estrella - Pantaleon Bridge Inauguration

WHAT'S ON VINCE DIZON'S TO-DO LIST

Secretary Vivencio "Vince" Dizon would probably be the best example of a multitasker, and an effective one at that. He wears many hats, so to speak, serving at the center of the government's COVID-19 response and the Build, Build, Build program.

He is the current Presidential Adviser on Flagship Programs and Projects, and the President and Chief Executive Officer of the Bases Conversion and Development Authority (BCDA). He is also the Deputy Chief Implementer of the National Action Plan Against COVID-19, the national government's Testing Czar, and the Chief Coordinator of the Test, Trace, Treat (T3) Program. Moreover, he is the Chairman of the Subic-Clark Alliance for Development and the Vice Chairman of Clark International Airport Corporation.

Every day at work has been a challenge, Secretary Vince said, especially since the country grappled with the pandemic. You would often see him in the news giving updates on the government's response against COVID-19. He is always on the go, attending important functions, inspecting various areas around the country, and speaking with leaders to ensure the smooth roll-out of the government's vaccination program.

On top of all these, he has a tough task at the BCDA, which is mandated to convert former military lands into productive civilian use. It is guided by the vision of transforming these properties into inclusive and sustainable premier centers of economic growth in partnership with the private sector. BCDA's developments include parts of Fort Bonifacio and Villamor Air Base, which are now known as Bonifacio Global City and Newport City, respectively.

Clark International Airport Inspection

In the first five years of the Duterte administration, BCDA, under the leadership of Secretary Vince, made a record-high contribution to the AFP of ₱17.81 billion. This is significantly higher than the ₱13.01 billion contributed during the six years of the previous administration.

So far, BCDA has generated about 400,000 jobs, attracted more than 1,000 locators, registered some $4 billion of investments in its special economic zones, and reported a combined asset value of around $10 billion.

As part of Build, Build, Build, one of BCDA's biggest undertakings is to transform the Clark Freeport and Special Economic Zone into the next big metropolis and major growth hub in the country. This is part of the Duterte Administration's strategy to develop alternative growth areas outside Metro Manila.

Clark is divided into four main districts—Clark Freeport Zone, Clark Global City, New Clark City, and Clark International Airport. Its development is expected to attract even more investments and spur inclusive economic growth in Central Luzon and across the country.

For instance, the New Clark City, a 9,450-hectare greenfield development, will be the country's first disaster-resilient, green, and inclusive city. It is the home of the National Government Administrative Center (NGAC), a recovery and back-up hub for the government in times of disasters and emergencies.

Secretary Vince said Clark gives him so much pride. The BCDA Group, he said, is determined to make Clark a model development for the entire country. In fact, the new Clark International Airport terminal building has been named as one of the six airport finalists at the 2021 Prix Versailles World Architecture and Design Award while the New Clark City Athletics Stadium has been shortlisted among the world's best completed buildings at the 2021 World Architecture Festival.

Clark International Airport

Clark is also a favorite place of Secretary Vince when he goes cycling, which usually serves as his bonding time with his wife.

With still a lot of work to do, he hopes the pandemic will be over soon so government can fast track infrastructure projects under Build, Build, Build.

After the Duterte Administration, retirement will not be an option for a public servant as young as Secretary Vince. If given the chance, however, he wants to go back to the academe to teach again.

He served as an assistant professor of Economics, research associate, and lecturer of Economics and Finance at De La Salle University, his alma mater. He completed his Bachelor of Arts degree in Economics and Bachelor of Science degree in Commerce-Management of Financial Institutions at DLSU.

He was also a senior lecturer in Economics, Finance and Statistics at the University of Northern Virginia in Prague, Czech Republic from 2005 to 2007.

With so much learned over the years, this student of public service definitely has so much to teach.

2019 Labor Day Tribute at the New Clark City Aquatics Center

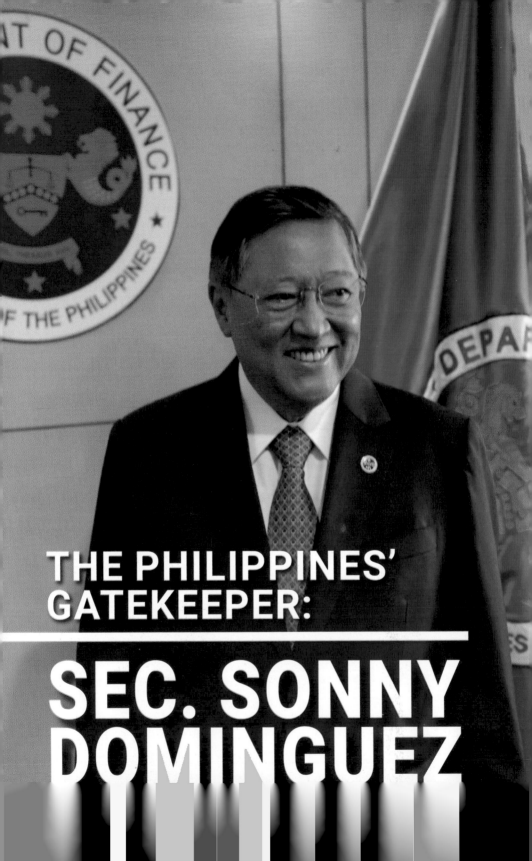

THE PHILIPPINES' GATEKEEPER:

SEC. SONNY DOMINGUEZ

When I asked Finance Secretary Carlos "Sonny" Dominguez III if he thought that the Philippines would become a trillion dollar economy, his answer was an emphatic, "Of course! And not in the distant future."

Statistics prior to the COVID-19 pandemic shows we are closer than we think. In 2018, the economy of the Philippines was already the 28th largest economy by GDP (Purchasing Power Parity) according to the International Monetary Fund. Under the administration of President Rodrigo Duterte, the Philippines recorded a GDP (PPP) of ₱956 billion in 2018.

Secretary Dominguez told me that while the Philippines, like other countries in the world, cannot operate in the normal way because of the pandemic, our economy will surge as soon as we are able to defeat the virus.

"I'm glad to have been part of the team of President Duterte that put our country in a good financial position not only to withstand the rigors of this pandemic, but also to be prepared to grow at a faster pace upon the control of the virus," he said.

In the second quarter of 2021, the Philippines' Gross Domestic Product (GDP) grew by 11.8 percent, the highest since the fourth quarter of 1988. The biggest contributor to the increase was the construction sector, which was pegged at 25.7 percent. It was followed by manufacturing at 22.3 percent and industry and services at 20.8 percent. In other words, the Philippines has ended its recession with the fastest year-on-year growth in 32 years.

State visit to China

In its August 2021 report, the International Monetary Fund predicted the recovery to gain momentum with Real GDP Growth expansion of 5.4 percent in 2021 and seven percent in 2022.

'Making the right decision'

People who work with Sec. Dominguez know he is not afraid to make unpopular decisions so long as they benefit the Filipino people in the long term.

"It is only during the time of President Duterte that the government was able to increase sin tax three times, and impose an excise tax on sugary drinks. The President isn't afraid to do the right thing even at the expense of his political capital," he said.

He says government programs should be able to increase its citizen's productivity and ability to create wealth. Taxes are necessary if we want to bring the Philippines from a tiger cub economy to a trillion dollar club member.

Prior to his stint as Secretary of the Department of Finance (DOF) under the Duterte Administration, Secretary Dominguez held a number of notable positions in both public and private sectors spanning over 40 years. He was Secretary of Agriculture and of Environment and Natural Resources during the Presidency of the late Corazon Aquino. He was President of leading Philippine corporations, such as the Philippine Airlines, the Philippine Associate Smelting and Refining Corporation, and the former Bank of the Philippine Islands Agricultural Bank.

Financing the Build, Build, Build projects

As Finance chief, his priority is to see to it that all of the government's tax reform programs and economic bills are passed. He makes sure to give his 100 percent in every task given to him and he is proud to have been able to build a good team within the DOF and its attached agencies, which allows them to efficiently work toward the achievement of goals.

He also enjoys working with the Build, Build, Build team. He explains that the Duterte Administration's most ambitious infrastructure program is not only about building roads, but also making sure these are properly financed and properly monitored, because the

worst thing that can happen is to start a project, then put a halt to it halfway through because of lack of funds.

As Finance Secretary, it is within his purview to ensure that financing for the Build, Build, Build projects is in place, and also to see to it that, through the implementing agencies, the projects are done on time, within budget, and properly monitored in every stage of project implementation.

According to Secretary Dominguez, Build, Build, Build is the main strategy of the Duterte Administration to reduce poverty because it creates jobs and makes logistics, doing business, and creating value chain much easier. But aside from infrastructure investment, the other strategies of the government to reduce poverty include investing in the human capital, primarily through huge investments in education and providing free college education, as well as sustainable financing plan through tax reforms.

Among the tax reforms implemented by the administration are the Tax Reform for Acceleration and Inclusion (TRAIN), which reduced the personal income taxes for 99 percent of taxpayers, and the more recent Corporate Recovery and Tax Incentives for Enterprises (CREATE) Law, which provides tax relief to businesses with the 10 percent reduction in the corporate income tax (CIT) rates of micro, small, and medium enterprises, as well as five percent reduction on CIT for bigger corporations.

He credits this to the President's political will and the ability to see far into the future, that is why the economic team was able to set a good foundation for the country's growth. He describes President Duterte as very analytical and one who sticks to his principles, especially against people who are violating the law. "It's very inspiring and uplifting to see a President act strictly in principle and in upholding the law," Secretary Dominguez said.

Secretary Dominguez realizes that there is still much to be done, but he also stresses that he and the DOF will work as hard as they always do, up to the last minute of this administration. And after that, maybe he can go back to doing the things he enjoys outside of work—shooting, hunting, and spending time with friends and family, especially his six grandchildren.

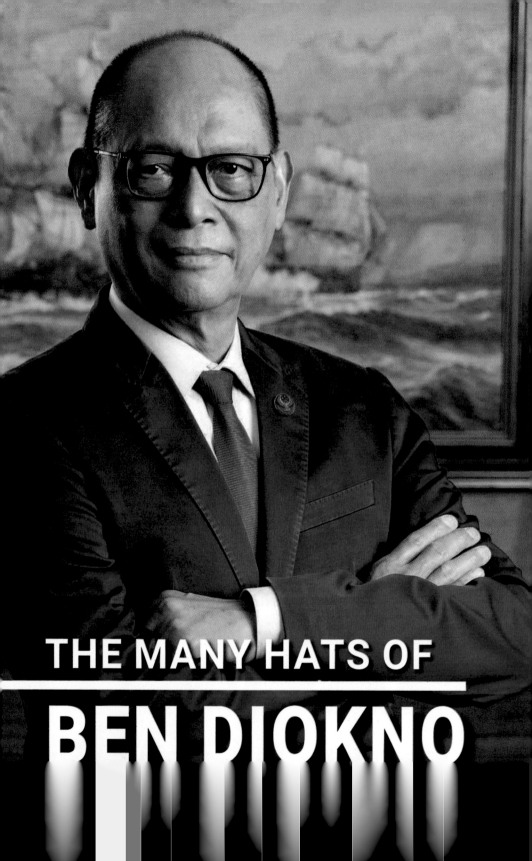

THE MANY HATS OF
BEN DIOKNO

The Economist. The Reformist. The Professor. While these may sound like characters in a television series, I'm just referring to only one real person. These could well describe the three main hats that Bangko Sentral ng Pilipinas (BSP) Governor Benjamin E. Diokno wears interchangeably or all at once, depending on his current position.

As an economist, his policy expertise and research contribution extend to various areas of public economics. He even served as adviser and consultant to institutions like the World Bank, Asian Development Bank, European Commission, and the USAID.

As a reformist, he was instrumental in crafting major policy reforms of the country, including the 1986 Tax Reform Program, the 1991 Local Government Code of the Philippines, and the Government Procurement Reform Act. During his term as Budget Secretary in 1998, he introduced a more transparent budget process with the introduction of the What-You-See-is-What-You-Get (WYSWYG) system. As Budget Secretary under the Duterte Administration, he introduced cash budgeting to replace obligation budgeting to promote budget accountability, simplify tracking of expenditures, and speed up fund utilization.

As a professor for over 40 years, he has taught courses such as public sector economics, microeconomics, macroeconomics, and development economics, among others. He is Professor Emeritus of the University of the Philippines-Diliman, his alma mater where he earned his Bachelor's Degree in Public Administration, as well as his

Oath taking of BSP Governor Ben Diokno

Master's Degree in Public Administration and in Economics. He also holds a Master of Arts in Political Economy from the Johns Hopkins University in Baltimore, Maryland, and a Ph.D. in Economics from the Maxwell School of Citizenship and Public Affairs, Syracuse University in New York.

Governor Diokno shares that he really wanted to go into government service. He thought it was logical because he came from a political family. While in college, his ultimate goal was to join one of the international development organizations. But when he got his Ph.D. in Economics, he was undecided whether to return to the Philippines, which was then under Martial Law, or stay in the US. He sought the advice of a former professor, who told him, "If you stay in the US, you'll be a small fish in a big pond, if you go back to the Philippines, you'll be a big fish in a small pond."

Ulat ng BSP sa Bayan

I could say we're lucky he heeded the advice to serve our country.

Governor Diokno was the one who fondly called the Duterte Administration's massive infrastructure program as the "Golden Age of Infrastructure", now known as Build, Build, Build, which he helped design and implement because he believes that the lack of public infrastructure has been a major challenge to the country's path to sustained inclusive growth.

As BSP Governor, his specific goals include keeping inflation manageable and having a cash-light economy, where at least half of all financial transactions are done digitally and at least seven out of ten households have a transaction account.

But if he was President, which he explains is not in his bucket list, he will focus on finding better ways of doing things to improve governance and the lives of the ordinary citizens. His bias would be on higher spending for social services and physical infrastructure.

He thanks President Duterte for choosing him in helping manage the country's finances as Budget Secretary, which he considers an extremely tough assignment. But he thinks being BSP Governor during this unprecedented crisis would be most unforgettable for him. He thought managing BSP would be a breeze, which it was, until COVID-19 came. But with the help of a supportive Monetary Board and professional staff, he maintains the BSP did well.

Under his leadership, the BSP was able to act swiftly and boldly to help the country during this pandemic. Through various monetary measures, the BSP released some ₱2.2 trillion into the system to calm the financial market, ensure adequate liquidity, and support the government in financing its COVID-19 related expenditures.

He goes on to assure the public that even if the current focus is on the health cum economic crisis, he won't let it distract them from realizing BSP's long-term reform agenda: digitalization and financial inclusion.

With the magnitude of his tasks, I wondered how he spends his free time, if any. He tells me he just finished reading Nudge by Richard H. Thaler and Cass R. Sunstein, and is now into First Friends by Gary Ginsberg. He just enjoys learning, reading, and writing. And with a mind like his, that answer does not come as a surprise to me, at all.

BONG GO

THE RISE OF THE PROBINSYANO

H e was initially identified as President Rodrigo Duterte's most trusted man, having served as the former Davao City Mayor's loyal and trustworthy aide for two decades. He was also referred to as the "People's bridge to the President," ensuring that the people's needs and concerns reach the Chief Executive's attention. But over the years, Senator Christopher Lawrence "Bong" Go has solidified his brand of service—one who is always ready and willing to serve the people.

In fact, President Duterte describes Senator Bong Go as the embodiment of a dedicated public servant who works tirelessly to make sure services reach those who need them the most.

As then Mayor Duterte's aide, he was tasked to attend to the needs of people who were seeking help from Davao's top leader. His role endeared him to the public, and it helped that he is also very approachable and sincere in his duty.

When he became Special Assistant to the President (SAP), and now Senator, he remained the same, the simple probinsyano who is always willing to go the extra mile just to help, especially those who have less in life.

As SAP, he prioritized the creation of Malasakit Centers all over the country to improve access to affordable and quality health services to the poor and

marginalized. The Malasakit Center aims to: (1) help reduce a patient's hospital bill to the lowest possible amount by covering various patient services and expenses, such as surgeries, laboratories, and medicines, through existing medical assistance programs under government agencies, such as the Department of Health (DOH), Department of Social Welfare and Development (DSWD), PhilHealth, and the Philippine Charity Sweepstakes Office (PCSO); and (2) bring together these aforementioned government agencies under one roof to hasten the delivery of the government's medical assistance programs for poor and disadvantaged Filipino patients.

The idea is simple—give help to those in need in the most efficient and convenient way. For Senator Go, we should not let those who are already suffering suffer further.

As Senator, he institutionalized the creation of these Malasakit Centers through Republic Act 11463, which he principally authored and sponsored in the Senate. As of September 3, 2021, there are already 138 Malasakit Centers nationwide.

Cavite Laguna Expressway Inauguration

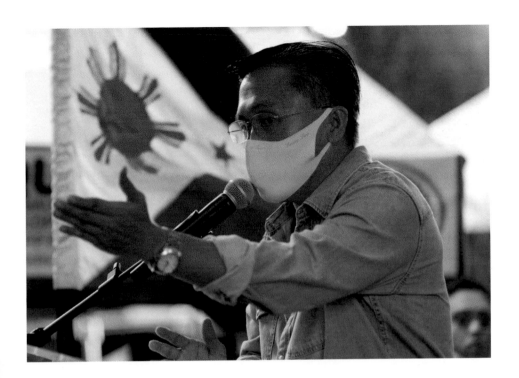

Senator Go has also filed many other proposed measures, particularly on health, salary increase for government employees, anti-illegal drugs and criminality, housing, education, immigration, long-term sports development, anti-corruption drive, fire protection and prevention, barangay welfare, labor, justice, migrant workers and overseas Filipinos, solo parents, disaster resilience, and e-governance, among other measures, which aim to improve Filipinos' quality of life. These measures aim to complement the programs of the Duterte Administration.

As a public servant and aware of the needs of our people having worked beside President Duterte for more than two decades, he also advocated for and supported measures on greater food security, localized peace talks, senior citizens, persons with disabilities, LGBTs, MSMEs and other local industries, and transport.

Asked what inspires him to work, Senator Go says, it is serving his fellow Filipinos. He shares that his decades of work with President Duterte have provided him a deeper understanding of what ails the country and what needs to be done. He considers the President his mentor who has taught him that public service is always prioritizing serving Filipinos and it should be done with "tapang at malasakit"—the Duterte brand of leadership.

Public service has long been ingrained in the mind and heart of Senator Go that when he wakes up, he always thinks of Filipinos who are suffering, those who are vulnerable, those whose lives revolve around the basic things in life—to be able to eat three times a day, to have a roof over their heads, to be able to send their children to school, and to be able to go to work and do their livelihoods safely.

"These are the people who need government services the most. As a servant of the people, it is my duty to ensure that these people are able to access quality services in a more convenient and timely manner," says the Senator.

Tarlac-Pangasinan-La Union Expressway

CHAPTER THREE
THE PHILIPPINES

The Philippines is no longer Asia's 'Sick Man'

Increased government spending, propelled by the Duterte Administration's Build Build Build program and strong household consumption drove the Philippine economy to grow by 6.8 percent in the first quarter of the Fiscal Year of 2018, surpassing World Bank's forecast of 6.7 percent and close to the lower end of the government's target of seven to eight percent. According to Department of Budget and Management (DBM) Secretary Ben Diokno, this growth rate makes the Philippines one of the fastest-growing economies in the fastest-growing region in the world.

According to the Department of Finance (DOF), National Government revenue rose by 16.4 percent in the first quarter of 2018 as the first phase of TRAIN took effect, almost doubling nominal GDP growth, which registered 9.7 percent during the quarter.

Due to improved tax administration, tax revenues grew by 18.2 percent with Bureau of Internal Revenue collections rising by 14.2 percent and Bureau of Customs collections rising by 24.7 percent.

In the first quarter, revenue effort rose by 0.91 percentage point and tax effort also increased by 1.03 percentage point — the highest first quarter tax effort ever achieved.

Expenditures grew by 27.1 percent, also outstripping the 9.7 percent nominal GDP growth due to the estimated 40.0 percent increase in capital outlays. Expenditure effort rose by 2.73 percentage point to 20 percent, the highest first quarter expenditure effort since 2003.

NLEX Connector

According to the Philippine Statistics Authority, Government Final Consumption Expenditure (GFCE) grew by 13.6 percent in Q1 2018, a marked improvement from the 0.1 percent growth in the same period of 2017.

The higher government spending is directly correlated with the Duterte Administration's Build, Build, Build program. Data on National Government Disbursements show a surge in Infrastructure and Other Capital Outlays by 33.7 percent year on year, reaching ₱157.1 billion. In fact, according to DBM, actual infrastructure disbursements exceeded the program by ₱13.7 billion, or 9.6 percent, in the first quarter of 2018.

The Gross Value-Added in Public Construction also showed optimistic results as it grew by 25.1 percent in the first quarter of the year, higher than the 2.1 percent growth recorded in the same period of 2017.

This is a result of the reforms, strategic policies imposed in agencies like Department of Public Works and Highways, Department of Transportation, and Bases Conversion and Development Authority to further improve infrastructure spending.

In DPWH, Secretary Mark Villar integrated physical and financial accomplishment to the existing monitoring system to ensure real-time reporting and revisited level of authorities provided based on performance and absorptive capacity. It also strictly imposed calibrated sanctions and penalties on contractors with negative slippages and strictly enforced uniform guidelines on suspension and blacklisting of contractors or suppliers or consulting firms.

Interestingly, the First Quarter 2018 Social Weather Survey, done on March 23 to 27, found that 30 percent of Filipino families, or one out of three, escaped poverty (18 percent usually non-poor, 12 percent newly non-poor) and that hunger has decreased by six percent, from 15.9 percent or an estimated 3.6 million families to 9.9 percent or an estimated 2.3 million families.

Clearly the Philippine Economy remains strong and will continue to grow with strong macroeconomic fundamentals backed by tax reform and the Build, Build, Build program.

Cavite Laguna Expressway

A counter-narrative of the Philippines

While attending the 6th ASEAN Connectivity Forum in Seoul, I learned that during the 1960s, the Philippines had the second highest per capita income in Asia, behind only Japan. A decade later, South Korea had passed our country in per capita income terms largely due to the successful implementation of the Economic Development Plan, where the government and public enterprises accounted for close to 40 percent of the total domestic investment in the period between 1963 and 1979 for the construction of infrastructure projects like highways, port facilities, electricity, etc.

On the other hand, the Philippines' infrastructure spending in the last five decades only averaged at 2.5 percent.

It was only in 2017, under the administration of President Rodrigo Duterte that the government budgeted around 5.4 percent of GDP for infrastructure development, which is more than twice the 2.5 percent average for the past six administrations in 50 years.

Since June 2016, DPWH has completed 29,264 kilometers of roads, 5,950 bridges, 11,340 flood control projects, 222 evacuation centers, 150,149 clssrooms, 214 airport projects, and 451 seaport projects.

In November 2018, the Philippine government laid the capsule, which marked the start of the construction of the 3.77-kilometer Panguil Bay Bridge connecting Tangub City in Misamis Occidental and Tubod in Lanao del Norte across Panguil Bay in Northern Mindanao.

Upon completion in November 2021 of the first bridge in the Mega Bridge Network, land travel between Tangub City in Misamis Occidental and Tubod in Lanao del Norte will only take seven minutes from the two to 2.5 hours travel at

status quo either via Roll-on, Roll-off (RORO) vessel or the 100-kilometer land travel through Panguil Bay Road.

The Panguil Bay Bridge, which is funded by a loan agreement between the Philippine government and the Korean Export Import Bank, will soon be the longest bridge in the country, exceeding by 1.61 kilometers with the 2.16-kilometer San Juanico Bridge connecting Samar and Leyte Provinces in Eastern Visayas.

The interest rate for the Panguil Bay Bridge Project is 0.15 percent per annum.

On Loans

Debunking the myth propagated by uninformed critics, Department of Finance Secretary Sonny Dominguez noted that the country's external debt is in fact low and declining, plunging from 66.6 percent of GDP in 2005 to 22.5 percent as of end of June 2018. Moreover, in comparison to our neighbors in Asia, the Philippines is still below the average of 30.9 percent of GDP. For instance, external debt ratio of Indonesia and Malaysia is at 41.4 percent (2017), and 68.7 percent (2017), respectively. The fiscal deficit of the country is also within the three percent deficit target at 2.2 percent of GDP in 2017.

In its Economic Bulletin, DOF also noted that borrowing is used to finance productive capital expenditures, which ensure that future servicing streams can be financed by revenues collected from a growing economy. In formulating the Public Investment Program (PIP), the economic internal rate of return (EIRR) of each project should at least be equal to 15 percent. Most of the projects approved have EIRRs exceeding 20 percent.

Build, Build, Build is a program that is not only necessary but is in fact long overdue.

Panguil Bay Bridge

Team Philippines

While in New York, I met with Ethel Capuno, a former colleague from the United Nations Development Program, whom I had the pleasure of working with in the Haiyan Response. She is now based in Headquarters as an Operations Specialist providing guidance to UNDP operations in Least Developed Countries in Asia and Africa.

We had a discussion as to whether the Philippines should still be referred to as a "third world country," a political term which was coined during the cold war to refer to non-allied countries, nations that were neither with the United States or with the Soviet Union.

She told me she had stopped thinking and referring to the Philippines as a third world country. To her, it is a developing country with mid-level human development index. To me, it is a country about to realize its full potential.

In the International Monetary Fund's World Economic Outlook, the Philippines ranked 39th out of 192 countries in terms of nominal Gross Domestic Product. It is expected to climb up by nine steps by 2023. The report predicts that the GDP of the country will increase to $523 billion (from $332 billion) in five years, securing the 30th place in the global ranking. Together with India, Thailand and Vietnam, the Philippines is classified as among the "emerging economies of Asia".

In the same report, the Philippines also ranked 29th out of 192 countries in terms of GDP when measured in purchasing power parity (PPP,) It is predicted to climb up to 25th by 2023.

Department of Finance Secretary Sonny Dominguez reported during the 'Tatak ng Pagbabago: Tatak ng Pag-unlad' Pre-SONA forum that in the first quarter of this year, the Philippine economy grew by 6.8 percent. This is far superior compared to the recorded average GDP growth of the country of 4.4 percent in the period of 2000 to 2009. It is also higher than the recorded average GDP growth of 4.9 percent for emerging market and developing countries in 2017.

In the last two years since President Rodrigo Duterte assumed position, the Philippine government has allotted 5.4 percent of its GDP in infrastructure development, which is more than double the 2.5 percent average of the last six administration in a span of five decades. Now, infrastructure spending under Build, Build, Build is 42 percent higher compared to last 2017.

The Philippines Investment Forum

Under the leadership of Department of Public Works and Highways Secretary Mark Villar, DPWH has completed 29,264 kilometers of roads.

Under the Tourism Road Infrastructure Program, a total of ₱121 billion was allocated from 2016 to 2021 for the construction, improvement, and upgrading of about 4,268 kilometers of roads leading to declared tourism destinations.

Under the Agri-Infrastructure Support program, a total of ₱38.6 billion was released from 2016 to 2020 for the construction of 3,859 kilometers of farm-to-market roads.

In the next four years, a total of 1,101 kilometers of High Standard Highways or Expressways in Luzon will be constructed — double the length of the existing expressway network spanning 382 kilometers. Once completed, travel time from Ilocos to Bicol will be reduced from 19 hours and 40 minutes to eight hours and 15 minutes.

Davao City Coastal Road Project

Bacolod - Negros Occidental Economic Highway

Infrastructure projects that will spur regional economic development and competitiveness, like the Bacolod-Negros Occidental Economic Highway, the Davao City Coastal Road, the Davao City By-Pass Road, and the Mindanao Road Development Network have also started construction.

The Inter-Island Linkage Project, a series of short and long-span bridges linking island provinces, is also in its advanced stages. The preparation of the Feasibility Study and Detailed Design of six bridges, namely the 22-kilometer Bohol-Leyte Bridge, the 5.5-kilometer Negros-Cebu Bridge, the 24.5-kilometer Cebu-Bohol Bridge, the 18.2-kilometer Luzon (Sorsogon)-Samar Bridge, the 4.4-kilometer Davao-Samal Bridge, and the 28-kilometer Bataan-Cavite Inter-Link Bridge will be undertaken under Asian Development Bank's Infrastructure Preparation and Innovation Facility (IPIF).

In 2018, the construction of the Panguil Bay Bridge, a 3.77-kilometer bridge connecting the city of Tangub in Misamis Occidental and the Municipality of Tubod in Lanao del Norte, started. This will reduce travel time between the two provinces from 2.5 hours to 10 minutes.

When completed, the Inter-Island Linkage network will connect Luzon, Visayas, and Mindanao via land travel.

The Philippines is on its way to realizing its full potential and while there may have been bumps in the road — "*Per aspera ad astra* (through hardship to the stars), as the old saying goes — the gem cannot be polished without trials.

The Philippines' PPP ranked 2nd
in The Economist's Asia Infrascope Index

In The Economist Intelligence Unit (EIU) 2018 Infrascope Report, the Philippines ranked second in the Asia Infrascope Index, "a benchmarking tool that evaluates the capacity of countries to implement sustainable and efficient public-private partnerships (PPPs)." Apart from Thailand, the Philippines was the only country in Asia that was considered "mature" as far as the regulatory environment is concerned.

The concept of Public-Private Partnerships (PPP) in the Philippines dates back to as early as 1986, when Proclamation No. 50 created the Asset Privatization Trust (APT) and the Committee on Privatization, and has evolved since with the enactment of several laws, including RA 6957, the Build-Operate-Transfer Law in 1991; RA 7718, and Memorandum Order No. 166 in 1993; Administrative Order 103 in 2000; Executive Order 144 in 2002; Executive Order No. 8 in 2010; and Executive Order No. 136 in 2013.

The current structure of PPP in the Philippines has been improved to streamline and clarify processes, including procedures for managing unsolicited proposals, joint-venture agreements, and appointment of probity advisors for PPP procurement.

According to the Public Private Partnership Center, there are at least 17 PPP projects in the Philippines under implementation, 15 of which are solicited and two are unsolicited. The total project cost is pegged at ₱328.67 billion.

These include Skyway Stage 3, an 18.68-kilometer elevated expressway stretched over Metro Manila from Buendia, Makati City to Balintawak, Quezon City; C5 South Link Expressway, a 7.7-kilometer expressway stretching from R-1 Expressway to SLEX/C5; and NLEX Harbor Spur Link, a 2.6-kilometer expressway connecting the existing 5.58-kilometer NLEX Harbor Link to Port Area in Manila.

Moreover, there are at least 41 projects in the pipeline, with unsolicited projects outnumbering solicited types. The 27 unsolicited projects currently cost over ₱3 trillion in comparison to the 14 solicited projects, which are currently at development stage.

During the administration of President Rodrigo Duterte, the government supported another type of modality, the hybrid PPP to complement the traditional PPP structure in the government's Build, Build, Build program. In this modality, the government builds and finances infrastructure projects and later on bids out the operation and maintenance aspects to the private sector.

So far, the government has two hybrid PPP projects – the Clark International Airport and the New Bohol Airport.

In December 2018, Bases Conversion and Development Authority (BCDA), in partnership with the Department of Transportation (DOTr), awarded the Clark International Airport's Operation and Maintenance contract to the four-member North Luzon Airport Consortium (NLAC). According to former Socioeconomic Planning Secretary Ernesto Pernia, NLAC's financial bid offer of 18.25 percent annual gross revenue percentage share is almost twice the minimum rate of 10 percent as approved by the NEDA Board. According to the Public-Private Partnership Center, the bid offer is more than 80 percent better than the minimum rate set.

The supplemental loan pact for the New Bohol Airport expansion project was signed in October 2018, only four months after the NEDA Board approved it on June 19, 2018.

Today, the economy of the Philippines is the world's 29th largest by GDP (Purchasing Power Parity), according to the 2021 estimate of the International Monetary Fund (IMF). In 2019, the Philippines breached the trillion mark after it recorded a GDP in purchasing power parity of $1.03 trillion. This is the first time that the tiger cub economy reached the trillion mark, alongside countries like the United States, China, India, Japan, Germany, Russia, Indonesia, Brazil, the United Kingdom, France, Mexico, Italy, Turkey, Korea, Spain, Saudi Arabia, and Canada.

NLEX Harbor Link

10 road trips to do in 2021

When I was in college, I dreamed about the Philippines I did not see. I wanted to explore the 81 provinces with my own eyes, to meet the Filipinos who lived there, to hear about their dreams and aspirations. As I jumped from one province to the other, I realized that traveling across the country was difficult. Even the trip to the airport could take two hours.

As a student, I dreamed of a nation without roadblocks. I didn't realize that 10 years after, I'd be part of President Rodrigo Duterte's Build, Build, Build team. And since July 2016, according to Secretary Mark Villar, DPWH has completed 25,343 kilometers of roads, and 5,271 bridges.

People would often ask — what is Build, Build, Build? It is a springboard, a chance to turn a dream of connecting Luzon, Visayas, and Mindanao into a reality. It means connecting 81 provinces, 146 cities, and 1,489 municipalities.

In case you're in the mood for a road trip, here's a list of projects you can try.

Sorsogon Coastal Road

01 Sorsogon City Coastal Bypass Road

If you want to explore Paguriran Lagoon, or go hiking on Mount Pulog, then you might want to drive through the scenic 5.52-kilometer Sorsogon City Coastal Bypass Road, which traverses seven barangays — Pangpang, Tugos, Cambulaga, Talisay, Sirangan, Sampaloc, and Balogo. The new expressway, equipped with bicycles lanes, starts at Daang Maharlika and ends at the existing transport terminal in Sorsogon City.

02 Tarlac-Pangasinan-La Union Expressway

If you are a thalassophile like me, then you'd love the Tarlac-Pangasinan-La Union Expressway (TPLEX), an 89.31-kilometer expressway connecting Tarlac, Pangasinan, and La Union.

Whether you're surfing in San Juan or cliff-diving in Tangadan Falls in San Gabriel or hanging by the kitchen bar of Flotsam & Jetsam, the completion of the new section from Pozorrubio in Pangasinan to Rosario in La Union will make your travel more efficient by almost 50 percent.

Now, travel time from Manila to Baguio has been reduced to only three hours.

03 Coron – Busuanga Road

If you are planning to hop from Coron to Busuanga, and to Calamian Islands, you may opt to take the newly widened 72.53-kilometer Coron-Busuanga Road.

Coron Busuanga Road

Alimusgan-Bai-Caganayan Road leading to Kaparkan Falls, Brgy. Caganayan, Tineg, Abra, CAR

04 Central Luzon Link Expressway

Want to visit Minalungao National Park in Nueva Ecija? It's closer with the opening of the 30-kilometer Central Luzon Link Expressway spanning from Tarlac City to Cabanatuan. Travel time between Tarlac and Nueva Ecija will be reduced from 70 minutes to only 20 minutes.

05 Boracay Circumferential Road, Region VI

Heading to Boracay? It would be hard to miss the newly widened 21.64-kilometer Boracay Circumferential Road. The new road has reduced travel time from Cagban Port or Tambisaan Port to Ilig-Iligan Beach by about 40 to 45 minutes.

06 Alimusgan-Bai-Caganayan Road leading to Kaparkan Falls, Brgy. Caganayan, Tineg, Abra, CAR

Never been to Kaparkan Falls in Tineg, Abra? Drive by the 11-kilometer Alimusgan-Bai-Caganayan Road to reach the waterfall plunging over limestone terraces.

Subic Freeport Expressway

07 Guindulman – Anda – Badiang – Cogtong Road

Want to swim in a limestone sinkhole or enjoy ancient cave paintings? Drive through the 12.84-kilometer Guindulman – Anda – Badiang – Cogtong Road. Nearby are the Combento Cave, the Cabagnow Cave Pool, and the Lamanok Island.

08 Urdaneta City Bypass Road

Heading to Pangasinan to visit the Manaoag Church and the Hundred Islands of Alaminos? Try the 7.2-kilometer Urdaneta Western Bypass Road, which serves as an alternate route to Manila North Road, Urdaneta-Dagupan Road, and Urdaneta-Manaoag Road.

09 Subic Freeport Expressway

Heading for Bataan or Zambales? Try the new 8.2-kilometer Subic Freeport Expressway, which connects Hermosa in Bataan to Subic in Zambales within a span of 10 minutes.

10 Davao City Coastal Road

The 18-kilometer Davao City Coastal Road passes through the coastal lines of Junctions Bago and Talomo, Matina Aplaya, Roxas Avenue, Sta. Ana Wharf, and R. Castillo. When completed, it is expected to reduce travel time from Davao-Cotabato Road to R. Castillo Avenue by about 30 minutes.

Daang Kalikasan

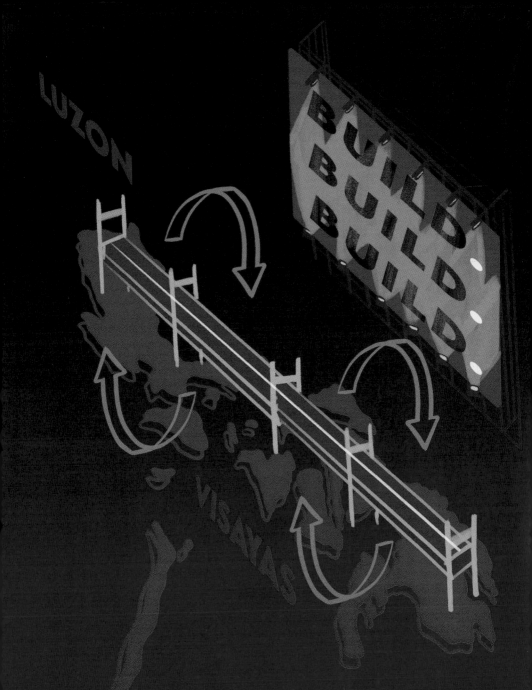

10 things to know about the plan to connect Luzon, Visayas, and Mindanao

The Philippines is an archipelago of 7,640 islands. Due to the lack of infrastructure investment in the last five decades, the cost to transport goods within the country has been expensive. The 2.1-kilometer San Juanico Bridge, which was built in 1969, is still the longest bridge 50 years later.

This will no longer be the case with President Rodrigo Duterte's Mega Bridge Project, a series of short and long-span bridges linking island provinces to eventually connect Luzon, Visayas, and Mindanao via land travel.

People would often ask — what is Build, Build, Build? It is a springboard, a chance to turn a dream of connecting Luzon, Visayas, and Mindanao into a reality. It means connecting 81 provinces, 146 cities, and 1,489 municipalities.

According to Department of Public Works and Highways Secretary Mark Villar, eight bridges under the Mega Bridge Masterplan are in the advanced stages: the Bataan-Cavite Interlink Bridge, the Panglao-Tagbilaran City Offshore Connector Bridge, the Guicam Bridge, the Panay-Guimaras Bridge, the Cebu-Mactan Bridge and Coastal Road Construction Project, the Panguil Bay Bridge, and the Samal Island-Davao City Connector Bridge.

Here are ten facts about the Mega Bridge Masterplan:

The 3.169-kilometer Panguil Bay Bridge will connect the city of Tangub in Misamis Occidental and the municipality of Tubod in Lanao del Norte. Once completed, travel time from Lanao del Norte to Misamis Occidental will be reduced from 2.5 hours (via the Tangub-Molave-Tubod Road or the Tangub – Kapatagan – Tubod Road) to only seven minutes.

The 3.98-kilometer toll-free Davao – Samal Island Bridge will serve about 25,000 vehicles a day and reduce travel time from Davao City to the Island Garden City of Samal from 30 minutes to only two to five minutes.

The 32.47-kilometer Panay Guimaras Negros Bridge will connect the islands of Iloilo, Aklan, Capiz, Antique, Guimaras, and Negros. When completed the travel time from Iloilo to Buenavista in Guimaras will be reduced from 45 minutes to only 10 minutes. Moreover, travel time from Guimaras to Pulupandan in Negros will be reduced from 60 minutes to only 15 minutes.

The 32.15-kilometer, four-lane Bataan-Cavite Interlink Bridge will start from Mariveles, Bataan and end in Naic, Cavite. It will involve the construction of two navigation bridges — the North Channel Bridge and the South Channel Bridge with main spans of 400 meters and 900 meters, respectively. When the Bataan-Cavite Interlink Bridge is completed, travel time between Bataan and Cavite will be reduced from nearly five hours to only 40 minutes.

The Cebu-Mactan Bridge and Coastal Construction Project will involve the construction of a 3.3-kilometer bridge with an elevated viaduct of 2.93 kilometers and a 4.9-kilometer coastal road expressway with a 4.57-kilometer elevated viaduct. When completed, travel time from Mactan Cebu International Airport to Cebu Port area will be reduced from 45 minutes to only 25 minutes.

The 1.2-kilometer four-lane Panglao–Tagbilaran City Offshore Connector Bridge will connect Bohol to the island municipalities of Dauis and Panglao. Construction of the two short span bridges spanning 42.7 meters and its 1.3-kilometer approach road started in 2018.

The Panglao – Tagbilaran City Offshore Connector Bridge bridge will reduce the travel time from Tagbilaran City Seaport to Panglao Island from 45 minutes to only 15 minutes.

In partnership with Asian Development Bank, three bridges in Tawi-Tawi will be constructed: the 540-meter Nalil – Sikkiat Bridge, the 569-meter Tongsinah – Paniongan Bridge, and the 680-kilometer Malassa – Lupa Pula Bridge.

The 1.208-kilometer Guicam Bridge will connect the Olutanga Island to Zamboanga Peninsula via the Canalizo Strait. This is part of the Improving Growth Corridors in Mindanao Road Sector Masterplan.

Also included in the Masterplan are the Bohol-Leyte Bridge, the Cebu-Bohol Link Bridge, and the Luzon – Samar Bridge.

Panguil Bay Bridge

Cebu - Mactan (4th Bridge)

Davao–Samal Island Bridge

Panglao-Tagbilaran City Offshore Connector

Skyway Stage 3

CHAPTER FOUR

EDSA DECONGESTION PROGRAM

Duterte's solution to EDSA traffic

Construction of Epifanio de Los Santos Avenue, more popularly known as EDSA, started in the 1930s. Initially, the project, which was named North-South Circumferential Road, only spanned from North Luzon Expressway to Magallanes Interchange. It was only in the 1960s that EDSA was extended to Taft, Roxas Boulevard, and Caloocan.

Mindanao Avenue Extension

Today, EDSA, the 23.8-kilometer circumferential highway, has become a source of frustration. The project, which was originally intended to accommodate a maximum capacity of 288,000 vehicles a day, is being used by 402,000 vehicles. In other words, EDSA has exceeded its capacity by about 39 percent.

In 2012, the Philippines lost ₱2.4 billion a day due to Metro Manila traffic. Six years later, a study conducted by Japan International Cooperation Agency said the number had gone up to ₱3.5 billion a day due to traffic congestion in Metro Manila. Now, road usage in Metro Manila is at about 13.4 million trips per day and could go as high as 16.1 million in 17 years. Economic losses could also rise up to ₱5.4 billion in 2035 without any infrastructure interventions.

From the onset of the administration, President Rodrigo Duterte and Public Works and Highways Secretary Mark Villar have been working on a plan to decongest EDSA through the Build, Build, Build program.

The EDSA Decongestion Program, which is composed of 23 projects amounting to over ₱383 billion is well underway. Secretary Villar is confident that President Duterte's promise of decongesting EDSA will be delivered before the end of his term.

Five years after, major road and bridge projects have already been completed including the NLEX Harbor Link Segment 10, the Radial Road 10 Exit Ramp, the

Mindanao Avenue Extension Segment 2C, the Metro Manila Skyway Stage 3, the Fort Bonifacio-Nichols Road (Lawton Avenue) Widening,the Estrella - Pantaleon Bridge and the Bonifacio Global City-Ortigas Center Link Road Project, among others.The R-10 Exit Ramp of NLEX Harbor Link is a 2.6-kilometer, four-lane elevated ramp extending NLEX Harbor Link Segment 10 to Radial Road 10 using C-3 road, effectively cutting travel time from Quezon City to Manila from two hours to only 20 to 30 minutes.

The Mindanao Avenue Extension is a 3.2-kilometer, four-lane divided highway from NLEX to Gen. Luis Avenue, connecting the areas of Valenzuela, North Caloocan, and NLEX. When completed, travel time between Quirino Highway and General Luis road will be reduced from one hour and 30 minutes to only 20 minutes.

The Metro Manila Skyway Stage 3 Project (MMSS3) is an 18.30-kilometer elevated expressway spanning from Buendia in Makati City to the North Luzon Expressway in Balintawak, Quezon City. The project is expected to decongest Metro Manila by at least 55,000 vehicles daily and reduce travel time from Makati to Quezon City from two hours to only 15 to 20 minutes.

Widening of the 3.3-kilometer Fort Bonifacio – Nichols Field Road from four lanes to six lanes will also be completed in 2020. It is expected to complement the Bonifacio Global City (BGC) – Ortigas Center Link Road Project, which effectively connects BGC and Ortigas Central Business within 12 minutes. The project is composed of the Sta. Monica-Lawton Bridge, a 440-meter, four-lane bridge across Pasig River connecting Lawton Avenue in Makati City and Santa Monica Street in Pasig City, and the Lawton Avenue – Global City Viaduct, a 565-meter four-lane viaduct structure traversing Lawton Avenue onwards to the entrance of BGC.

DPWH is also set to begin civil works on the following projects: NLEX Harbor Link Segment 8.2 from Mindanao Avenue to Commonwealth Avenue in Quezon City and six bridges under the Metro Manila Logistics Network, namely: North and South Harbor Bridge, the Palanca-Villegas Bridge, the East Bank-West Bank Bridge 2, the Marcos Highway - St. Mary Avenue Bridge, Homeowner's Drive - A Bonifacio Bridge, and Kabayani St - Matandang Balara Bridge.

Sec Mark Villar takes a selfie with Build, Build, Build team.

EDSA decongestion masterplan:
Connecting NLEX and SLEX in 30 minutes

The problem surrounding the 90-year-old Epifanio de los Santos Avenue (EDSA), a 23.8-kilometer circumferential highway, needs no introduction. The project, which was started in the 1930s, has long exceeded its maximum capacity of 288,000 vehicles a day. Now, there are about 402,000 vehicles using the alignment every day, 39 percent more than its intended capacity.

Inevitably, the absence of any substantial infrastructure intervention has resulted in a congestion level of about 71 percent, the second worst traffic congestion in the world. In other words, drivers in Metro Manila would need to spend an average of 71 percent extra travel time in traffic.

But the congestion dilemma has also become a source of economic frustration. In 2012, the Philippines lost ₱2.4 billion a day due to Metro Manila traffic. Six years later, a study conducted by the Japan International Cooperation Agency said the number had gone up to ₱3.5 billion.

This is about to change with the completion of the EDSA Decongestion Masterplan, a network of 23 infrastructure projects meant to connect the northern and southern most parts of Manila within a span of 20 to 30 minutes.

From the onset of the Duterte administration, Public Works and Highways Secretary Mark Villar has been working on a plan that would divert about 200,000 vehicles away from EDSA, C5, and other major thoroughfares.

One of the 23 projects under the EDSA Decongestion Masterplan is the Metro Manila Skyway Stage 3 Project, an 18.30-kilometer elevated expressway from Buendia in Makati City to the North Luzon Expressway (NLEX) in Balintawak, Quezon City.

The project, which is composed of five sections, is expected to decongest traffic on EDSA, C5, and other major thoroughfares (e.g. Quezon Avenue, Araneta Avenue, Nagtahan Avenue, and Quirino Avenue) by at least 55,000 vehicles daily.

Now that the project is completed, travel time from Makati to Quezon City has been reduced from two hours to only 15 to 20 minutes. Travel time from NLEX to SLEX has been shortened from 2.5 hours to only 30 minutes. Residents of Quezon City will also be able to reach NAIA in just 20 minutes.

Makati to Manila

The opening of the Skyway Stage 3 project is only a precursor to the completion of a network of big-ticket projects, which will all be completed by 2022.

For instance, Skyway will eventually connect to the newly opened NLEX Harbor Link Segment 10 and NLEX Radial Road 10 ramp, effectively creating a direct route from Makati to Manila via the NLEX SLEX Connector, an eight-kilometer elevated expressway spanning from C3 Road in Caloocan City to PUP Sta. Mesa in Manila.

This connection will effectively create a loop within Metro Manila where every city is connected within a 20 to 30-minute timeframe.

The EDSA Decongestion Masterplan also includes the BGC-Ortigas Link Bridge, the Pantaleon-Estrella Bridge, the Binondo-Intramuros Bridge, the Katipunan Extension, the Laguna Lake Expressway, and the Mindanao Avenue Extension, among others.

Inspection of the NLEX Harbor Link Project

25 Build, Build, Build projects to decongest Metro Manila

The story of EDSA need not be told. Anyone who has set foot in Manila would know — and would have complained at some point — about the world's worst city for drivers.

While other nationalities would ask about the weather, Filipinos would talk about the traffic. This is not at all surprising. The debate about Metro Manila's "true midpoint" is not new. It happens almost every day — over family dinners, coffee meet-ups, high school reunions, and even on dates. I remember one friend who broke up with his boyfriend because she could not handle a "long distance relationship". The five-hour travel time to and from Parañaque and Fairview took a toll on their relationship. And honestly, no one could blame them. EDSA has become a source of frustration for many, if not all drivers, commuters, and passengers.

The problem, however, is expected. Metro Manila is one of the world's most densely populated cities with over 42,000 inhabitants per square kilometer. But EDSA, the 23.8-kilometer circumferential highway stretching from Taft to Caloocan, has not been extended after the 1960s. The project, which was originally intended to accommodate a maximum capacity of 288,00 vehicles a day, is being used by 402,000 vehicles. In other words, EDSA has exceeded its capacity by about 39 percent.

The absence of a genuine infrastructure intervention has already caused the Philippines billions of pesos. In 2012, the Philippines lost ₱2.4 billion a day due to Metro Manila traffic, according to Japan International Cooperation Agency. Six years later, the number had gone up to ₱3.5 billion a day due to traffic congestion in Metro Manila. Now, road usage in Metro Manila is at about 13.4 million trips per day and this could go as high as 16.1 million in 17 years.

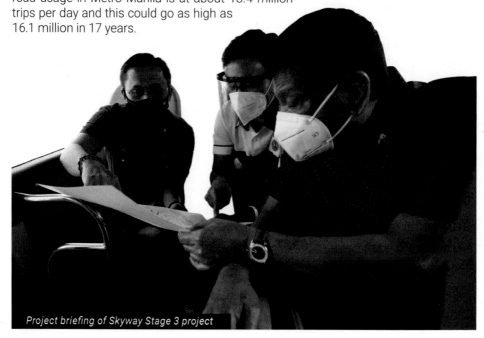

Project briefing of Skyway Stage 3 project

EDSA Decongestion Master Plan

Since 2016, President Rodrigo Duterte and Public Works and Highways Secretary Mark Villar have embarked on a plan to decongest EDSA and solve traffic through the Build, Build, Build program.

According to Villar, the EDSA Decongestion Program, which is composed of 23 projects amounting to over ₱383 billion, is well underway. President Duterte's promise of decongesting EDSA is at hand.

Six big-ticket projects in Metro Manila were made accessible to the public in 2020. These include the NLEX Harbor Link R-10 Exit Ramp, the Mindanao Avenue Extension Segment 2C, Metro Manila Skyway Stage 3, Fort Bonifacio-Nichols Road (Lawton Avenue) Widening, and the Bonifacio Global City – Ortigas Center Link Road Project.

Manila to QC in 15 minutes

The NLEX Harbor Link Segment 10 is a 5.58-kilometer, six-lane divided elevated expressway utilizing the existing PNR railroad tracks connecting McArthur Highway, C-3 road in Caloocan and Malabon. The project, when completed, effectively shortens travel time from Valenzuela City to C3 in Caloocan from one hour to only five minutes.

Skyway Stage 3

Estrella Pantaleon Bridge

The NLEX Harbor Link Segment 10 will extend and connect to the Radial Road 10 Exit Ramp, a 2.6-kilometer, four-lane elevated ramp, which connects Caloocan, Malabon, and Valenzuela to Manila. When the project is completed, travel time from Port Area in Manila to NLEX will be reduced from two hours to only 10 to 15 minutes.

Quirino Highway to Gen. Luis Road in 20 minutes

Another project that eases the travel in the east-west thoroughfare and targets to decongest and connect Quirino Highway and General Luis Road is the Mindanao Avenue Extension Segment 2C project, which was started in the 1980s.

The Mindanao Avenue Extension Segment 2C project is a 3.2-kilometer, four-lane divided highway from NLEX to Gen. Luis Avenue, connecting the areas of Bulacan, Valenzuela, North Caloocan, and Quezon City. When completed, travel time between Quirino Highway and General Luis Road will be reduced from one hour and 30 minutes to only 20 minutes.

Makati to QC in 20 minutes

The main line of the Metro Manila Skyway Stage 3 Project (MMSS3), an 18.30-kilometer elevated expressway spanning from Buendia in Makati City to the North Luzon Expressway in Balintawak, Quezon City, was inaugurated in January 2021. It will have several access ramps or interchanges, namely Buendia Avenue (South Super Highway, Makati City), Pres. Quirino Avenue (Malate, Manila), Plaza Dilao (Paco, Manila), Nagtahan/Aurora Boulevard (Manila), E. Rodriguez Avenue (Quezon City), Quezon Avenue (Quezon City), Sgt. Rivera St. (Quezon City), and NLEX.

The project is expected to decongest Metro Manila by at least 55,000 vehicles daily and reduce travel time from Makati to Quezon City from two hours to only 15 to 20 minutes.

Estrella Pantaleon Bridge Inauguration

*Inspection of the **BGC Ortigas Link Bridge Project***

BGC to Taguig in 12 minutes

Widening of the 3.3-kilometer Fort Bonifacio – Nichols Field Road from four lanes to six lanes will also be completed in 2022.

It is expected to complement the newly completed Bonifacio Global City (BGC) – Ortigas Center Link Road Project, which effectively connects BGC and Ortigas Central Business within 12 minutes. The project is composed of the Sta. Monica-Lawton Bridge, a 440-meter, four- lane bridge across Pasig River connecting Lawton Avenue in Makati City and Santa Monica Street in Pasig City, and the Lawton Avenue – Global City Viaduct, a 565-meter four-lane viaduct structure traversing Lawton Avenue onward to the entrance of BGC.

Civil works to begin this year

DPWH is also set to begin civil works on the following projects this year: NLEX Harbor Link Segment 8.2 from Mindanao Avenue to Commonwealth Avenue in Quezon City; the Metro Manila Priority Bridges Seismic Improvement Project covering the retrofitting of Guadalupe and Lambingan Bridges; and the Pasig River & Manggahan Floodway Bridges Construction Project inclusive of five bridges — North & South Harbor Bridge, Palanca-Villegas Bridge, Blumentritt-Antipolo Bridge, Beata-Manalo Bridge crossing Pasig River, and the Eastbank-Westbank Bridge 2 crossing Manggahan Floodway.

Other projects

Apart from these, the EDSA Decongestion Masterplan also includes the following projects: Radial Road 10, NLEX-SLEX Connector Road, Katipunan Avenue Extension, Southeast Metro Manila Expressway (C6 Phase 1), Samar Street, Laguna Lake Highway, C5 South Link Expressway, NAIA Expressway Phase 2, Binondo-Intramuros Bridge, Estrella-Pantaleon Bridge, Marcos Highway - St. Mary Avenue Bridge, Homeowner's Drive - A. Bonifacio Bridge, Kabayani Street-Matandang Balara Bridge, and the Bataan-Cavite Interlink Bridge.

EDSA
DECONGESTION
PROJECTS
(AN OVERVIEW)

Radial Road 10

Project Description: The 9.7-kilometer road traversing the old Smokey Mountain area congested by Informal Settlers is now a high-capacity highway that will offset the heavy volume of vehicles on major highways like EDSA and C5.

NLEX-SLEX Connector Road

Project Description: An eight-kilometer, all-elevated, four-lane toll expressway extending the NLEX southward from the end of Segment 10 in C3 Road, Caloocan City to PUP Sta. Mesa, Manila and connecting to the Skyway Stage 3, and mostly traversing along the PNR rail track. The project includes two interchanges located at C3 Road/5th Avenue, Caloocan and España Avenue, Manila.

NLEX Harbor Link C3-R10 Section

Project Description: It is a 2.60-kilometer, four-lane (initial) elevated ramp extending the NLEX Harbor Link Segment 10 exit to Radial Road 10 (R-10), using C-3 Road as its route.

NLEX Harbor Link Segment 8.2

Project Description: It is an 8.30-kilometer, four-lane divided (2x2) expressway from Segment 8.1 at Mindanao Avenue, traversing westward to Republic Avenue and turning right to Luzon Avenue up to Commonwealth Avenue in Quezon City.

NLEX Harbor Link Segment 10

Project Description: It is 5.58-kilometer, six-lane divided (2x3) elevated expressway connecting McArthur Highway and C-3. It will utilize the existing PNR railroad tracks that cut across Valenzuela City and Malabon City.

Samar Street

Project Description: The widening of the 1.2-kilometer Samar Street will connect Timog Avenue and Mother Ignacia in Quezon City to EDSA.

7

Mindanao Avenue Extension

Project Description: It is a 3.2-kilometer, four-lane divided highway from intersection of NLEX to Gen. Luis Avenue that will connect the areas of Valenzuela, North Caloocan, Quezon City (Novaliches), and NLEX. Travel time between Quirino Highway and General Luis Road will be reduced from one hour and 30 minutes to 20 minutes.

9

Metro Manila Skyway Stage 3

Project Description: It is an 18.83-kilometer elevated expressway from Buendia in Makati City to the North Luzon Expressway (NLEX) in Balintawak, Quezon City. The project will connect the northern part of Metro Manila to the southern portion within a span of 30 minutes.

8

Kabayani Street-Matandang Balara Bridge

Project Description: It is a 414.9-meter bridge crossing Marikina River connecting Kabayani Road, Stockholm Street, and Delhi Street.

10

Homeowners Drive - A Bonifacio Bridge

Project Description: It is a 594-meter steel arch bridge connecting JP Rizal Street and Lopez Jaena Street in Marikina City.

11

Southeast Metro Manila Expressway (C6 Expressway)

Project Description: It is a 32.664-kilometer toll road from Skyway/FTI in Taguig City to Batasan Complex in Quezon City, which will reduce travel time from Bicutan to Batasan in Quezon City from 1.5 hours to only 26 minutes.

12

Bonifacio Global City - Ortigas Center Link Road Project (Kalayaan Bridge)

Project Description: The 1.3-kilometer bridge and viaduct structure will connect the cities of Pasig, Makati, and Taguig within a span of 12 minutes.

13

Marcos Highway - St. Mary Avenue Bridge

Project Description: It is a 2.1-kilometer bridge crossing Marikina River connecting J.P. Rizal Street and A. Bonifacio Avenue.

14

East Bank - West Bank Bridge

Project Description: The 933-meter bridge will connect the cities of Pasig and Cainta over the Manggahan Floodway.

15A

Retrofitting of the Guadalupe Bridge

Project Description: The Guadalupe Bridge will be retrofitted to seismic bridge design specifications for the safety of about 365,000 motorists who use it daily.

15B

Retrofitting of the Lambingan Bridge

Project Description: The Lambingan Bridge will be rehabilitated to meet improved seismic bridge design specifications necessary to strengthen the resilience of the transport network in Metro Manila.

16

Fort Bonifacio - Nichols Field Road (Lawton Avenue)

Project Description: The project involves the widening of the 3.3-kilometer Nichols Field Road from four lanes to six lanes. It will reduce travel time between SLEX and EDSA or C5 from one hour to only 30 minutes.

17

Sucat - Alabang Skyway Extension

Project Description: It is a three-lane additional carriageway parallel to the existing viaduct alignment. The northbound expansion will start from the midpoint of Susana Heights and Mandarin Overpass and will end at the existing ramp leading to the Skyway near Sucat Interchange with a total length of 3.993 kilometers. The southbound expansion, also a three-lane additional carriageway, will stretch almost parallel to the northbound alignment with a total length of 3.773 kilometers. The project is expected to reduce travel time by at least 50 percent.

NAIA Expressway

Project Description: It is 14.85-kilometer, four-lane elevated expressway from the end point of NAIA Expressway Phase I to PAGCOR Entertainment City. It now provides access to NAIA Terminals 1, 2, and 3 as well as an interface with the Skyway and Cavitex.

Laguna Lake Highway

Project Description: It is 6.94-kilometer, four-lane divided highway with a three-meter-wide segregated bike lane, which has reduced travel time from Taytay to Bicutan from one hour to only 30 minutes.

C5 South Link Expressway

Project Description: It is a 7.70-kilometer, six-lane expressway, which will reduce travel time between R-1 Expressway and SLEX/C5 from 40 minutes to only 10 minutes.

Bataan-Cavite Interlink Bridge

Project Description: The project involves the construction of a 32.15-kilometer, four-lane bridge starting from Barangay Alas-asin in Mariveles, Bataan, crossing Manila Bay, and terminating at Barangay Timalan, Naic, Cavite. It also involves the construction of two navigation bridges, the North Channel Bridge and South Channel Bridge with main spans of 400 meters and 900 meters, respectively. Travel time between Bataan and Cavite will be reduced from nearly five hours to less than two hours.

22

Estrella-Pantaleon Bridge

Project Description: The existing bridge will be replaced by pre-stressed concrete rigid frame bridge (V-shape piers) with corrugated steel webs with four-lane concrete deck slab of approximately 506.46 lineal meters to connect Estrella Street on Makati side to Barangka Drive on Mandaluyong side. Now, travel time between Makati and Mandaluyong is only ten minutes.

24

Binondo - Intramuros Bridge

Project Description: The 680-meter basket-handle tied steel arch bridge connecting Intramuros at Solana Street and Riverside Drive and Binondo at San Fernando Bridge will divert about 29,992 vehicles from Roxas Jr. Bridge and Jones Bridge.

23

Palanca-Villegas Bridge

Project Description: The 225-meter bridge crossing over Pasig River in Manila will accommodate at least 2,900 vehicles every day.

25

North & South Harbor Bridge

Project Description: The 799-meter, four-lane bridge located in Port Area, Manila will divert at least 5,800 vehicles daily.

A few years back while attending the Leaders in Development program of Harvard Kennedy School, our professor asked us to write one thing we aspired to achieve in the next ten years. We wrote it on a piece of paper and placed it beside our name card. I thought for a moment and scribbled — the Philippines achieving its full potential.

In the 1960s, the Philippines had the second highest per capita income in Asia, behind only Japan. A decade later, South Korea had passed our country in per capita income terms largely due to the successful implementation of the Economic Development Plan, where the government and public enterprises accounted for close to 40 percent of the total domestic investment in the period between 1963 and 1979 for the construction of infrastructure projects like highways, port facilities, and bridges.

Prior to the term of President Rodrigo Duterte, average infrastructure spending for the past five decades was only at 2.5 percent of the country's GDP. The 2015 IMF report found that the Philippines had a lower public investment in comparison to other members of ASEAN.

We all know that Build, Build, Build is a program that is not only necessary but is in fact long overdue.

If the Philippines is to achieve its full potential, then it must do something to cut losses due to traffic congestion in Metro Manila, which has gone up to ₱3.5 billion a day. It was at this point that Secretary Mark Villar presented the plan to decongest the 90-year-old EDSA, a 23.8-kilometer circumferential highway, which has long exceeded its maximum capacity of 288,000 vehicles a day.

The plan was not well received at the onset. Few believed it could be done. One critic at one point said "Ambisiyosa. Nasobrahan ang tama sa utak". My reply was brief, "Our leaders ought to be more ambitious about what it plans, commits, and does. Filipinos have long deserved this. If we fail, it is our heads on the line".

Four years later, with the completion of several big-ticket projects in Metro Manila, including the Skyway Stage 3, the NLEX Harbor Link, the Radial Road 10 Spur Link, the Laguna Lake Highway, the promise of returning EDSA back to its 1930 form is within arm's reach.

NLEX Harbor Link Segment 10

The EDSA Decongestion Program
FACT SHEET

01 Metro Manila is one of the world's most densely populated cities with over 42,000 inhabitants per square kilometer. EDSA has not been extended since the 1960s and has already exceeded its capacity by about 39 percent.

02 The EDSA Decongestion Program is composed of 25 projects, which include 14 expressways spanning 121 kilometers and 11 bridges spanning 9.3 kilometers.

03 The mainline of the 18-kilometer Skyway Stage 3 has already been opened to the public alongside 10 ramps: Buendia (northbound on-ramp & southbound off-ramp), Osmena-Quirino (northbound off-ramp), Plaza Dilao (southbound on-ramp), Quezon Avenue (northbound off-ramp and southbound off-ramp), Talayan-Quezon Avenue (northbound on-ramp and southbound off-ramp), and NLEX (northbound off-ramp and southbound on-ramp).

04 Skyway Stage 3 was not completed using its original alignment, which was approved in 2014. Due to right-of-way difficulties, it had to be realigned following the San Juan River alignment. This was approved via Memorandum of Agreement, which was signed on October 25, 2018. Prior to this, site possession for the entire project was only at 8.64 percent.

05 The Memorandum of Agreement signed by San Miguel Corporation included an interconnection structure between Metro Manila Skyway Stage 3 and the NLEX-SLEX Connector. This is the first time in Philippine history that expressways operated by different concessionaires — as in this case, San Miguel Corporation and Metro Pacific — will interconnect.

Metro Manila Skyway Stage 3

06 Ten ramps of Skyway Stage 3 are still being constructed: Quirino (northbound on-ramp), Plaza Dilao (southbound off-ramp), United Nations (southbound off-ramp), Nagtahan (northbound off-ramp, northbound on-ramp), Araneta (northbound on-ramp, southbound off-ramp), and C3 (northbound off-ramp, southbound on-ramp and southbound off-ramp).

07 The NLEX Harbor Link Segment 10, a 5.58-kilometer expressway connecting MacArthur Highway and C3 road will interconnect with the Skyway Stage 3 via the NLEX-SLEX Connector Road, an eight-kilometer expressway connecting the end of Segment 10 in C3 Road in Caloocan to PUP Sta Mesa in Manila.

NLEX Harborlink
(C3 R10 Section)

08 The 2.6-kilometer NLEX Harbor Link C3-Radial Road 10 Spur Link spanning from C3 road in Caloocan to Radial Road 10 in Manila was the first project to be completed following the new COVID-19 protocol. It has effectively reduced travel time from Quezon City to Manila from two hours to only 20 minutes.

09 The NLEX - SLEX Connector is utilizing the Super T Technology, which would reduce construction schedule by about one year. The first five-kilometer segment spanning from C3 road to Espana is expected to be completed within the year.

10 The extension of Harbor Link Segment 10 to R-10 in Manila was strategic following the completion of the 4.75-kilometer Radial Road 10 expansion, a project which spanned seven presidents due to right-of-way issues.

11 The NLEX Harbor Link Segment 8.2 is an 8.35-kilometer, four-lane divided expressway spanning from Segment 8.1 at Mindanao Avenue to Commonwealth Avenue.

12 The Alabang-Sucat Skyway Extension will build two additional lanes from Sucat Main Toll Plaza to Susana Heights. The project is now at 47 percent and will be delivered within the year.

13 The first segment of the 7.7 km C5-South Link Expressway Project spanning from Merville to C5 or SLEX has been completed in July 2019. This will eventually interconnect to Radial Road 1, Sucat Interchange and E. Rodriguez.

Skyway Extension

18 The widening of the 1.086-kilometer Samar Street was completed in December 2018.

19 The 680-meter Binondo-Intramuros Bridge, which will connect Intramuros and Binondo via a viaduct, will be equipped with pedestrian infrastructure.

14 The Southeast Metro Manila Expressway is a 32.664-kilometer toll road expressway spanning from Taguig to Batasan Complex in Quezon City. It will reduce travel time from Bicutan to Batasan from one hour and 50 minutes to only 26 minutes.

20 The BGC-Ortigas Link Bridge, also known as the Kalayaan Bridge, will connect the cities of Taguig, Makati, and Pasig. Now, travel time between the central business districts of BGC and Ortigas has been reduced to only 12 minutes.

15 The 6.94-kilometer Laguna Lake Highway is the first toll-free expressway in Metro Manila with segregated bicycle lanes. It has effectively reduced travel time from Taytay in Rizal to Bicutan from one hour to only 30 minutes.

21 The 506-meter Estrella - Pantaleon Bridge will link Estrella Street in Makati and Barangka Drive in Mandaluyong within a span of 10 minutes.

16 The Fort Bonifacio-Nichols Field Road (Lawton Avenue) involves the widening of the 3.3-kilometer Nichols Field Road. The project which is already at 60 percent is expected to be completed in 2021.

Estrella Pantaleon Bridge

17 The Mindanao Avenue Extension is a 3.2-kilometer highway, which will reduce travel time from Quirino Highway to General Luis Avenue from one hour and 30 minutes to only 20 minutes.

To dream the impossible dream: Connecting NLEX to SLEX in 30 minutes

I n 2016, when we started Build, Build, Build, critics said that the EDSA Decongestion Program is mathematically impossible, that it could not be done, that President Rodrigo Duterte was overpromising, and that Google Maps did not support such assertion. They failed to see the bigger picture — the possibility of a 90-year-old EDSA back to its original 1930s form, a future where Filipinos do not have to debate about Metro Manila's "true midpoint" and a reality wherein every city in Metro Manila can be accessed within a 20 to 30 minute time frame.

I could not blame them. The odds were not in our favor. I could still remember the first time Department of Public Works and Highways Secretary Mark Villar presented the plan to decongest EDSA, a 23.8-kilometer circumferential highway, which has long

Skyway Stage 3

exceeded its maximum capacity of 288,000 vehicles a day. At that time, the congestion level was already at 71 percent — the second worst traffic congestion in the world. In other words, drivers in Metro Manila would need to spend 71 percent extra travel time in traffic.

This has become a source of frustration. I remember one friend who'd complain about being in a long distance relationship because her boyfriend was living in Quezon City. It would take them four hours to travel for a two-hour date. The north and south divide was even becoming more pronounced.

Main alignment of Skyway Stage 3 now open

Since 2016, DPWH has been working on a plan composed of 25 projects that would divert about 200,000 vehicles away from EDSA, C5, and other major thoroughfares.

One of the 25 projects under the 132-kilometer EDSA Decongestion Masterplan is the Metro Manila Skyway Stage 3, an 18-kilometer expressway spanning from Buendia in Makati to Balintawak in Quezon City. The main alignment of the project has already been opened to the public and has effectively reduced travel time from North Luzon Expressway (NLEX) to South Luzon Expressway (SLEX) from two hours to only 30 minutes.

To reach this stage, however, much had to be done. Prior to May 2017 — not even one of 47 National Grid Corporation Poles and 1,312 Meralco poles had been relocated. Site possession for the entire alignment was only at 8.64 percent. No right-of-way was acquired for Section 2A and 2B. Section 3 and Section 4 were only at 2.86 percent and 5.5 percent, respectively.

It was clear that the original alignment had to be revised. In May 2017, Secretary Villar received a proposal from San Miguel Corporation to realign Section 2B to utilize the San Juan River alignment. This was approved via a Memorandum of Agreement, which was signed on October 25, 2018, to include an interconnection structure between Metro Manila Skyway Stage 3 and the NLEX-SLEX Connector.

This is the first time in Philippine history that expressways operated by different concessionaires — as in this case, San Miguel Corporation and Metro Pacific — will interconnect.

And who are the biggest victors of this arrangement? The Filipino people.

For the first time in decades, Filipinos may opt to bypass EDSA and C5. Soon, Filipinos would be able to travel to any city in Metro Manila within a 20 to 30-minute time frame. In a few more months, we will effectively connect the 16 cities and one municipality of Metro Manila — Caloocan, Las Piñas, Makati, Malabon, Mandaluyong, Manila, Marikina, Muntinlupa, Navotas, Parañaque, Pasay, Pasig, Pateros, San Juan, Taguig, Quezon City and Valenzuela — seamlessly via a network of high standard highways and bridges.

Solving the ₱3.5 billion problem in Metro Manila

Back in 2016, when Build, Build, Build was just starting, a lot of people had doubts. One friend looked me in the eye and said, "This was another campaign promise meant to be broken." We were likened to ardent suitors prepared to say anything. We could not blame them. At that time, it did seem impossible. Traffic in Metro Manila was costing us ₱3.5 billion a day. EDSA has exceeded its capacity by over a hundred thousand vehicles. Government projects were delayed for years — with some projects implemented only after several decades. But while we were all very familiar with this reality, it was not a reality we were prepared to accept. The Philippines was far from its full potential. To many of us, it was a chance to realize a dream. It was a chance to shape history and usher in the Golden Age of Infrastructure.

When Secretary Mark Villar first laid out the plan for the Luzon Spine Expressway, a 1,101-kilometer network of high-standard highways in Luzon, about twice the existing network of 382 kilometers, the objective was to ensure every major city in Metro Manila would be connected within a 20 to 30-minute timeframe and that travel time from Ilocos to Bicol would be reduced by half, from 19 hours and 40 minutes to eight hours and 15 minutes.

So when President Duterte exclaimed about cutting travel time from Buendia to Cubao to only five minutes, a number thought it was impossible. For the Build, Build, Build team, this has always been the target. Since the start of the administration, Sec. Villar has instituted a number of reforms founded on basic premises of science and technology — the creation of masterplans, decentralization of right-of-way authority, drone monitoring, and geo-tagging, among others.

For instance, just this year, a number of game-changing projects will be opened to the public.

Skyway Stage 3

The Plaza Dilao Ramp of Skyway Stage 3, an 18.68-kilometer elevated expressway stretched over Metro Manila from Buendia, Makati City, to Balintawak, Quezon City, will be opened to the public this July. It will reduce travel time from Buendia, Makati City to Balintawak, Quezon City, from the current two hours to just 15 to 20 minutes.

The project, which was inaugurated in January 2021, will have several access ramps/interchanges, including Buendia Avenue (South Super Highway, Makati City), Pres. Quirino Avenue (Malate, Manila), Plaza Dilao (Paco, Manila), Nagtahan/Aurora Boulevard (Manila), E. Rodriguez Avenue (Quezon City), Quezon Avenue (Quezon City), Sgt. Rivera St. (Quezon City), and NLEX.

Section 1 from Buendia Avenue in Makati City to Quirino Avenue in Nagtahan, Manila, is now 83 percent completed, while Section 3 from Ramon Magsaysay Avenue to Balintawak is 81 percent completed.

C5 Southlink

Phase 1 of C-5 South Link Expressway, a 7.7-kilometer expressway stretching from R-1 Expressway to SLEX/C5, was made accessible to the public in July 2019.

Segment 3A1, which spans two kilometers from Merville to C5/SLEX, will reduce travel time from Paranaque to Taguig and Makati from one hour to only 10 to 15 minutes.

NLEX Harbor Spur Link

Also expected to be completed within the year is the 2.6-km NLEX Harbor Spur Link, which connects to the existing 5.58-kilometer NLEX Harbor Link connecting Karuhatan in Valenzuela City to C3 Road in Caloocan City. The first truck-graded expressway is expected to reduce travel time from Port Area in Manila to Quezon City from 1.5 hours to only 10 minutes.

John Lennon was right — A dream you dream alone is only a dream. A dream you dream together is a reality.

Inspection of Skyway Stage 3

9 new bridges across Pasig River

The land area of Tokyo is thrice the size of Metro Manila but the vehicle density in Manila is higher. There are about 9.3 million vehicles competing in the Philippines' limited road network. In 2016, majority of the 32,770 kilometers of national roads are at saturation levels — with EDSA exceeding its road capacity of 288,000 vehicles a day.

Metro Manila alone accounts for about 13.4 million trips per day. Studies show that this can increase to as high as 16.1 million in 17 years.

Due to the traffic congestion brought about by the lack of infrastructure, JICA estimated losses in Metro Manila at about ₱2.4 billion pesos a day or about 0.8 percent of our GDP.

The instruction of President Rodrigo Duterte from the onset has been very clear. Put an end to EDSA traffic.

The first area to be surveyed by drone was the Pasig River alignment. This was the start of what Secretary Mark Villar would later call the Metro Manila Logistics Improvement Network.

In addition to the 26 existing bridges crossing Pasig River, Marikina River, and Manggahan Floodway, which cater to about 1.30 million vehicles daily, nine new bridges in the area will be constructed to provide alternative linkages between major thoroughfares and increase the number of usable roadways that would decongest traffic in EDSA and other major roads in Metro Manila.

Three bridges under the masterplan will be completed within the year: the BGC-Ortigas Link Road Project, the Binondo-Intramuros Bridge, and the Estrella-Pantaleon Bridge Project.

The Bonifacio Global City – Ortigas Center Link Road Project involves the construction of a 440-meter Sta Monica to Lawton Bridge and a 565-meter viaduct structure, which will connect Lawton Avenue in Makati to BGC.

When completed by the third quarter of this year, traveling between the central business districts of Taguig and Pasig will only take 12 minutes, and traffic congestion at EDSA and C-5 Road, particularly along Guadalupe Bridge and Bagong Ilog Bridge, will be alleviated by about 25 percent.

On the other hand, the Estrella-Pantaleon Bridge is a 506-meter, four-lane prestressed concrete rigid frame bridge with corrugated steel webs, to connect Estrella Street in Makati to Barangka Drive in Mandaluyong. The project is expected to alleviate EDSA and C5 by about 30,000 vehicles per day.

Moreover, the 680-meter Binondo-Intramuros Bridge is a basket-handle tied steel arch bridge, which connects Intramuros at Solana Street and Riverside Drive and Binondo at San Fernando Street with a viaduct structure over Estero de Binondo.

Filipinos could also opt to walk as the bridge is equipped with pedestrian walkways.

Also included in the Metro Manila Logistics Network are six bridges crossing Pasig River, Marikina River, and Manggahan Floodway: 1.582-kilometer Marcos Highway - St. Mary Avenue Bridge, the 691-meter Homeowner's Drive - A. Bonifacio Bridge, the 723-meter Kabayani Street - Matandang Balara Bridge, the 2.026-kilometer North and South Harbor Bridge, the 438-meter Palanca - Villegas Bridge, and the 932.78-meter Eastbank - Westbank Bridge 2.

Ultimately, by 2022, the goal is to ensure that every city in Metro Manila is connected within a 20 to 30-minute time frame.

BGC Ortigas Link Bridge

Right-of-way reforms critical in Skyway Stage 3 completion

When the construction of Skyway Stage 3 started, I was a freshman at law school. Almost every day, I'd pass by the same alignment which, if completed, would cut travel time from North Luzon Expressway to South Luzon Expressway from 2.5 hours to only 30 minutes. At the time, I was still working for United Nations and our Manila Office was located at the RCBC Plaza on HV dela Costa on Ayala Avenue. There were many days I hoped they'd fast-track the construction. The promise of reduced travel time from Makati to QC meant more time to study, dine, shower, or sleep. Little did I know that I'd be part of the project about two years later.

Skyway Stage 3 is an 18-kilometer expressway from Buendia in Makati to Balintawak in Quezon City. The problem was delayed due to difficulty in acquiring the right-of-way required for the original alignment, specifically at Section 2B from Pandacan to Sta. Mesa.

Since the project was started until November 2017, accomplishment on right-of-way activities had been almost nil. For instance, site possession for the entire alignment was only at 8.64 percent. Before the issuance of Department Order 65, only Section 1 had substantial right-of-way acquisition, which was only at 34.85 percent. No right-of-way was acquired for Section 2A and 2B. Section 3 and Section 4 were only at 2.86 percent and 5.5 percent, respectively.

Relocation of the 47 National Grid Corporation poles and 1,312 Meralco poles only started in May 2017.

It was clear that the original alignment that was proposed had to be revised. In May 2017, Department of Public Works and Highways Secretary Mark Villar received a proposal from San Miguel Corporation to realign Section 2B to utilize the San Juan River alignment. The Memorandum of Agreement was signed on October 25, 2018, which included the construction of an interconnection structure between Metro Manila Skyway Stage 3 and the NLEX-SLEX Connector, an eight-kilometer elevated four-lane toll expressway from NLEX Harbor Link Segment 10 in C3 Road, Caloocan City, to PUP Sta. Mesa in Manila.

Twelve months later, civil works construction for the main span of Skyway Stage 3 has been completed. By December, travel time from NLEX to SLEX will be reduced from two hours to only 30 minutes. Makati to Quezon City will only be 20 minutes.

The problem of Skyway Stage 3 is not an isolated incident. The problem of right-of-way has hounded many infrastructure projects for decades. Mindanao Avenue Extension, a project which connects North Caloocan to both the North Luzon Expressway and Quezon City has been delayed for about 40 years. It took six presidents to complete Radial Road 10, a 9.7-kilometer expressway from Delpan Bridge, Tondo, Manila, to the mouth of the Malabon River at Bangkulasi Bridge, C-4 Road, in Navotas City.

In Mindanao, we also opened Cagayan de Oro Coastal Road, a project which was first funded in 1997. Now, the 12.77-kilometer stretch serves as a bypass road starting from Brgy. Gusa in the eastern side all the way to the western side in Brgy. Igpit, Opol, in Misamis Oriental, connecting six barangays in the city and two barangays in Opol.

Inspection of NLEX Connector Project

Reforms in DPWH

As early as 2016, when the Duterte administration launched the Build, Build, Build program, Department of Public Works and Highways (DPWH) Secretary Mark Villar instituted key reforms in the right-of-way processes, including the issuance of an administrative order creating Right-of-Way Task Forces for each of the projects being implemented. He also decentralized the ROW acquisition functions and delegated the duties and responsibilities to various implementing units. Prior to this, regional offices were not capacitated with their own right-of-way divisions and were dependent only on legal support provided by the Central Office.

Moreover, DPWH institutionalized the use of Infra-Track App, which detects ghost project real time through geotagging.

As early as when the system detects a five percent negative slippage, the contractor involved in the project is given a warning and required to submit a "catch-up program" to eliminate the slippage or delay.

If such slippage furthers to at least 10 percent, he will be given a second warning and required to submit a detailed action program on a two-week basis, which commits him to accelerate the work and accomplish specific physical targets, which should reduce the slippage over a defined time period. The contractor will be instructed to specify the additional input resources – money, manpower, materials, machines, and management – which he should mobilize for this action program.

At any point the contractor incurs a delay of at least 15 percent, he will be given a final warning and required to come up with a more detailed program of activities with weekly physical targets, together with the required additional input resources. On-site supervision will be intensified, and evaluation of project performance will be done at least once a week. At the same time, the project manager, district engineer, or regional director will be tasked to prepare a contingency plan for the termination or rescission of the contract and/or takeover of the work by administration or contract.

All contractors with ongoing DPWH contracts, which have incurred negative slippages of 15 percent or more, will automatically be pre-disqualified from future biddings until after the negative slippage have been reduced to less than 15 percent. No time suspensions are provided without the prior approval of the secretary or the undersecretary in charge. Negligence or inexcusable failure of the contractor to provide the required equipment, supplies, or materials are also not tolerated.

Reimagining the Smokey Mountain alignment

The right-of-way problem, which delayed Radial Road 10, spanned six presidents. The road traversing the old Smokey Mountain area was congested by informal settlers. It was only in January 2017 that the Department of Public Works and Highways, under the leadership of Secretary Mark Villar, was able to complete the conversion of the 9.7-kilometer road section into a high-capacity highway, which helped offset the usual heavy volume of vehicles in major thoroughfares like EDSA and C5.

When it opened, the Radial Road 10 stretching from Delpan Bridge in Tondo, Manila, to the mouth of the Malabon River at Bangkulasi Bridge, C-4 Road in Navotas City showed a lot of potential. Extending the current alignment of NLEX Harbor Link Segment 10 to Radial Road 10 was strategic. An additional exit ramp to the 5.58-kilometer six-lane divided elevated expressway spanning from McArthur Highway and C3 Road will provide a direct access between the port area and the northern provinces of Luzon.

In September 2018, the construction of the 2.6-kilometer, four-lane elevated ramp

Inspection of NLEX Harbor Link Project

began. Twenty one months later, on June 15, 2020, the R-10 Spur Link was opened to the public, benefitting a total of 30,000 vehicles, 70 percent of which are truckers and cargo haulers.

Now, travel time from Quezon City to Port Area in Manila has been reduced from two hours to only 15 to 20 minutes.

Within the next two years, the NLEX Harbor Link alignment will be connected to three major infrastructure projects: NLEX Harbor Link Segment 8.2, Skyway Stage 3, and NLEX-SLEX Connector.

Mindanao Avenue to Commonwealth Ave in 10 minutes

The NLEX Harbor Link Segment 8.2 is an 8.35-kilometer, four-lane divided expressway from Segment 8.1, which will start at Mindanao Avenue and traverse Republic Avenue, Luzon Avenue and Commonwealth Avenue in Quezon City. When completed, the project is expected to benefit 45,000 motorists per day and reduce the travel time from Mindanao Avenue to Commonwealth Avenue from 45 minutes to only 10 minutes.

Makati to Quezon City in 20 minutes and SLEX to NLEX in 20 minutes

The main line of the Metro Manila Skyway Stage 3 Project (MMSS3), an 18.30-kilometer elevated expressway spanning from Buendia in Makati City to the North Luzon Expressway in Balintawak, Quezon City, will also be connected to the high standard highway network. This is the first time in Philippine history that an interconnection agreement has been signed allowing Skyway Stage 3, NLEX Harbor Link, and NLEX-SLEX Connector to connect.

The NLEX-SLEX Connector Project is an eight-kilometer, four-lane expressway, spanning from C3 Road in Caloocan City to PUP in Sta. Mesa in Manila.

When the interconnection is completed, every city in Metro Manila will be connected in a 20 to 30-minute time frame. Travel time from the northernmost part of Metro Manila to the southernmost portion will be reduced to only 30 minutes.

The project is expected to decongest EDSA and C5 by at least 55,000 vehicles daily and reduce travel time from Makati to Quezon City from two hours to only 15 to 20 minutes.

Reforms in Right-of-Way

Since 2016, DPWH instituted key reforms in the right-of-way processes, including the issuance of an administrative order creating Right-of-Way Task Forces for each of the projects being implemented, which effectively decentralized ROW acquisition functions. This is complimented by the Infra-Track App, a fully automated monitoring system utilizing geotagging feature, satellite technology, and drone monitoring.

The truth about two Build, Build, Build projects

Critics of the administration recently pointed out that over 180,000 families will be displaced in Metro Manila should the NLEX-SLEX Connector Road Project and the North-South Commuter Railway (NSCR) Project push through. This claim is fictitious, inaccurate, and misleading.

For example, based on the census and tagging conducted by the National Housing Authority, the government agency mandated to relocate and resettle Informal Settler Families (ISFs) affected by the construction of national infrastructure projects, the estimated number of likely affected ISFs in the NLEX – SLEX Connector Road Project is only 1,700.

When completed, the NLEX-SLEX Connector Project, an eight-kilometer expressway from C3 Road in Caloocan City to PUP in Sta. Mesa, Manila, to the common alignment of Skyway Stage 3, will reduce travel time between SLEX and NLEX from two hours to only 20 minutes.

Moreover, according to the Department of Transportation (DOTr), what critics appear to lump together as the NSCR Project consists of four different projects, namely: PNR Clark 1 (38-kilometer, Tutuban-Malolos), PNR Clark 2 (51-kilometer, Malolos-Clark), PNR Calamba (56-kilometer, Manila-Calamba), and PNR Bicol (653-kilometer, Manila-Matnog; Batangas).

Currently, the Philippines only has 76.9 kilometers of operational railways. The government targets to build and lay the groundwork for approximately 1,900 kilometers of railways by 2022 and beyond, which will benefit around 4.5 million passengers per day.

In a joint statement, the Department of Public Works and Highways and DOTr noted that ISF affected by the NSCR projects are not confined to 38 barangays in Manila, but are rather spread across Region III (Central Luzon), National Capital Region, Region IV-A (Calabarzon), and Region V (Bicol).

It is also stressed that contrary to the figure presented by certain critics, the estimated number of likely affected ISFs is 344 for PNR Clark 1; 1,173 for PNR Clark 2; 11,384 for PNR Calamba; and 1,700 for the NLEX-SLEX Connector Project. For PNR Bicol, the previous estimate of 79,531 ISFs will be greatly reduced because of the DOTr and PNR's approach of exploring re-alignments to avoid displacement of persons, to minimize conflict with road traffic and structures, and to straighten curves to achieve faster operating speeds.

Even assuming the number of affected ISFs for PNR Bicol is not reduced (which it will), the total number of affected ISFs at 94,132 across four regions is far apart from the estimation provided.

Further, all four phases of the NSCR Project are separately financed by the Asian Development Bank (ADB), the Japan International Cooperation Agency (JICA), and China.

As with other ADB and JICA financed projects, borrower countries such as the Philippines are required to ensure compliance not just with all applicable local laws and regulations on land acquisition and resettlement, but also with the ADB's Safeguard Policy Statement and JICA's Guidelines for Social Considerations. This means that part of project preparation and implementation is a comprehensive evaluation of the project's potential social impact, and the implementation of measures that will ensure that affected persons are left "no worse off," as required under ADB and JICA Social Safeguards.

It bears repeating that these projects are long overdue, and are ultimately meant to alleviate the decades-long suffering of thousands of Filipino commuters in Luzon. Moreover, these projects are poised to economically transform the regions, ferrying in commerce, and increasing incomes faster than before.

The DOTr and the DPWH, under the Duterte administration, remain steadfast in their goal of giving a better life for all Filipinos, and will not be diverted by criticisms anchored on false and misleading data.

NLEX Connector Project

Daang Kalikasan

CHAPTER FIVE

LUZON

Reimagining Luzon

Atotal of 939.38 kilometers of High Standard Highways/Expressways in Luzon are targeted to be implemented/constructed in Luzon. The target is twice the 382.26 kilometers of existing expressways. Once completed, the travel time from Metro Manila to La Union will be reduced from six hours and 55 minutes to three hours and 10 minutes. Moreover, travel time from Ilocos to Bicol will be reduced from 19 hours and 40 minutes to eight hours and 15 minutes.

In 2019, DPWH under the leadership of Secretary Mark Villar broke ground and opened critical sections of the following projects.

1. NLEX Harbor Link Segment 10
The 5.58-kilometer, six-lane elevated NLEX Harbor Link, Segment 10 connecting McArthur Highway and C-3 will decongest Metro Manila by providing access to NLEX without passing through EDSA or the Balintawak Toll Plaza. It will reduce travel time from Valenzuela City to C-3 Caloocan City from more than one hour to only five minutes, benefitting 20,000 motorists per day.

2. NLEX Harbor Link, R-10 Segment
The 2.60-kilometer, four-lane elevated ramp extending the NLEX Harbor Link Segment 10 exit to Radial Road 10 (R-10), using C-3 Road will shorten travel time from Manila to NLEX from one to one and a half hour to only 10 minutes.

3. Metro Manila Skyway Stage 3
The 17.973-kilometer elevated expressway connecting Skyway Stage 1 in Buendia, Makati City to the North Luzon Expressway in Balintawak, Quezon City will reduce travel time from Alabang to Quezon City from two hours to only 20 minutes.

4. Tarlac-Pangasinan-La Union Expressway (TPLEX)
The 89.31-kilometer expressway from Tarlac City to Rosario, La Union will reduce travel time between Tarlac City and Rosario, La Union from 3.5 hours to only one hour.

Tarlac-Pangasinan-La Union Expressway

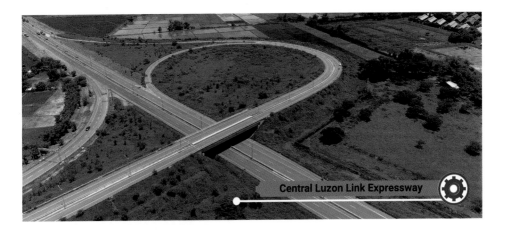

Central Luzon Link Expressway

5. Central Luzon Link Expressway, Phase I, Tarlac-Cabanatuan, Nueva Ecija

The 30-kilometer, four-lane expressway will reduce travel time between Tarlac City and Cabanatuan City from 70 minutes to 20 minutes, decongesting traffic passing through Daang Maharlika by about 48 percent.

6. Manila Cavite Toll Expressway Project, C-5 South Link Expressway

The 7.70-kilometer, six-lane divided expressway, stretching from R-1 Expressway to SLEX/C5 will reduce travel time from R-1 Expressway to SLEX/C5 from 40 minutes to 10 minutes.

7. NLEX - SLEX Connector

The eight-kilometer, four-lane expressway, spanning from C3 Road in Caloocan City to PUP, Sta. Mesa, Manila to the common alignment of Skyway Stage 3, will reduce travel time between SLEX and NLEX from 1.5 to two hours to 15 to 20 minutes. It will reduce travel time between Clark and Calamba from three hours to one hour and 40 minutes.

8. South Luzon Expressway (SLEX) Toll Road 4 (TR4)

The 66.74-kilometer South Luzon Expressway (SLEX) Toll Road 4 expressway extension from Sto. Tomas, Batangas to Tayabas/Lucena (Mayao), Quezon will facilitate faster and safer travel to Laguna, Batangas, Quezon, and the Bicol Region, reducing travel time from four hours to one hour. To be completed in 2021, the project will benefit 17,000 travelers per day.

9. Cavite-Tagaytay-Batangas Expressway (CTBEX)

An approximate 50-kilometer tollway consists of a two-by-two lane carriageway traversing mostly the rural areas of Silang, Tagaytay, Amadeo, Mendez, Alfonso, and Magallanes, all in the Cavite province, and Nasugbu in Batangas.

10. Arterial Plaridel Bypass Road

The 24.61-kilometer bypass road traverses the municipalities of Balagtas, Guiguinto, Plaridel, Bustos, and San Rafael in Bulacan and connects NLEX in Balagtas, Bulacan with Maharlika Highway in San Rafael, Bulacan. When completed, the road project will reduce average travel time between Burol, Balagtas and Maasim, San Rafael in Bulacan from 69 minutes to 24 minutes.

1,101 KILOMETERS

HIGH STANDARD
HIGHWAYS / EXPRESSWAYS

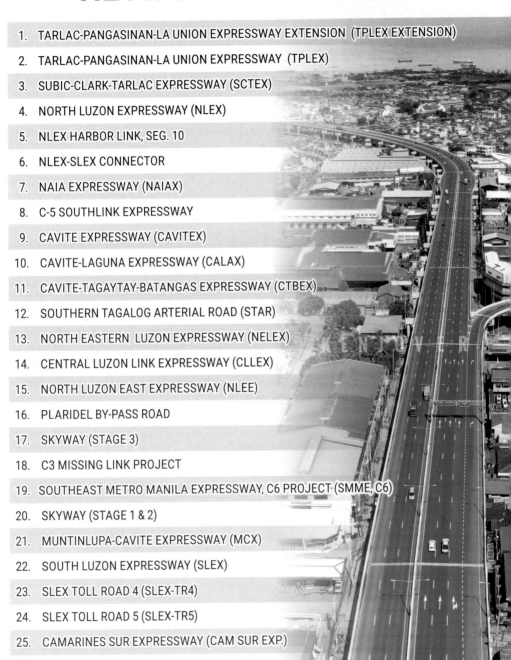

LUZON SPINE EXPRESSWAY NETWORK PROGRAM

1. TARLAC-PANGASINAN-LA UNION EXPRESSWAY EXTENSION (TPLEX EXTENSION)
2. TARLAC-PANGASINAN-LA UNION EXPRESSWAY (TPLEX)
3. SUBIC-CLARK-TARLAC EXPRESSWAY (SCTEX)
4. NORTH LUZON EXPRESSWAY (NLEX)
5. NLEX HARBOR LINK, SEG. 10
6. NLEX-SLEX CONNECTOR
7. NAIA EXPRESSWAY (NAIAX)
8. C-5 SOUTHLINK EXPRESSWAY
9. CAVITE EXPRESSWAY (CAVITEX)
10. CAVITE-LAGUNA EXPRESSWAY (CALAX)
11. CAVITE-TAGAYTAY-BATANGAS EXPRESSWAY (CTBEX)
12. SOUTHERN TAGALOG ARTERIAL ROAD (STAR)
13. NORTH EASTERN LUZON EXPRESSWAY (NELEX)
14. CENTRAL LUZON LINK EXPRESSWAY (CLLEX)
15. NORTH LUZON EAST EXPRESSWAY (NLEE)
16. PLARIDEL BY-PASS ROAD
17. SKYWAY (STAGE 3)
18. C3 MISSING LINK PROJECT
19. SOUTHEAST METRO MANILA EXPRESSWAY, C6 PROJECT (SMME, C6)
20. SKYWAY (STAGE 1 & 2)
21. MUNTINLUPA-CAVITE EXPRESSWAY (MCX)
22. SOUTH LUZON EXPRESSWAY (SLEX)
23. SLEX TOLL ROAD 4 (SLEX-TR4)
24. SLEX TOLL ROAD 5 (SLEX-TR5)
25. CAMARINES SUR EXPRESSWAY (CAM SUR EXP.)

Build Build Build: From 385 kilometers to 1,101 kilometers of high standard highways in Luzon

n 2016, the Duterte Administration embarked to build the Luzon Spine Expressway Network — a 1,101-kilometer expressway network which would connect the northern and southern most part of Luzon. By building a total of 25 expressways with a total road length of 716 kilometers, Department of Public Works and Highways Secretary Mark Villar aims to complement the existing expressway network spanning 385 kilometers. Once completed, the travel time from Metro Manila to San Fernando, La Union will be reduced from six hours and 55 minutes to three hours and 10 minutes. Moreover, travel time from La Union to Bicol will be reduced from 19 hours and 40 minutes to eight hours and 15 minutes.

Included in the expressway network are the NLEX Harbor Link Project, Tarlac-Pangasinan-La Union Expressway, Central Luzon Link Expressway, Plaridel Bypass Road Phase II, Metro Manila Skyway Stage 3, NLEX-SLEX Connector Road, among others.

The NLEX Harbor Link Project, a 5.7-kilometer expressway, which traverses Karuhatan

SLEX Toll Road 4

in Valenzuela City, Governor Pascual Avenue in Malabon City, and C3 road in Caloocan City, will reduce travel time from Manila Port to NLEX to only 10 minutes.

The Central Luzon Link Expressway (CLLEX) is a 30-kilometer expressway, which traverses the municipalities of La Paz, Zaragosa, Aliaga, and Caalibangbangan, to connect two large cities of Tarlac and Cabanatuan. The CLLEX, which originates from the connection of SCTEx and of TPLEx in Balincanaway, Tarlac City, is expected to decongest traffic in Pan Philippine Highway by 48 percent and reduce travel time between Tarlac City and Cabanatuan City from 70 minutes to 20 minutes.

Section 3 of the Tarlac-Pangasinan-La Union Expressway is a 25.83-kilometer expressway, which extends the existing 63.02-kilometer alignment traversing Tarlac, Rosales and Urdaneta to Binalonan, Pozzurobio, and La Union, creating an 88.85-kilometer stretch. The Urdaneta-Binalonan segment, which was operational since September of 2016, has reduced travel time from Tarlac City to Urdaneta from two hours and 30 minutes to about 40 minutes. Upon completion, TPLEX is expected to benefit over 100,000 vehicles per day and will cut travel time to Gerona, Paniqui, Rosales, Urdaneta, and Rosario.

The NLEX-SLEX Connector Road, which will traverse 5th Avenue/C3 Road in Caloocan City passing through Blumentrit and España, is expected to decongest Metro Manila traffic and provide better access to seaports and airports. It will reduce travel time from NLEX to SLEX from two hours to only about 20 minutes.

DPWH is now updating the High Standard Highway Network Development Masterplan which would expand the coverage from the sphere of 200 kilometers to 300 kilometers radius around Metro Manila.

Cavite Laguna Expressway

ILO

COS
REGION

ACCOMPLISHMENTS

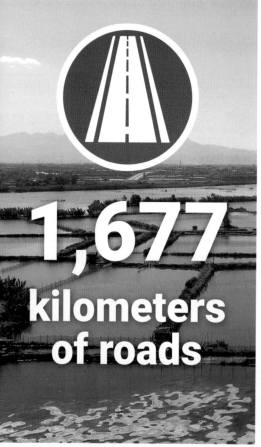

1,677
kilometers of roads

399
bridges

1,251
flood mitigation structures

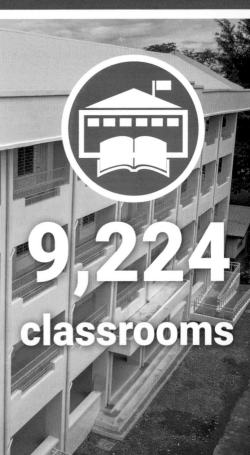

9,224
classrooms

Almost four years after President Rodrigo Duterte launched the Build, Build, Build program, the Philippine government's most ambitious infrastructure plan, computer-generated images which were once used to present a vision, began turning into actual roads and bridges.

Since July 2016, DPWH has completed a total of 29,264 kilometers of roads and 5,950 bridges.

Critics have said it cannot be done and yet the output of 6.5 million workers involved in the Build, Build, Build program has proved them wrong.

Another misconception was that most projects are only situated in Metro Manila or are operated under the modality of public private partnership. This is far from the truth. In fact, less than five percent of the Build, Build, Build projects charge toll or operate under a concession agreement.

To correct this misinformation, I will take you to at least 10 big-ticket projects in all 17 regions. We'll explore the northwestern section of Luzon, Region 1, or Ilocos Region, which is composed of four provinces — Ilocos Norte, Ilocos Sur, La Union, and Pangasinan.

Since 2016, DWPH has completed 1,677 kilometers of roads, 399 bridges, 1,251 flood control projects, and 9,224 classrooms in Ilocos Region.

Urdaneta Bypass Road

Heading to Pangasinan to visit the Manaoag Church and the Hundred Islands of Alaminos? The 7.17-kilometer Urdaneta City Bypass Road traverses eight barangays namely Nancayasan, Sto. Domingo, Sta. Lucia, Nancamaliran East, Mabanogbog, San Vicente, Camantiles, and Anonas. It serves as an alternate route to the existing Manila North Road, Urdaneta-Dagupan Road, Urdaneta-Manaoag Road, and the Tarlac-Pangasinan-La Union Expressway. Now, travel time from Villasis to Binalonan has been reduced from one hour to only 30 minutes.

Candon City Bypass Road

The 7.3-kilometer Candon City Bypass road traverses the eastern side of the city to decongest the Manila North Road and improve the connectivity of Manila to Ilocos Sur, Ilocos Norte, and Abra. Its completion reduced the travel time from Sta. Lucia in Ilocos Sur to Santiago from 40 minutes to only 20 minutes. It is expected to benefit 13,061 motorists per day.

Laoag City Bypass Road

The 7.9-kilometer Laoag City Bypass Road starts at Brgy Buttong in Laoag City and ends in Barangay Pasiocan in Ilocos Norte. It includes the construction of an 805-meter Laoag Bridge and a 129-meter Casili Bridge. When completed, travel time from Laoag to Ilocos Norte will be reduced from 45 minutes to only 10 minutes.

Tarlac-Pangasinan-La Union Expressway

Whether you're surfing in San Juan, or cliff-diving in Tangadan Falls in San Gabriel, or hanging by the kitchen bar of Flotsam & Jetsam, the completion of the 89.31-kilometer TPLEX has made your travel more efficient by almost 50 percent. Now, travel time from Manila to Baguio has been reduced to only three hours.

Bantay - San Ildefonso Bypass Road

Going to Vigan? The 10.97-kilometer Bantay - San Ildefonso Bypass Road starts at the junction of the Manila North Road from Barangay Taleb in the municipality of Bantay through the barangays of Tay-ac, Bongro, Binongan, Sto. Domingo, Arnap, Belen, Bungro, and Poblacion East at San Ildefonso.

When completed, it will reduce travel time from Bantay to San Ildefonso from one hour to only 15 to 20 minutes.

Daang Kalikasan

Up for some soul searching against the scenic mountain range? The 19.89-kilometer Daang Kalikasan Road will reduce the travel time from Mangatarem in Pangasinan to Sta. Cruz in Zambales from two hours and 30 minutes to only one hour.

Laoag - Ilocos Norte Connector

Heading to the Paoay Sand Dunes or Paoay Lake? Check out the 3.6-kilometer Laoag - Ilocos Norte Connector, which traverses Darayday in Laoag City and San Nicolas in Ilocos Norte.

Daang Katutubo

Want to explore the Ylang ylang plantation? Check out the 27.55-kilometer Daang Katutubo Road, which serves as an access road to the Mapita Tribal Community and the view deck in Nayong Aguilar.

8

Lingayen Bypass Road

The 6.2-kilometer Lingayen Bypass Road starts at the intersection of Pangasinan-Zambales Road and Lingayen Labrador Diversion Road and traverses along Lingayen proper to Barangay Poblacion in Binmaley. The project is expected to benefit 18,492 motorists every day.

9

Apayao - Ilocos Norte Road

The 65.58-kilometer Apayao - Ilocos Norte Road connects the towns of Conner, Kabugao, and Calanasan in Apayao to the municipality of Solsona and the city of Laoag in Ilocos Norte. It serves as an alternate route to motorists coming from the Cordillera Administrative Region going to Laoag International Airport and the Manila North Road in Ilocos Region.

10

CORDI
ADMINIS
REGION

LLERA
TRATIVE

Cordillera Administrative Region
ACCOMPLISHMENTS

1,304
kilometers of roads

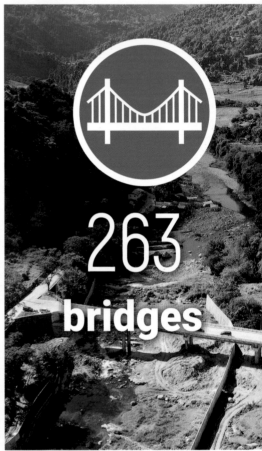

263
bridges

434
flood mitigation structures

2,570
classrooms

Back in 2016, no one knew what Build, Build, Build meant or what it stood for. Critics had very little expectation of the team. They wagered against our success, not knowing that when they did, they gambled against the future of their country. They were certain that the infrastructure projects would never materialize — that blueprints would remain as drawings. They didn't expect 6.5 million Filipinos to stand and work behind it.

While we were doing our 100-day report, Secretary Mark Villar and I talked on the kind of projects he wanted to pursue. He was a visionary who dreamed of great things for the Philippines and was willing to work 16 hours a day for it.

One of the first masterplans to materialize was the Luzon Spine Expressway Network, a blueprint whose aim was to increase the high standard highway network in Luzon by threefold and connect the northern and southernmost parts of Luzon. Ultimately, the goal was to cut travel time from Ilocos to Bicol from 20 hours to only nine hours.

I could still remember, the first time we told the public of the plan to connect Manila to Baguio within 3.5 hours. No one believed us. They said it was mathematically impossible but the Build, Build, Build team carried on to realize a future that the next generation deserves.

Now, DWPH has completed 1,304 kilometers of roads, 263 bridges, 434 flood control projects, 2,570 classrooms, and 23 evacuation centers in the Cordillera Administrative Region.

Let's explore 10 Build, Build, Build projects in CAR, a region composed of six provinces — Abra, Apayao, Benguet, Ifugao, Kalinga, and Mountain Province.

Baguio-La Trinidad-Itogon-Sablan-Tuba-Tublay (BLISTT) Outer Ring Circumferential Road

When the 154-kilometer BLISTT Outer Ring Circumferential Road project is completed, traffic in highly urbanized centers of Baguio, La Trinidad, Itogon, Sablan, Tuba, and Tublay will be reduced by about 50 to 60 percent.

Apayao-Ilocos Norte Road

The Apayao-Ilocos Norte Road is the missing link of the Cordillera Roads Improvement Project (CRIP), which will be the region's backbone that will connect all provincial and major growth centers. It will also serve as a lateral access road for Regions I and II to the Cordillera. The 65.58-kilometer road network with 12 bridges will reduce travel time from the capital town of Kabugao, Apayao to Laoag City, Ilocos Norte via Calanasan, Apayao from 6.5 hours to 3.5 hours when completed by the end of 2022. Barely three kilometers out of the 65.58 kilometers remain unpaved and have been included in the FY 2022 Regional Budget Proposal.

Kennon Road rehabilitation

Since its closure in 2018 due to the devastation brought by several typhoons, DPWH has spent more than ₱3 billion for the rehabilitation of Kennon Road, a 116-year-old infrastructure. Of the identified 21 critical sections that required immediate and comprehensive repairs, 11 sections are undergoing construction works. The agency will need additional allocation for the remaining five erosion-prone sections to be fixed before the 33.7-kilometer stretch can be fully opened to the public. Once repairs are finished, Kennon Road will still need to be converted into an all-weather road through a public-private partnership after the completion of its feasibility study.

Balili-Suyo-Sagada Road

The 9.446-kilometer Balili-Suyo-Sagada Road, which starts at the end of the Dantay-Sagada Road in Barangay Ambasing, Sagada and ends at Baguio-Bontoc Road (Halsema Highway) in Barangay Balili, Bontoc, Mt. Province, is already 85 percent complete.

Great Wall of Baguio City

Dubbed as the "Great Wall of Baguio City", this 4.6-kilometer bypass road under construction to connect Major Mane Road to Kennon Road is underway, expected to be fully operational by 2023. The region is now on its Phase 4 of implementation after 3.07 kilometers of the said road were finished under the first three phases of the project.

The ongoing two-lane project has unexpectedly become a local tourist destination as it provides a breathtaking 360-degree view of Benguet mountain ranges. Aimed also to decongest traffic in the Central Business District, this bypass road will serve as an additional safe route to travelers from Kennon Road going to EPZA, the Philippine Military Academy, Balatoc, and Philex Mines.

Sabangan-Sagada Provincial Road

When completed, the 9.85-kilometer Sabangan-Sagada Provincial Road will serve as an alternate route leading to the famous Sagada Caves, Hanging Coffins, Kiltepan Peak, and other well-known tourist destinations in the area like the Banao Lake, Bokong Lake, Latang Lake, Aguid and Fidelisan Water Falls, Bumod-ok Waterfalls, and many more.

Alimusgan-Bai-Cagayanan Road

In Tineg, Abra, DPWH is fast-tracking the implementation of the 11-kilometer tourism road leading to Kaparkan Falls. The Alimusgan-Bai-Cagayanan Road project is now at 41 percent. It is expected to increase economic activity in the area through transport and tourism-related activities.

Benguet Sports Complex and Facilities

The completion of the largest sports facility in Benguet will create opportunities for the province to host annual local, regional, and national sports events such as the Palarong Pambansa or even a potential venue for bigger international competitions and tournaments.

Chico River Embankment Dike

The 18-kilometer embankment dike along the Chico River spans from Calanan, Tabuk City to Magaogao, Pinukpuk in Kalinga. This ₱5.462-billion flood control structure expects to preclude the loss of lives and properties within the 18 barangays that are being affected.

Chico Karayan Bridge

The 215-meter bridge, which was partially damaged by Typhoon Lawin in 2016, is finally completed. Now, the eastern barangays of Mountain Province are more accessible to market centers.

CAG

AYAN
VALLEY

REGION II (Cagayan Valley)
ACCOMPLISHMENTS

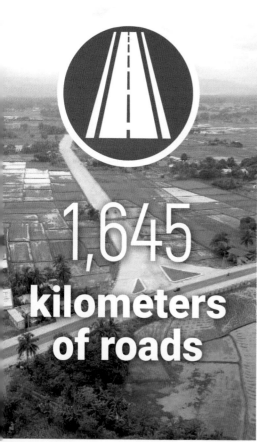

1,645
kilometers of roads

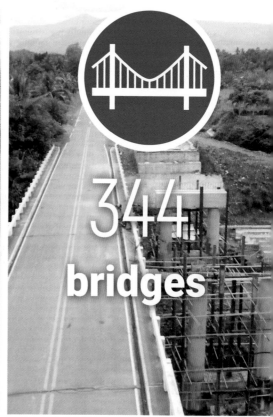

344
bridges

BY THE NUMBERS

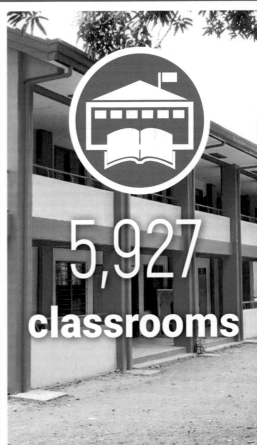

411
flood mitigation structures

5,927
classrooms

When Pigalo Bridge in Isabela was devastated by typhoons Pedring and Quiel in 2011, farmers who wanted to deliver their agricultural products to Manila or Tuguegarao had to take a 76-kilometer detour via Alicia-Angadanan-San Guillermo-Naguilian Road.

Residents of Isabela had to cross the Cagayan River whenever they had to go to school or sell their produce. Small boats have become a principal mode of transportation. However, villages are isolated during the rainy season when boats are prohibited.

The Pigalo Bridge is only one of 344 bridges completed in Region 2.

According to Department of Public Works and Highways Secretary Mark Villar, under the term of President Rodrigo Duterte, a total of 1,645 kilometers of roads, 344 bridges, 411 flood mitigation structures, and 5,927 classrooms have been completed in the Cagayan Valley Region.

Let's explore ten big-ticket projects in Cagayan Valley, a region composed of five provinces — Batanes, Cagayan, Isabela, Nueva Vizcaya, and Quirino.

Pigalo Bridge in Isabela

The Pigalo Bridge, which was started in April 10, 2017, was completed in a span of two years and was formally inaugurated in June 2019. It replaced the old dilapidated overflow structure, which posed a danger to motorists and pedestrians for at least eight years.

To secure access of pedestrians, sidewalks with concrete railings were also included in the 450-meter Pigalo Bridge, which established access of San Guillermo, Echague, and San Mateo in Isabela to Tuguegarao City and Manila via Daang Maharlika and Junction Angadanan.

Racuh-a-idi Batanes Access Road

The 273-meter Racuh-a-idi Batanes Access Road will enhance the access of locals whose farms and pasturelands are located along the road section as well as those who wish to visit the Racuh-a-idi (Old Settlement).

Bayombong - Solano Bypass in Nueva Ecija

The 6.202-kilometer Bayombong - Solano Bypass will reduce travel time from Bayombong in Nueva Ecija to Manila by about 60 minutes.

Abusag Bridge in Cagayan

The 511-meter Abusag Bridge will reduce travel time from Tuguegarao City and Baggao from two hours and 30 minutes to only one hour and 30 minutes. It will benefit 15,000 travelers per day.

Cabagan Bypass Road in Isabela

The 1.7-kilometer, four-lane Cabagan Bypass Road traverses Barangays Ngarag, Poblacion, and Ugad in Cabagan, Isabela. Travel time from Tuguegarao City in Cagayan and Ilagan City in Isabela will be reduced by at least 20 minutes. It will benefit about 15, 000 motorists per day.

Disiluad Bridge in Quirino

The 161-meter Disiluad Bridge along Cordon-Aurora Boundary Road will connect the municipalities of Diffun and Maddela in Quirino.

Alicia-Angadanan-San Guillermo-Cauayan City-Naguilian Bypass

The 77-kilometer Alicia-Angadanan-San Guillermo-Cauayan City-Naguilian Bypass involves the construction of four bridges — Colorado, Dioton, Macalauat, and San Luis. The project, which was partially opened in June 2021, will connect the municipalities of Alicia, Angadanan, San Guillermo, Cauayan, and Naguilan in Isabela.

Roxas Bypass Road

The 4.9-kilometer Roxas Bypass Road will traverse Barangay San Antonio along Santiago-Tuguegarao Road and intersect the Roxas Paracelis Road. It will reduce travel time from Sotero to Poblacion in Roxas, Isabela from 30 minutes to only 10 minutes.

Bambang Bypass Road in Nueva Vizcaya

The 5.57-kilometer Bambang Bypass Road traverses Barangay Almaguer North, Buag Calaocan, Homestead, and Macate. It will reduce travel time along Daang Maharlika Road.

Claveria Diversion Road

The 4.55-kilometer Claveria Diversion Road will traverse Barangays Kilkiling, Bilibigao, Pinas, and San Antonio. It will also connect the National Highway from Brgy. Kilkiling to the Claveria-Calanasan Road, a road going to the upper Province of Apayao, within a span of eight to ten minutes.

CENTRAL
LU

ZON

REGION III (Central Luzon)

ACCOMPLISHMENTS

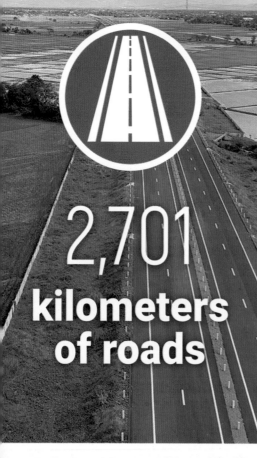

2,701
kilometers of roads

507
bridges

BY THE NUMBERS

1,770 **flood mitigation structures**

13,822 **classrooms**

According to the Philippine Statistics Authority, the economy of Central Luzon grew by 5.6 percent in 2019. Service had the largest share in the region's economy, accounting for 45.1 percent. Industry accounted for 42.6 percent while agriculture, forestry, and fishing were responsible for 12.3 percent.

Despite this, Central Luzon remains to be the "Rice Granary of the the Philippines." Out of the country's total rice yield of 18.81 million metric tons, 3.72 million metric tons or 19.8 percent come from Region 3.

The increase in road connectivity in Central Luzon is expected to improve the net profit to cost ratio of agricultural products and transform the regional economies of Aurora, Bataan, Bulacan, Nueva Ecija, Pampanga, Tarlac, and Zambales.

One of the big-ticket projects in the Build, Build, Build program is the Bataan-Cavite Interlink Bridge, a 32.15-kilometer, four-lane bridge, which aims to connect Central Luzon, CALABARZON, and Metro Manila.

The inter-island bridge, which is 15 times longer than San Juanico Bridge, is part of the Mega Bridge Masterplan, a blueprint institutionalized by the Duterte Administration to eventually connect Luzon, Visayas, and Mindanao via land travel.

According to Build, Build, Build czar Mark Villar, Department of Public Works and Highways has completed 2,701 kilometers of roads, 507 bridges, 1,770 flood mitigation structures, and 13,822 classrooms in Central Luzon.

Bataan - Cavite Interlink Bridge

The 32.15-kilometer inter-island bridge will start from Barangay Alas-asin in Mariveles, Bataan, cross Manila Bay, and terminate in Barangay Timalan, Naic, Cavite. When completed, the project will reduce travel time from Bataan to Cavite from five hours to only 20 to 30 minutes.

The detailed engineering design of the project will be carried out within a 15-month period with the support of Asian Development Bank.

It will include the construction of two navigation bridges — the North Channel Bridge and the South Channel Bridge — and six viaducts.

Plaridel Bypass

The Plaridel Bypass Road project, a new arterial road traversing the municipalities of Balagtas, Guiguinto, Plaridel, Bustos, and San Rafael in the province of Bulacan, has been opened.

Funded by the government of the Philippines (GOP) and government of Japan through Japan International Cooperation Agency (JICA), the recently completed highway shortened travel time to and from North Luzon Expressway via a new interchange at Brgy. Burol 2nd, Balagtas to the Philippines-Japan Friendship Highway in Brgy. Maasim, San Rafael, Bulacan.

The infrastructure project is expected to accommodate 15,000 vehicles per day and cut travel time between NLEX-Balagtas and Maharlika Highway in San Rafael by as much as 30 minutes.

Central Luzon Link Expressway

The first 18-kilometer segment of the 30-kilometer Central Luzon Link Expressway was opened to travelers in July 2021. Travel time from Tarlac City to Cabanatuan City in Nueva Ecija will be reduced to just 20 minutes.

Pandi National High School

The newly completed Pandi National High School adds 80 more classrooms in Bulacan. Since July 2016, 13,822 classrooms have been completed in Region 3.

Ciudad de Victoria Interchange

The Manila North Road in Bocaue, Bulacan will soon be connected to the town of Sta. Maria without passing the Governor Halili Road with the completion of the Ciudad de Victoria Interchange Bypass Road. Within the year, travel time from Bocaue to Sta. Maria in Bulacan will be reduced from 50 minutes to only 15 minutes.

Pulilan - Baliuag Diversion Road

Travel time between the towns of Baliuag and Pulilan in Bulacan has been reduced by half, from one hour to only 30 minutes with the opening of the 9.6-kilometer Pulilan - Baliuag Diversion Road. The project also includes the construction of bicycle lanes.

Capas - Botolan Road

The 84.47-kilometer Capas-Botolan Road will serve as a direct link between the provinces of Tarlac and Zambales, and will further provide access to the New Clark City. It starts in Olongapo - Bugallon Road in Zambales and ends at Manila North Road in Tarlac.

Bagac - Mariveles Road

The project, which starts at Barangay Paysawan in Bagac and ends at Mariveles in Bataan, serves as an alternate route to SCTEX and Roman Expressway. It is expected to benefit about 1,000 motorists per day and reduce travel time from two hours to only 40 minutes.

Sta. Cruz - Mangatarem Road

The 19.45-kilometer Daang Kalikasan Road will start at Tarlac - Pangasinan Road and end at Sta. Cruz, Zambales. When completed, it will reduce travel time from Mangatarem in Pangasinan to Zambales from two hours and 30 minutes to only one hour.

Subic Freeport Expressway

Despite the pandemic, the ₱1.57-billion capacity expansion project along Subic Freeport Expressway (SFEX), which started construction in May 2019, is now open to the public. The toll road, which is operated by NLEX Corporation, includes a 108-meter tunnel and two bridges — the 23.7-meter Argonaut Bridge and the 181.2-meter Jadjad Bridge.

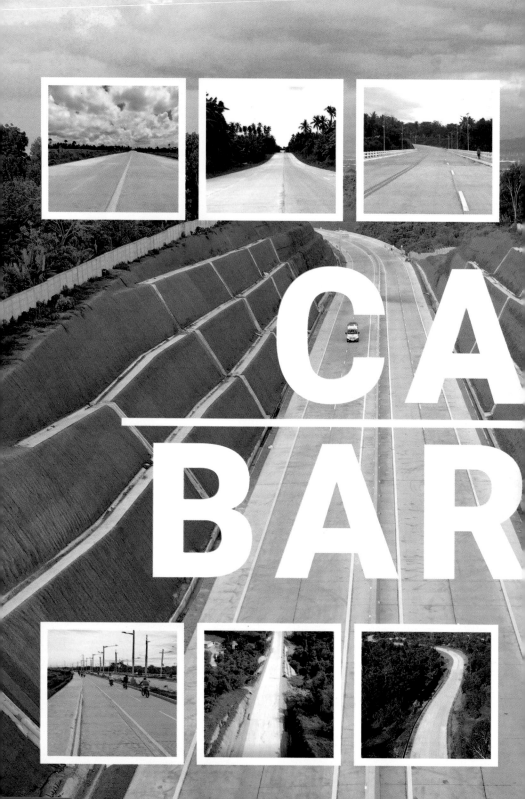

CA
BAR

LA
ZON

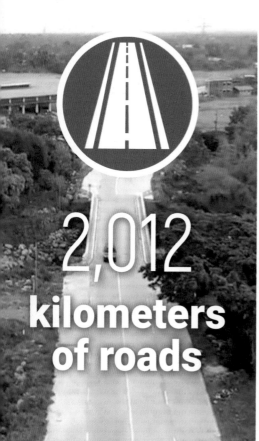

2,012 kilometers of roads

499 bridges

BY THE NUMBERS

1,042
flood
mitigation
structures

19,735
classrooms

During our first few months in DPWH, we received the most number of complaints on Circumferential Road 6, a toll-free expressway we now call Laguna Lake Highway. At that time, it was full of potholes, so large that we would get reports of dented exhaust pipes, mufflers, or catalytic converters. It would scrape against bumpers, side skirts, and undercarriages. When it rained, the problem was even aggravated by mud and flooding.

It was at this point that Secretary Mark Villar decided to call everyone involved in the project. It was then that we realized that Circumferential Road 6 only had the specifications of a dike rather than an all-weather national highway. The project was primarily a flood control program and the road was only meant to provide access for light vehicles. It was clear, the road needed to be upgraded.

This was the start of a movement that would lead to the construction of the 10.7-kilometer Laguna Lake Highway, the first toll-free expressway with protected bicycle lanes.

We'll explore 10 big-ticket projects in Calabarzon, a region composed of five provinces — Batangas, Cavite, Laguna, Quezon, Rizal, and one highly urbanized city, Lucena.

Since July 2016, DPWH has completed a total of 2,012 kilometers of roads, 499 bridges, 1,042 flood mitigation structures, and 19,735 classrooms in CALABARZON.

Sariaya Bypass

Heading to Mt. Banahaw? Try the 7.42-kilometer Sariaya bypass road, which starts at MSR Daang Maharlika Road and ends in Quezon Eco-tourism Road. The project has reduced the traffic volume along Daang Maharlika and Manila South Road by 40 percent. It also provides an alternate route for motorists going from Sariaya to Lucena.

Alaminos - San Pablo City Bypass

The 12.85-kilometer Alaminos-San Pablo City Bypass Road starts at the junction of Pan Philippine Highway, traverses the junction of Alaminos - Lipa City Road, and terminates in Barangay San Vicente, San Pablo City. The project, which was partially opened in March 2020, will cut travel time between the towns by as much as 40 minutes.

Tayabas Bypass Road

The Tayabas Bypass Road is part of the Luzon Spine Expressway Network, which will provide an alternate route to motorists coming from the provinces of Quezon and Bicol through the Pagsanjan - Sta Cruz - Los Banos - Calamba corridor. The 6.05-kilometer project will also provide a direct route from Lucena and Tayabas toward Sariaya, Candelaria, and San Juan, saving as much as 30 minutes of travel time.

The East West Expressway

The 41.67-kilometer East West Expressway will provide the missing gaps to connect two national roads — Cavite - Batangas Road in the East and Ternate - Nasugbu Road in the West. It will traverse the municipalities of Silang, Amadeo, Indang, Maragondon, General Aguinaldo, Magallanes in Cavite, and Nasugbu in Batangas.

Tagaytay Bypass Road

The 8.6-kilometer Tagaytay Bypass Road will connect two national roads: Indang Alfonso Road via Luksuhin Road and Tagaytay - Batangas Arterial Highway. The project, which was partially opened in October 2020, will reduce travel time from Alfonso to Tagaytay from 53 minutes to only 33 minutes.

Kaykulot Diversion Road

Heading to Picnic Grove or People's Park in The Sky? Check out the 1.7-kilometer Kaykulot Diversion road, which will connect Sta. Rosa - Ulat - Tagaytay Road and Tagaytay - Laguna via Calamba Road.

Laguna Lake Highway

The four-lane, 10.7-kilometer Laguna Lake Highway will connect the province of Rizal to Metro Manila. The project, which was opened in November 2018, has effectively reduced travel time from Bicutan to Taytay in Rizal from one hour to only 30 minutes.

The Star Tollway - Pinamucan Bypass Road

The 19-kilometer bypass road will connect high growth potential areas, such as Pinamucan in Batangas City to Star Tollway, easing current traffic congestion within Batangas, and lessening travel time by as much as 50 minutes. The project will also provide an alternate access from Star Tollway toward Taysan and Lobo, Batangas via Batangas – Lobo Road and Batangas – Tabangao – Lobo Road.

Batangas City - San Pascual - Bauan Diversion Road

When completed, the 10.88-kilometer Batangas City - San Pascual - Bauan Diversion Road will reduce travel time between Batangas City and Bauan from two hours to only 30 minutes.

Lobo - Malabrigo - Laiya - San Juan Road

Heading to the beach? Check out the the 22.16-kilometer Lobo - Malabrigo - Laiya - San Juan Road, which will connect the municipalities of San Juan and Lobo in Batangas.

MIMA

ROPA

1,310
kilometers of roads

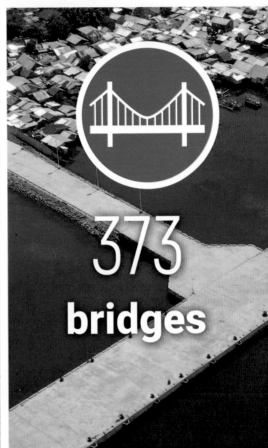

373
bridges

BY THE NUMBERS

377
flood mitigation structures

6,792
classrooms

Of all the places, Palawan is one of the most memorable. The first time I went there, my boat sank and for almost an hour, we clung to a bamboo pole in the middle of the sea to survive. Ten years have passed and yet, I couldn't forget that fateful night in 2012.

It was one of the most beautiful things I've seen. Every inch of the sky was filled with fireflies and stars. As you hopped from one island to the other, you'd realize — each one had a different character. And Palawan, it had more or less 1,780 islands.

The archipelagic nature of the Philippines posed a number of difficulties in the monitoring and implementation of Build, Build, Build projects.

How do we monitor 20,000 projects simultaneously in a country composed of roughly 7,640 islands? How do we get rid of ghost projects? How do we minimize discretion at DPWH?

Secretary Mark Villar was adamant to find a solution, one that was progressive, forward thinking, and feasible. First, he introduced an automated monitoring system called the Infra-Track App, which utilizes geo-tagging, satellite technology, and drone monitoring.

In 2019, DPWH completed the transition. Now, the Infra-Track App is able to detect ghost projects real time as the new application plots photos inputted in the system for monitoring in the exact geographic coordinates where it was taken. The system, through geographic identification of photos, videos, and other posts, automatically alerts key DPWH officials when a project is misreported from a different location.

This is one of the many reforms initiated in the department following President Rodrigo Duterte's mandate of increasing transparency and accountability in government.

Let's explore Region 4B or Mimaropa, composed of five provinces — Occidental Mindoro, Oriental Mindoro, Marinduque, Romblon, and Palawan.

Since 2016, DPWH has completed a total of 1,310 kilometers of roads, 373 bridges, 377 flood mitigation structures, and 6,792 classrooms in Region 4B or MIMAROPA.

Puerto Princesa Cruise Port and Facilities

The Puerto Princesa Cruise Port will put the province of Palawan on the map of international cruise destinations. The 500-meter wharf and docking facility will also serve as a gateway to El Nido, San Vicente, and Taytay in Palawan.

Access Road from Coron Town to Borac Roro Port

The access road from Coron Town to Borac Roro Port will traverse the barangays of Decabobo, Buenavista, Turda, Guadalupe, and San Nicolas. When completed, it will support Coron's trade industry through easier access to and from the new Port of Borac.

Coron - Busuanga Road

Heading to Kayangan Lake, Twin Lagoons, or Malcapuya Island? Explore the newly widened 72.53-kilometer Coron - Busuanga Road.

Calintaan Bypass in Occidental Mindoro

Heading to Salugsog Falls or Makatiklas Falls in Calintaan? Explore the 1.3-kilometer Calintaan Bypass Road in Occidental Mindoro.

Magarwak Bridge

Heading to Mt. Magarwak trail or the Magarwak Eco-Park? Traverse the newly widened Magarwak Bridge along the Puerto Princesa North Road in Palawan.

Access Road leading to Simbahang Bato

Heading to the Bancuro Church Ruins? Take the 5.564-kilometer access road leading to Simbahang Bato in Naujan, Oriental Mindoro.

Tabigue Flood Control Project along Boac River

The 640-meter Tabigue Flood Control Project will help mitigate flooding in low lying barangays along the Boac River, such as Barangay Tabigue, Poras, and Lupac.

Boac - Mogpog Bypass in Marinduque

The 2.25-kilometer Boac Mogpog Bypass in Marinduque will benefit about 2,048 motorists per day. It is connected to the Mogpog - Balanacan Port Road and will serve as an access road to various barangays located at Mogpog riverside.

Panangcalan Evacuation Center

The one-story evacuation center is equipped with comfort rooms, shower stalls, hand washing area, prayer room, clinic, kitchen, reception area, and an administrative office.

Boac Bypass Road in Marinduque

The 2.5-kilometer Boac Bypass road is connected to the Marinduque Circumferential Road and benefits 1,985 motorists per day. It serves as an access road to various barangays located at the Boac Riverside.

MET
MA

RO

NILA

877
kilometers of roads

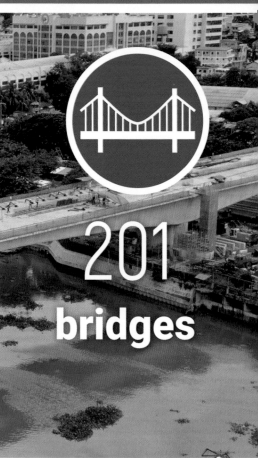

201
bridges

BY THE NUMBERS

1,746
flood mitigation structures

10,169
classrooms

As we prepared for the inauguration of the Pantaleon-Estrella Bridge in July 2021, a project bombarded by criticism and fake news since it started construction in January 2019, I remember announcing the closure, dismantling, and transfer of the mobile bridge to Pangasinan and receiving a lot of personal attacks and insults thereafter for what they thought was a useless exercise of government power.

But no Filipino on her right conscience, after reading the technical report of the bridge, the traffic monitoring survey, and the traffic management study, would recommend the retention of a structure with a utilization level well above its maximum intended capacity. Would it be able to withstand the "Big One" when its utilization rate was five times more than its actual capacity? No. There was a moral obligation to upgrade the structure to what it is today — a bridge capable of handling 50,000 vehicles.

Did we inconvenience the public for 19 months? Yes, but the new 506-meter bridge connecting Makati City at Estrella Street and Mandaluyong City at Barangka Drive, will provide a safer route for Filipinos for at least two decades.

Did we take loans with usurious interest rates to put it up? No, the ₱1.47 billion bridge project was funded under a grant from the Chinese government.

Were Filipinos not allowed to work on the bridge project? No, at least 350 Filipino workers were hired for the project.

Were Chinese experts present during project implementation? Yes, to oversee the use of form travelers systems in the construction.

Was this peculiar? Of course not. You'd find Korean engineers in Panguil Bay Bridge and Japanese engineers in Plaridel Bypass. This is a technical requirement usually found in Official Development Assistance (ODA) Projects to ensure that bridges are built on the right specifications and that there is proper knowledge transfer of the technology.

Will this aid in decongesting EDSA? Yes, as part of a masterplan composed of 25 projects, which include 14 expressways spanning 121 kilometers and 11 bridges spanning 9.3 kilometers.

Have we finally solved Metro Manila traffic? Not yet. The battle to decongest EDSA started in July 2016 and it has been fought every single day since. From the first time Build, Build, Build Czar Mark Villar laid out the masterplan up to now, not a day has been wasted to actualize it.

Let's explore the ninth most populous metropolitan area in Asia and the fifth most populous urban area in the world — National Capital Region, a region composed of 16 cities and one municipality.

According to Secretary Villar, DPWH has completed 877 kilometers of roads, 201 bridges, 1,746 flood mitigation structures, and 10,169 classrooms in National Capital Region.

Estrella-Pantaleon Bridge

To improve the existing bridge network consisting of 30 bridges crossing Pasig River, Marikina River, and Manggahan Floodway, which caters to about 1.3 million vehicles daily, the 506-meter Estrella-Pantaleon Bridge is constructed to connect Makati and Mandaluyong. Upon completion, it is expected to decrease traffic congestion at Makati-Mandaluyong Bridge by up to 3,360 vehicles per day and at Guadalupe Bridge by up to 4,474 vehicles per day.

Kalayaan Bridge

The 961-meter Bonifacio Global City-Ortigas Center Link Road Project involves the construction of a four-lane bridge across Pasig River connecting Lawton Avenue in Makati City and Sta. Monica Street in Pasig City, and a viaduct structure spanning from Lawton Avenue to Bonifacio Global City. When completed, travel time from Taguig to Makati or Pasig Cities will be reduced from one hour to only 12 minutes. Traffic congestion at EDSA and C-5 Road, particularly along Guadalupe Bridge and Bagong Ilog Bridge, will be alleviated by about 25 percent.

Skyway Stage 3

The 18-kilometer Skyway Stage 3 was not completed using its original alignment, which was approved in 2014. Due to right-of-way difficulties, it had to be realigned following the San Juan River alignment. This was approved via a Memorandum of Agreement, which was signed on October 25, 2018. Prior to this, site possession for the entire project was only at 8.64 percent. The project is expected to decongest EDSA and C5 by at least 55,000 vehicles daily and reduce travel time from Makati to Quezon City from two hours to only 15 to 20 minutes.

NLEX Harbor Link Segment 10

The 5.58-kilometer NLEX Harbor Link Segment 10, the first truck graded expressway in the country, will connect to four other expressways: The NLEX Connector Project, the Skyway Stage 3, the Radial Road 10, and the NLEX Harbor Link C3 Radial Road 10.

A 5.58-kilometer expressway connecting MacArthur Highway and C3 road will interconnect with the Skyway Stage 3 via the NLEX-SLEX Connector Road, an eight-kilometer expressway connecting the end of Segment 10 in C3 Road in Caloocan to PUP Sta. Mesa in Manila.

NLEX Harbor Link C3 Radial Road 10 Spur Link

The 2.6-kilometer NLEX Harbor Link C3-Radial Road 10 Spur Link spanning from C3 road in Caloocan to Radial Road 10 in Manila was the first project to be completed following the new COVID-19 protocol. It has effectively reduced travel time from Quezon City to Manila from two hours to only 20 minutes.

Pasig-Marikina Flood Control Project

Phase III of the Pasig-Marikina River Channel Improvement Project (PMRCIP), which spans from the Lower Marikina River (Napindan Channel to the downstream of Manggahan Floodway) to Delpan Bridge, is already complete. Revetments, parapet walls, dike embankment, sluice structures, and bridge foundation protection were

constructed and installed along priority critical sections of the Pasig-Marikina River.

The civil works for Phase IV are currently ongoing to address the downstream of Manggahan Floodway to Marikina Bridge. This would also include the construction of the Marikina Control Gate Structure and further decrease flooding inundation by 7.5 percent.

Binondo-Intramuros Bridge

The 680-meter Binondo Intramuros Bridge, which will connect Intramuros and Binondo through a viaduct, will be equipped with pedestrian infrastructure.

Skyway Extension

The Alabang-Sucat Skyway Extension will build two additional lanes from Sucat Main Toll Plaza to Susana Heights. The project is now at 47 percent and will be delivered within the year.

Mindanao Avenue Extension

The Mindanao Avenue Extension is a 3.2-kilometer highway, which will reduce travel time from Quirino Highway to General Luis Avenue from one hour and 30 minutes to only 20 minutes.

NLEX Connector

The eight-kilometer NLEX-SLEX Connector, spanning from C3 Road in Caloocan to Sta. Mesa in Manila, is utilizing the Super T Technology, which would reduce construction schedule by about one year. The first five–kilometer segment from C3 road to España is expected to be completed in 2022.

METRO MANILA LOGISTICS NETWORK

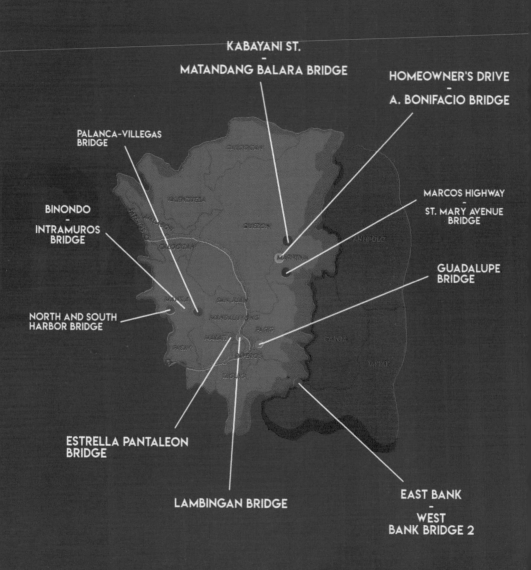

KABAYANI ST.
-
MATANDANG BALARA BRIDGE

HOMEOWNER'S DRIVE
-
A. BONIFACIO BRIDGE

PALANCA-VILLEGAS
BRIDGE

MARCOS HIGHWAY
-
ST. MARY AVENUE
BRIDGE

BINONDO
-
INTRAMUROS
BRIDGE

GUADALUPE
BRIDGE

NORTH AND SOUTH
HARBOR BRIDGE

ESTRELLA PANTALEON
BRIDGE

LAMBINGAN BRIDGE

EAST BANK
-
WEST
BANK BRIDGE 2

Metro Manila Logistics Infrastructure Network

According to the National Statistics Authority, there are about 9.3 million vehicles competing for space within the Philippines' limited road network. Vehicle density in Manila is higher than Singapore or Tokyo. Majority of the 32,770 kilometers of national roads are at saturation levels — with EDSA exceeding its road capacity of 200,000 vehicles a day — by almost 600 percent.

According to the 2012 study of the Japan International Cooperation Agency (JICA), it was estimated that Metro Manila was losing ₱2.4 billion a day or 0.8 percent of the GDP. The loss did not account for time lost that should have been spent with family or friends.

Five years after President Rodrigo Duterte laid out Build, Build, Build, the Department of Public Works and Highways has identified and started major road networks, which the Filipino People need in order to achieve seamless travel and connectivity. In fact by that time, DPWH Secretary Mark Villar had completed the master plan and started the implementation of the Metro Manila Logistics Improvement Project.

In addition to the 26 existing bridges crossing Pasig River, Marikina River, and Manggahan Floodway, which cater to about 1.3 million vehicles daily, 11 new bridges in the area will be constructed to provide alternative linkages between major thoroughfares and increase the number of usable roadways that would decongest traffic in Epifanio de los Santos Avenue (EDSA) and other major roads in Metro Manila.

Included in the Metro Manila Logistics Network are three bridges crossing Marikina River, namely the 1.582-kilometer Marcos Highway - St. Mary Avenue Bridge, the 691-meter Homeowner's Drive - A. Bonifacio Bridge, and the 723-meter Kabayani Street - Matandang Balara Bridge.

Three additional bridges crossing Pasig River and Manggahan Floodway are also underway. These are the 2.026-kilometer North and South Harbor Bridge, the 438-meter Palanca - Villegas Bridge, and the 932.78-meter Eastbank - Westbank Bridge 2.

The 961-meter Bonifacio Global City — Ortigas Center Link Road Project involves the construction of a four-lane Sta Monica to Lawton Bridge across Pasig River connecting Lawton Avenue in Makati City and Sta. Monica Street in Pasig City and a viaduct structure traversing Lawton Avenue onward to the entrance of Bonifacio Global City. Now, traveling between the central business districts of Taguig and Pasig Cities will only take 12 minutes and traffic congestion at EDSA and C-5 Road, particularly along Guadalupe Bridge and Bagong Ilog Bridge, will be alleviated by about 25 percent.

The Binondo-Intramuros Bridge, spanning 807 meters, is a ₱4.61-billion four-lane, steel bowstring arch bridge project, which is expected to connect Intramuros at Solana Street and Riverside Drive and Binondo at San Fernando Street.

The Estrella-Pantaleon Bridge, a ₱1.37-billion project, replaced the existing bridge with a four-lane twin spine steel box girder bridge, spanning 560 meters, to connect Estrella Street in Makati to Barangka Drive in Mandaluyong. The project was inaugurated in July 29, 2021.

The Duterte Administration spent about ₱3.4 trillion in infrastructure projects or about 4.93% of our GDP from 2016 to 2019. This is higher than the combined infrastructure spending of four prior Presidents.

COL
REGION

REGION V (Bicol Region)

ACCOMPLISHMENTS

1,769
**kilometers
of roads**

319
bridges

BY THE NUMBERS

751

flood mitigation structures

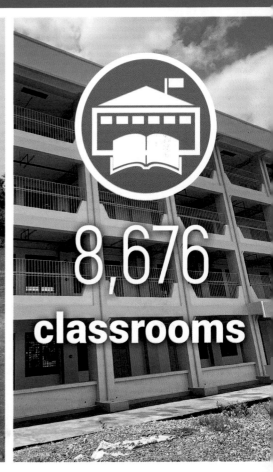

8,676

classrooms

The first time I joined the President's delegation, we were in the Bicol region. Typhoon Nina, internationally known as Nock-ten, entered the Philippine Area of Responsibility (PAR) on December 23. It intensified into a typhoon on December 24 and made landfall over Catanduanes province on the evening of December 25. At about 3 p.m., on Christmas Day, I received a message asking me to report back to central office and prepare a report on the damages sustained by the provinces affected by Typhoon Nina. We were informed that the President wanted it on his desk the following day, including actions already undertaken by the department.

As soon as it was safe for our ground personnel, Sec. Mark Villar ordered the dispatch of our prepositioned equipment and to proceed with the clearing of debris so as to facilitate rescue operation and give way for the distribution of relief goods.

By December 27, we were already on the ground with Mayor Duterte— first in Catanduanes, and then in, Camarines Sur. He skipped the gift-giving ceremonies and called it "corny" and "over-dramatic". But behind the doors, away from the camera, he met his men and asked them to deliver. For DPWH, we only had 48 hours to ensure that roads are passable and cleared.

I soon regretted the fact that we didn't bring any food. It was very different from what I originally expected it to be. I remember how an entire plane shared two pieces of Skyflakes brought by Sec. Briones.

We'll explore Bicol Region, a project composed of six provinces — Albay, Camarines Norte, Camarines Sur, Sorsogon, Catanduanes, and Masbate.

Since 2016, DPWH has completed a total of 1,769 kilometers of roads, 319 bridges, 751 flood mitigation structures, and 8,676 classrooms in Region 5.

Imelda Boulevard in Catanduanes

The 6.532-kilometer Imelda Boulevard, which leads to Virac Port in Catanduanes, also serves as a flood control structure which will mitigate the impact of storm surges.

San Fernando - San Jacinto - Monreal Road in Masbate

The 24.50-kilometer expressway, which includes the construction of five bridges, will traverse the municipalities of San Fernando, San Jacinto, and Monreal in Masbate.

2

Esperanza - Placer Road Leading to Pasiagon Beach Front in Masbate

Heading to Balay na Bato or Pasiagon Beach Front? Drive through the 30.56-kilometer road network, which will also aid in transporting aquatic and agriculture products.

3

Camarines Sur Expressway Project

The four-lane, 15.21-kilometer Camarines Sur Expressway Project will reduce travel time from San Fernando to Pili from 51 minutes to only 11 minutes.

4

Pasacao - Balatan Tourism Coastal Highway in Camarines Sur

The 40.69-kilometer coastal expressway will traverse the municipalities of Pasacao, San Fernando, Minalabac, Bula, and Balatan in Camarines Sur. The project, which serves as an alternate route to Daang Maharlika, will traverse 15 barangays and benefit about 8,000 motorists a day.

Legazpi City Coastal Road

Want to enjoy the panoramic view of Mt. Mayon? Drive through the 3.10-kilometer Legazpi City Coastal Road, which traverses four barangays in Albay — Baybay, Rawis, San Roque, and Bonot.

Albay - Sorsogon Connector

The 15.87-kilometer Albay - Sorsogon Connector, which follows the east coast, links two national roads — the Legazpi - Punta de Jesus Road in Albay and the Junction Sorsogon - Bacon Manito Road in Sorsogon. It is expected to benefit about 5,000 travelers per day.

Cagraray Island Cirumferential Road in Albay

Heading to the beach? Try the 40-kilometer Cagraray Island Circumferential Road, which connects four barangays in Cagraray Island to Bacacay town proper via land.

Sorsogon City Coastal Bypass Road

The 5.52-kilometer, four-lane Sorsogon Coastal Road, which includes a jogger's lane and a bicycle lane, serves as a diversion road when going to the municipalities of Casiguran, Gubat, and Castilla.

Matnog - Sta. Magdalena - Bulusan Road

The 31.41-kilometer highway will connect three municipalities in Sorsogon (Matnog, Sta. Magdalena, and Bulusan) and facilitate the transport of farm and marine products within the region.

Take me home, country roads
Eight provinces are now closer to Metro Manila, thanks to Build, Build, Build

I n 2016, President Rodrigo Duterte embarked to build the Luzon Spine Expressway Network, a 1,101-kilometer expressway network, which would connect the northernmost and southernmost parts of Luzon.

By building a 655-kilometer expressway network, Department of Public Works and Highways Secretary Mark Villar aims to complement the existing expressway grid spanning 385 kilometers. The goal is to increase the road network by threefold.

Included in the masterplan, which will eventually reduce travel time from La Union to Bicol by half, are the NLEX Harbor Link Project, the Tarlac-Pangasinan-La Union Expressway, the Urdaneta Bypass Road, the Radial Road 10, the Central Luzon Link Expressway, the Plaridel By-Pass Road, the Metro Manila Skyway Stage 3, the NLEX-

BLISTT Outer Ring Circumferential Road

SLEX Connector Road, among others. While 2020 might be remembered as the year international travel ground to a halt, with hope by the latter part of 2021, domestic travel will begin to recover.

With the completion of 26,494 kilometers of roads and 5,555 bridges nationwide—eight provinces in the North are now closer to Metro Manila.

01 Benguet

Baguio, La Trinidad, Itogon, Sablan, Tuba, and Tublay (BLISTT) are now more accessible with the opening of the Tarlac-Pangasinan-La Union Expressway (TPLEX) and the BLISST Outer Circumferential Road.

The BLISTT Outer Circumferential Road is a 144-kilometer road network, which provides access to the northern areas of the Cordillera Administrative Region to the Cagayan Valley Region via the Benguet-Vizcaya Road.

The Philippine Military Academy can also be accessed from this route via the Baguio-Bua-Itogon-Dalupirip Road.

02 Ilocos Sur

The completion of the 7.13-kilometer Candon City Bypass has reduced travel time from Sta. Lucia and Santiago, Ilocos Sur from 40 minutes to only 20 minutes. Motorists headed to the northern part of Ilocos Region may now use this alternate road that begins at Barangay Ayudante and ends at Barangay Tablac.

Other big-ticket projects in the region include the Bantay-San Ildelfonso Bypass Road, the Bantay-Vigan Diversion Road, and the Tagudin Bypass Road.

Candon City Bypass Road

Tarlac-Pangasinan-La Union Expressway

03 Pangasinan

Pangasinan is only two hours away from Manila with the opening of the 88-kilometer TPLEX.

Travel time from Villasis to Binalonan has also been reduced to only 30 minutes via the newly opened Urdaneta Bypass Road. Heading to Aguilar in Pangasinan? Check out the 24.22-kilometer scenic Daang Katutubo Road, which should be completed in 2022.

04 Bulacan

The completion of the 24.61-kilometer Plaridel Bypass Route will ease the traffic congestion in Daang Maharlika by providing a direct route from NLEX to San Rafael in Bulacan. The completion of the project, having diverted about 15,000 vehicles on Pan-Philippine Highway, provides an alternate route to Angat, Balagtas, and Pandi in Bulacan.

Travel time from Manila to San Rafael has been reduced by about 45 minutes.

05 Ilocos Norte

The completion of the Sicapo, Tabbayagan, and Madduang Bridges along Apayao-Ilocos Norte Road in Apayao Province has reduced travel time from the provinces of Apayao and Ilocos Norte by at least three hours. Now, travel time from Cordillera Administrative Region (CAR) to Ilocos Norte has been reduced from six hours and a half to only three hours.

The Apayao-Ilocos Norte Road connects the towns of Conner, Kabugao, and Calanasan in Apayao to the municipality of Solsona and the city of Laoag in Ilocos

Apayao - Ilocos Norte Road

Norte. It serves as an alternate route to motorists coming from CAR going to Laoag International Airport and the Manila North Road in Ilocos Region.

06 Mountain Province

Heading to Sagada to break across Echo Valley or explore Mt. Kiltepan? Try the 9.44-kilometer Balili-Suyo-Sagada Road and the 9.85-kilometer Sabangan-Sagada Road leading to the hanging coffins, Bomo-ok Falls, and Sumaguing cave.

07 La Union

With the completion of the last section of the 88.85-kilometer Tarlac-Pangasinan-La Union Expressway, travel time from Manila to Rosario in La Union has been reduced from six hours and 30 minutes to only three hours and 30 minutes.

08 Nueva Ecija

With the opening of the first 18-kilometer section of the 30-kilometer Central Luzon Link Expressway this year, travel time from Tarlac to Nueva Ecija will be reduced from 70 minutes to only 20 minutes. The toll-free expressway can be accessed via the interconnection structure of SCTEX and TPLEX in Balingcanaway in Tarlac City. CLLEX is expected to decongest traffic in Pan Philippine Highway by 48 percent and reduce travel time by 70 percent.

Going to the Ditabuyan Falls in Pantabangan, Nueva Ecija? Try the newly completed two-kilometer access road in Barangay Cadaclan.

Cebu Cordova Link Expressway

CHAPTER SIX

VISAYAS

WESTERN VISA

YAS

REGION VI (Western Visayas)

ACCOMPLISHMENTS

**2,193
kilometers
of roads**

**467
bridges**

BY THE NUMBERS

508
flood mitigation structures

11,556
classrooms

When I was still in elementary, my father Manuel and mother Elnora would tell me about the San Juanico Bridge, a 2.16-kilometer bridge connecting the island provinces of Samar and Leyte. Whenever we went home to Iloilo, I'd often wonder why we had to take boats or airplanes to travel to nearby Negros Occidental. There were not many bridges at that time.

The 2.1-kilometer San Juanico Bridge, which was built in 1969, is still the longest bridge 50 years after. The Build, Build, Build team has worked since 2016 on a masterplan — the Mega Bridge Project — a series of short and long-span bridges linking island provinces to eventually connect Luzon, Visayas, and Mindanao via land travel.

Rumors have circulated that the 32-kilometer Panay-Guimaras-Negros Project has been shelved. Is this true? No. Have there been challenges? Yes. After all, the inter-island bridge is 15 times the length of San Juanico Bridge.

Panay-Guimaras-Negros Bridge was never meant to be fully constructed within the term of President Rodrigo Duterte. What we aimed for from the beginning was a blueprint that would turn this dream into a reality.

Has the work on the project continued since 2016? Yes. In fact, the feasibility study, which was completed in November 2019, was evaluated and approved by the Investment Coordination Committee and the NEDA Board for possible financing through Official Development Assistance (ODA).

The Detailed Engineering Design Cost Appraisal, which was initiated by Korea Eximbank and completed in March 24, 2021, is now with NEDA.

If there was one thing I could attest from one Ilonggo to another, Mark Villar and the DPWH team worked hard to ensure this project didn't end up as lip service. Prior to his term, this project was not even on the table.

Today, we'll explore 10 big-ticket projects in Western Visayas Region, a region composed of six provinces — Aklan, Antique, Capiz, Iloilo, Guimaras, and Negros Occidental.

Since 2016, DPWH has completed a total of 2,193 kilometers of roads, 467 bridges, 508 flood mitigation structures, and 11,556 classrooms in Region 6 or Western Visayas.

Iloilo River Esplanade

The 8.25-kilometer Iloilo River Esplanade is a tide embankment project aimed to control sedimentation and erosion along riverbanks while providing much needed urban green space in the metro.

Boracay Circumferential Road

Heading to the best beach in the world? Walk, cycle, or ride through the newly widened 21.64-kilometer Boracay Circumferential Road. The new road has reduced travel time from Cagban Port or Tambisaan Port to Ilig-Iligan Beach by about 40 to 45 minutes.

Panay East West Highway

The 41-kilometer Panay East West Highway will complement the existing routes of the Strong Republic National Highway leading to Culasi Port in Ajuy in Iloilo. It traverses along existing national secondary road linking the Iloilo towns of Calinog, Passi, Lemery, Sara, and Concepcion toward Culasi in Ajuy, thereby complementing the Panay East-West Lateral Highway. It starts from Brgy. Ilaures in Bugasong in Antique and ends at Valderrama in Antique and Lambunao in Iloilo.

Iloilo Bypass Road

The 14.3-kilometer Iloilo Radial Road 1 Bypass Road is an alternate route starting at C-1 Avenue and ends at Tigbauan - Cordova - Leon Junction Road.

Aganan Bridge

The Aganan Bridge will reduce travel time from the Municipality of Maasin to the Municipalities of Alimodian and San Miguel and the Southern part of Iloilo Province by about 15 minutes.

Antique Esplanade

Heading to Antique? Catch the sunset from the Antique Esplanade located along the coastline of barangays Comon and San Pedro in San Jose de Buenavista.

Tumagbok Bridge

The Tumagbok Bridge along Iloilo - Antique Road will ease traffic mobility for 5,807 motorists per day and provide better access along the main thoroughfare connecting the provinces of Iloilo and Antique.

Kalibo Bridge in Aklan

Attending the Ati-atihan Festival? Explore the 770-meter Kalibo Bridge connecting Kalibo and Caticlan. This is part of the 15.81-kilometer Kalibo Circumferential Road, which will provide an alternate route from Aklan West Road and a direct link to Kalibo Airport.

8

Bacolod-Negros Occidental Economic Highway

9

The 49-kilometer Bacolod-Negros Occidental Economic Highway, which is now 41 percent completed, will reduce travel time from Victorias City to Bacolod-Silay Airport by 40 minutes.

Negros Connector

The 33-kilometer Candoni - Gatuslao - Basay Road will connect the provinces of Negros Occidental and Negros Oriental. It will link the municipalities of Candoni and Hinoba-an in Negros Occidental to the municipalities of Basay in Negros Oriental.

10

Six months to save Boracay

Sustainable Tourism Development has been the subject of both international and domestic discourse. It is particularly important when the life cycle of many tourist destinations, including Boracay, is at risk of irreversible collapse. In his study, "A New Approach to Sustainable Tourism Development," Frederico Nato has cautioned developing countries and pointed to evidence how over-exploitation and over-development have caused many tourist destinations irreversible damage arising from environmental degradation and consequent loss of revenues.

The problem hounding Boracay has been persistent for over two decades. The presence of algal bloom along Boracay's shoreline has become more frequent and pronounced. At the onset, the phenomenom would be observed only for two weeks, but now it would be around for months.

At least 200 businesses and thousands of local residents had not installed pipelines connecting to the province's septage and sewage treatment plant.

In 2015, the Department of Environment and Natural Resources (DENR) Environmental Management Bureau (EMB) noted that coliform bacteria levels in a drainage outlet that emptied into the sea in Sitio Bulabog in Boracay had exceeded safe standards by at least 47x, or 47,460 most probable number (mpn) per 100 milimeter (ml). The safe level for swimming is 1,000 mpn per ml.

In 2018, the Department of Public Works and Highways (DPWH) started the demolition of structures that occupied the 12-meter government road right-of-way and cleaning or declogging of existing drainage lines along Boracay Circumferential Road.

Boracay Circumferential Road

Secretary Mark Villar said that rehabilitation would be carried out, strictly following the 6.10-meter carriageway standard on both sides, a standard consistent with the 2008 municipal ordinance imposing a minimum setback requirement of at least six meters from the center of the road.

The Boracay Circumferential Road, spanning 21.64 kilometers from Cagban Port in Barangay Manoc-Manoc to Ilig-iligan Beach in Brgy. Yapak, will connect two main entry and exit points of the island and reduce travel time by about 40 to 45 minutes.

The project would also have sidewalks for pedestrians and bike lanes.

Roads on the island were narrow due to road right-of-way violations, with structures closely built along national roads, resulting in carriageways being shared by vehicles, pedestrians, and merchants.

The project would incorporate an improved drainage and sewerage system along the main road to contain in-land flooding and waste discharge.

DPWH employed at least 150 construction workers and 18 heavy equipment to start the demolition. The order was to implement a 24/7 construction schedule to meet the six-month deadline posed by President Rodrigo Duterte.

Boracay

Boracay: A case of political will

Before the six-month closure, coliform bacteria in Bolabog reached as high as one million most probable number (MPN) per 100 mililiter (ml). The streets were so narrow and cars could not pass through. Pedestrians competed with pedicabs and tricycles for whatever little space was left on the street. There were no sidewalks. Establishments encroached on the shoreline, with some sections left with barely any sand.

Six months later, water quality had significantly improved — with a recorded value of only 19 to 20 MPN/100 ml, according to Department of Environment and Natural Resources Secretary Roy Cimatu. This was even lower than the acceptable threshold of 100 MPN/100 ml for swimming areas and 200 MPN/100 ml for areas of non-contact sport.

A total of 1,438 structures, which had been built within easement areas, have been removed. The streets, which were once too narrow for cars to even enter, can now accommodate two-way traffic. PWD-friendly sidewalks have been constructed for pedestrians. Tourists will now enjoy a wider beach front following the imposition of a rule requiring a 30-meter easement from the water's edge.

At the onset, critics pointed out that Boracay beach closure seemed to be a drastic move, an isolated strategy. But the statement was nothing but a myth.

When I visited Florida as part of the US Department of State's International Visitor Leadership Program (IVLP), I learned that beach closures were part of a standard operating procedure relevant to Algal Bloom Monitoring. Recently, it closed Jupiter Beaches on Palm Beach County, Hobe Sound Beach, and Bathtub Beach in Martin County.

In Rhode Island, the moment the concentration of Enterocci bacteria in beach water exceeds 60 colony-forming units per 100 mililiters, they issue a temporary closure. In 2018 alone, there were at least 40 beach closures in Rhode Island, including Briar Point Beach in Coventry, Camp Beach in Kingston, Bristol Town Beach, Oakland Beach in Warwick, and Sandy Point Beach in Portmount. More recently, Thailand's Maya Bay, made famous by Leonardo DiCaprio's film "The Beach," was also closed indefinitely.

When Boracay opened in October 2018, Department of Public Works Secretary Mark Villar noted that Phase 1 of the 4.1-kilometer Boracay Circumferential Road and Flood Control Project also opened.

Now, the alignment, which was recovered after full implementation of the 12-meter road setback rule, will have a dual function as a traffic mitigation measure and a flood control project.

The roadway plan, which includes the installation of a total of 1,273 pieces of high-density polyethylene pipes (HDPE), construction of loading and unloading bays, sidewalks, and plant strips, was made accessible in December 2018.

The first two phases of the 21.64-kilometer Boracay Circumferential Road were completed in December 2020. The project will connect the main entry points of Boracay and reduce travel time by at least 75 percent. It also provides access to the Ati Community Village.

The author after the reopening of Boracay

CENTRAL
VISA

YAS

ACCOMPLISHMENTS

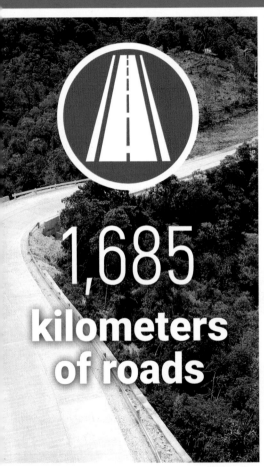

1,685
kilometers of roads

346
bridges

BY THE NUMBERS

596
flood mitigation structures

7,912
classrooms

In the Roadmap Study for Sustainable Urban Development in Metro Cebu, Japan International Cooperation Agency predicted the increase of economic activity in the province by 15 times its 2010 level and the creation of one million jobs should the blueprint be implemented by 2050.

One of the key recommendations of the agency was the strengthening of the Mactan - Cebu Link through the creation of another bridge infrastructure between Mandaue and Mactan and another that would link Cebu to Cordova.

The Cebu-Cordova Link Expressway, operated by the Metro Pacific, is now at 70 percent. It should be completed by 2022.

The governments of the Philippines and Japan have also formalized the loan agreement involving the fourth Cebu-Mactan Bridge while construction on the 73.75-kilometer Metro Cebu Expressway has also started.

Since the start of President Rodrigo Duterte's term, DPWH under the leadership of Secretary Mark Villar has completed 1,685 kilometers of roads, 346 bridges, 596 flood mitigation structures, and 7,912 classrooms in Region 7.

Let's explore Central Visayas, a region composed of four provinces — Cebu, Bohol, Negros Oriental, and Siquijor — and three highly urbanized cities: Cebu City, Lapu-Lapu, and Mandaue.

Cebu-Mactan Bridge (4th) and Coastal Road Construction Project

To respond to the increasing traffic demand in Metro Cebu, DPWH, in partnership with the Japanese government, will construct the fourth long span bridge that would connect Cebu and Mactan Island. This will complement three bridges that span across the Mactan Channel — the Marcelo Fernan Bridge, the Sergio Osmena Bridge, and the about to be completed Cebu-Cordova Link Expressway.

The project involves the construction of a 3.3-kilometer bridge with an elevated viaduct of 2.86 kilometers and a 4.9-kilometer coastal road with a 4.751-kilometer elevated viaduct.

Metro Cebu Expressway

The Metro Cebu Expressway is a 73.75-kilometer high standard arterial road that would serve as an alternative north-south backbone highway. It would connect Naga City to Danao City in Cebu and improve Metro Cebu's seamless east-west, south-north urban inter-modal transport.

The project is composed of three segments. The first segment, which spans 26.8 kilometers, will connect Minglanila, Talisay, Cebu City, Mandaue, and Consolacion in Cebu. The 29.799-kilometer second segment will expand it to Danao City. The final 17.15 kilometers section will connect it to Naga City.

Cebu-Cordova Link Expressway (CCLEX)

The 8.5-kilometer Cebu-Cordova Link Expressway will connect mainland Cebu from Cebu City via the Cebu South Coastal Road to Cordova Town in Mactan Island. Implemented by the Cebu Cordova Link Expressway Corporation (CCLEC), a subsidiary of Metro Pacific Tollways Corporation, the infrastructure has a navigational clearance of 51 meters for shipping traffic. It is expected to serve at least 50,000 vehicles daily.

Access Road to Madridejos

Fond of Danggit? Drive through the recently completed 5.9-kilometer access road, which connects the three municipalities on the Island of Bantayan - Santa Fe, Bantayan, and Madridejos. Don't forget to drop by the Virgin Island.

Montana - San Juan Buenaventura Road

Heading to Baclayon in Bohol? Why don't you try the 3.5-kilometer Montana - San Juan Buenaventura Road.

Panglao - Tagbilaran City Offshore Connector Bridge

The 2.71-kilometer inter-island bridge is part of the Mega Bridge Master Plan, which aims to connect Luzon, Visayas, and Mindanao via land travel. The project will connect Bohol to the island municipalities of Dauis and Panglao through the construction of a 1.2-kilometer, four-lane bridge, two short span bridges, and a 1.3-kilometer access road.

Slope Protection along Dumaguete North Road

The installation of a rockfall barrier along Dumaguete North Road has reduced the hazard for rockfall and landslides due to slope instabilities caused by loose, disintegrated, and weathered surfaces as well as debris flows.

Candoni - Gatuslao - Basay Road

The 33-kilometer Candoni – Gatuslao – Basay Road, or the "Negros Connector" will connect the provinces of Negros Occidental and Negros Oriental. It will link the municipalities of Candoni and Hinoba-an in Negros Occidental to the municipality of Basay in Negros Oriental.

Maria Flood Control Project

The installation of 2,057 hexapods have minimized inundation in the coastal areas of Maria in Siquijor, which would often experience flooding and storm surges. The project also included the construction of two bridges that would allow residents to pass through even during the high tide.

Alcoy Seawall

The Alcoy Seawall was constructed together with a wave deflector and an embankment to prevent flooding and protect the shoreline from erosion and scouring.

EASTERN
VISA

YAS

1,548
kilometers
of roads

598
bridges

BY THE NUMBERS

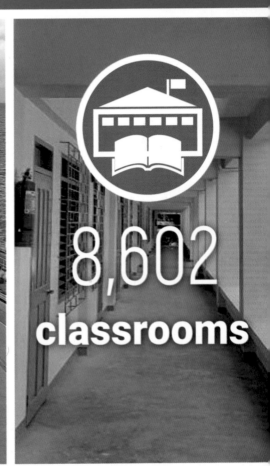

648
flood
mitigation
structures

8,602
classrooms

10

Before my stint at Build, Build, Build, I worked with the United Nations Development Program and Food and Agriculture Organization on their Typhoon Haiyan Response (locally known as Typhoon Yolanda).

The first time I saw Tacloban (after the onslaught of Yolanda), I was crying. Cadavers were in black plastic bags and the streets smelled of death and decay. In several barangays, not a single house survived.

In one of our visits, I met a fourth-year high school student, who was three months shy from graduation. Before Yolanda hit, he was studying for his exams with his girlfriend. It was supposed to be the last Christmas they would be dependent on their allowances.

They dreamed of traveling together after college. It was going to be their first time. They never had money to spare before. But in three months, they thought, everything would be all right. They only had to wait a few more months. After all, they had already waited for four years.

What he didn't expect was the fact that the storm would be so strong he would have to choose between saving his girlfriend and her one-year-old niece. For months, he would stare longingly at the sea, at the exact same spot he found his girlfriend, with a piece of galvanized iron that was used for roofing pierced through her stomach.

It was a relief that one of the first projects we started under DPWH Secretary Mark Villar was the Leyte Tide Embankment, a storm surge protection structure that would serve as the first line of defense for residents of Tacloban, Palo, and Tanauan in Leyte should another typhoon hit the region.

Let's explore ten Build, Build, Build projects in Region 8 or Eastern Visayas, a region composed of six provinces, one independent city, and one highly urbanized city.

According to Sec. Villar, a total of 1,548 kilometers of roads, 598 bridges, 648 flood mitigation structures, and 8, 602 classrooms have been completed under the term of President Rodrigo Duterte.

Leyte Tide Embankment Project

The height of the tide embankment project is set from a storm surge simulation of a 50-year return period. The project will include a promenade, a bicycle lane, an early warning tower, a view deck, and a fish landing. It is expected to protect at least 33,185 houses and an area of 33.7 square kilometers.

Palo West Bypass Road Project

The 2.956-kilometer Palo West Bypass is a six-lane-wide highway and will include the construction of two bridges – the 20.8-meter Caloogan Bridge and the 48.80-meter Bangon Bridge. The project will decongest traffic from Tacloban City to Palo, Leyte from 30 minutes (via Daang Maharlika Road) to only 15 minutes. The project will benefit about 1,500 motorists per day and decongest traffic in the junction of Palo-Carigara-Ormoc Road and Daang Maharlika - Tacloban - Baybay South Road - Government Center Road Network.

Tacloban City Bypass Road Project

The Tacloban City Bypass will start from Brgy. Nula - Tula and end at Brgy Caibaan along Daang Maharlika. The project will improve accessibility of the road network and reduce travel time from 1.5 hours (via Daang Maharlika) to only 30 minutes. The project is expected to benefit about 1,000 motorists per day.

Tacloban City Bypass Road Extension

The 33-kilometer, six-lane expressway will decongest traffic along Tacloban - Babatngon Road going to Tacloban City shortening travel time from 1.5 hours to only 45 minutes. This will complement the proposed international seaport that will be constructed in Babatngon, Leyte.

Mahaplag - Hilongos Road

The 48.20-kilometer Mahaplag - Hilongos Road starts at Brgy. San Isidro, Mahaplag, Leyte, along Daang Maharlika, and ends in Brgy. San Roque, Hilongos, Leyte along Ormoc-Baybay-Southern Leyte Road. The project will reduce travel time from Maasin City to Tacloban City from four hours to only 1.5 hours.

Maasin Coastal Bypass Road

The 4.7-kilometer Maasin Coastal Bypass Road will connect Tomas Oppus Street to Maasin City Port to Boundary Southern Leyte - Maasin - Macrohon - Daang Maharlika Road.

Ormoc City Diversion Road

The 4.3-kilometer Ormoc City Diversion Road will speed up movement of people, goods, and services between Brgy San Juan and Naungan in Ormoc City.

Divisoria - Langit - San Antonio Farm - San Diego - Sto. Nino Road

The 12-kilometer road project in Alang-alang is included in "ROLL IT," a convergence program between the Department of Trade and Industry (DTI) and the Department of Public Works and Highways (DPWH), which aims to improve access to areas with processing activities or raw materials.

8

San Roque Bypass

9

The San Roque Bypass in Northern Samar, which is already at 78.01 percent, includes the construction of a 2.4-kilometer concrete road and a 450-square-meter concrete bridge.

Calbayog City Coastal Road

10

The 4.32-kilometer Calbayog City Coastal Road will minimize traffic congestion in the city property by diverting traffic from Daang Maharlika to the Coastal Diversion Road.

Davao Coastal Road

CHAPTER SEVEN

MINDANAO

Surpassing the invisible line

A few years back, as my travel to Mindanao became more frequent with the construction of the Mindanao Road Network Development, a 2,567-kilometer road network in Northern Mindanao, Davao, SOCCSKSARGEN, and CARAGA Regions, I developed a more nuanced view of Islam which opposed the image constructed in binary public discourse. To me, it did not reflect the multi-faceted reality of Muslims, the spectrum of personalities, and the diversity that existed within the religion.

One of my closest friends in law school, Farahnaz Ali Ghodsinia, is a Muslim. After one of our classes, while walking to the parking lot of Malcolm Hall, we saw a caterpillar by her windshield. My immediate reaction was to fold one of our cases into a roll and hand it over. Instead of using it to kill the caterpillar, she carefully assisted it back to the grass. She told me that in a few weeks, that caterpillar would turn into a butterfly. Admittedly, I was surprised and soon realized it was a representation of Islam that needed to be told.

A 2015 survey conducted by Pew Research noted that most people in several countries with significant Muslim populations had an unfavorable view of ISIS. This would include Lebanon, Israel, Jordan, Palestinian Territory, Indonesia, Turkey, Nigeria, Malaysia, and Senegal. It also noted that 92 percent of Muslims in Indonesia and 91 percent of Muslims in Iraq believed that suicide bombings and other forms of violence against civilians in the name of Islam were rarely or never justified.

The study also showed that, in many cases, people in countries with large Muslim populations like Nigeria and Lebanon were as concerned as other countries about the threat of Islamic extremism.

Violence or hatred is not a function of religion. It is unfair to criticize Muslims for the crime committed by a handful. As Farah would often tell me over dinner, the killing of an innocent person has no place in genuine Islam.

A few weeks back, we attended the US-ASEAN Women Leaders Academy in Indonesia, the country with the world's largest Muslim population. There was no substantial difference, except that their drawers bore arrows known as Qibla pointers, which indicate the direction of Kaaba, Islam's holiest place in Mecca. It was also my first time to visit Istiqlal (Independence) Mosque, the largest mosque in Southeast Asia built in a span of 17 years and designed by Frederich Silaban, a Christian architect from North Sumatra. Our tour guide told us that the mosque had come to be a bastion of religious tolerance as it stood right in front of the Jakarta Cathedral, the oldest Roman Catholic cathedral in Jakarta built in neo-gothic style. In fact, whenever there is a large Muslim or Christian celebration as in Christmas or Eid Al-Fitr, each institution opens up its parking space for the worshipers of the other.

The United Nations has often defined culture as being created, contested, and recreated within the social praxis of diverse groups in economic, social, and political arenas. There is no point to segregation — to further an invisible line dividing Christians and Muslims. Just as men need to stand up for women in gender rights, Catholics must stand with our Muslim brothers and sisters for sustainable peace. We must be the first to oppose whenever Muslims are branded and discriminated against. As the old Chinese proverb say — Just as a fence has to be built with pegs, an able person needs the help of three others.

Zamboanga Connector

ZAMBO
PENI

ANGA
NSULA

1,817
kilometers of roads

269
bridges

289
flood mitigation structures

7,308
classrooms

I f you are in any way part of Build, Build, Build, be strong and steadfast. The truth will not change only because alternate realities are repeated, or that facts are often ignored. The attacks will be more vicious and it will be at a rate that we have never seen before. Do not be disheartened. There is work to be done still. While we are already able to complete 29,264 kilometers of roads, 15,134 kilometers are still ongoing. While we have already built 5,950 bridges, we still have 1,859 bridges to build.

Build, Build, Build is a springboard, a chance to turn a dream of connecting Luzon, Visayas, and Mindanao into a reality. It means linking 81 provinces, 146 cities, and 1,489 municipalities. It means bridging people together from different classes, dialects, ethnicities, and religions.

Your sacrifices gave us a chance for peace. Without you, we would not have been able to implement a 280-kilometer masterplan in Zamboanga Peninsula and residents of far flung areas would still have no access to basic social services.

It does not matter how projects are financed. Whether you are working on a project, which received external financing from Asian Development Bank such as the Alicia - Malangas Road in Zamboanga Sibugay, or one that was locally funded, such as the Sindangan Bayog Lakewood in Zamboanga del Norte, you have made a dent in the Philippine narrative.

The ongoing debate to differentiate Build, Build, Build and Public Private Partnerships (PPPs) serve no real value, except to those who want to sow discord or confusion. PPPs are only a subset of Build Build Build, as the former is only a financing modality of the latter.

Contrary to what some purport it to be, Public Private Partnerships in the Philippines date back as early as 1986, when Proclamation No. 50 created the Asset Privatization Trust (APT) and the Committee on Privatization. It has evolved since with the enactment of several laws, including RA 6957 or the Build-Operate-Transfer Law in 1991, RA 7718 and Memorandum Order No. 166 in 1993, Administrative Order 103 in 2000, Executive Order 144 in 2002, Executive Order No. 8 in 2010, and Executive Order No. 136 in 2013.

And while there are many motivations in entering PPPs such as broader sector reform, efficient and effective use of available resources, or mobilization of capital investment, it is not a viable financing option for all the regions in the Philippines. In fact, less than five percent of Build, Build, Build projects are financed via PPPs considering the revenue percentage share expectation of private concessionaires.

For instance, DPWH has not implemented a PPP project in Zamboanga Peninsula, a region composed of three provinces — Zamboanga del Norte, Zamboanga del Sur, and Zamboanga Sibugay — and the highly urbanized city of Zamboanga City.

According to Build, Build, Build Czar Mark Villar, DPWH has completed 1,817 kilometers of roads, 269 bridges, 289 flood mitigation structures, and 7,308 classrooms in Region 9.

Alicia - Malangas Road Province in Province of Zamboanga Sibugay

Eight bridges will be built along the 23.7-kilometer Alicia - Malangas Road Project, which traverses 15 barangays of the municipalities of Alicia and Malangas. These are the 40.94-meter Logpond Bridge, the 35.94-meter Tigabon Bridge, the 30.94-meter Ilisan Bridge, the 40.94-meter Bella Bridge, the 25.94-meter Payag Bridge, the 60.94-meter Lipacan Bridge, the 25.94-meter Sinusayan Bridge, and the 40.94-meter Lapirawan Bridge.

The project is part of the Improving Growth Corridors in Mindanao Road Sector Project, a 280-kilometer masterplan financed jointly by the Asian Development Bank and the government of the Philippines.

Tampilisan - Sandayong Road Project

The ₱623.260 million Tampilisan - Sandayong Road Project covers the upgrading of 15.07 kilometers of combined existing barangay or municipal roads generally made up of gravel with three to four meters wide to standard specifications of a secondary national road. When completed, the Tampilisan- Sandayong Road will provide a direct link between Dipolog and Pagadian Cities bypassing Ipil, which is the capital town of Zamboanga Sibugay.

The start of the project road is at the junction of the Dipolog-Ipil National Highway and the Sto. Nino barangay road traversing Barangays New Dapitan, Poblacion, Farmington, Situbo. It ends at Barangay Sandayong's road crossing over to Naga town proper, Zamboanga Sibugay.

Guicam Bridge Project

The 540-meter Guicam bridge will link Barangay Lutiman, Alicia in Zamboanga Sibugay and Olutanga port.

Lutiman - Guicam - Olutanga Road

The ₱989.69 million Lutiman – Guicam – Olutanga Road involves the concrete paving of 29.10 kilometers of national tertiary road made up of gravel and the construction of a 60.98-lineal-meters bridge following the existing alignment traversing the municipalities of Alicia, Mabuhay, Talusan, and Olutanga, Zamboanga Sibugay Province. It leads to a ferry operation at Guicam Channel about 440 meters wide to connect Guicam and Mabuhay on Olutanga Island.

Western Mindanao Command Hospital

Through the convergence program between the DPWH and the Department of National Defense under the Tatag ng Imprastraktura para sa Kapayapaan at Siguridad (TIKAS), a hospital will be built to complement the existing health system and provide health services to our men in uniform.

Buenavista - Bolong Coastal Bypass Road

Looking for a hidden paradise? Head to Bolong Island Beach in Zamboanga City and try the Buenavista - Bolong Coastal Road. Nearing its completion, it is expected to benefit 4,200 motorists daily. Once completed, it will reduce travel time from Buenavista to Bolong from one hour to only 15 minutes.

Up for a longer stay? The road connects to the wharf that ferries tourists to Once Islas, 11 islands on the Moro Gulf that are guaranteed to satisfy your cravings for fine white sand and pristine blue water.

Sindangan - Bayog - Lakewood Road

Out of 79.346 kilometers, 50.640 kilometers of the Sindangan - Bayog - Lakewood are already complete. The road network, which begins at the junction of Dipolog - Sindangan - Liloy Road in Zamboanga del Norte and terminates at the junction of Tubod - Lakewood Road in Zamboanga del Sur, will reduce travel time between the two provinces by over 66 percent from six hours to only two hours.

Zamboanga Connector

The 68.295-kilometer Siocon - Sirawai - Sibuco - Limpapa Road will connect three municipalities of Zamboanga del Norte to Zamboanga City. When the project is completed, travel time from Siocon to Zamboanga City will be reduced from five hours to only 1.5 hours.

Junction National Highway to Ayala - La Paz Road

Heading to Nancy Falls? Drive through the 28.482-kilometer road network, which will connect Ayala - La Paz Road to the national highway. When completed, travel time from Ayala to La Paz will be reduced from two hours to only 30 minutes. It is expected to benefit at least 1,100 motorists daily.

Barra Bridge

The Barra Bridge provides the shortest and fastest way to travel from Dipolog City to the city airport.

NORTHERN
MIND

ANAO

ACCOMPLISHMENTS

2,972
kilometers of roads

431
bridges

BY THE NUMBERS

413
flood mitigation structures

9,540
classrooms

When Secretary Mark Villar first assumed position in DPWH, he did not have a lot of public inspections. He would quietly go from one province to another without any notice or advice. He would always tell us it was important to put the proper systems in place so as to address the root cause of the problem. One of our first unannounced inspections was in Northern Mindanao. Cagayan de Oro Coastal Road, a project which was first funded in 1997, was still incomplete almost two decades later.

The problem of right-of-way has hounded many infrastructure projects for decades. Now, a right-of-way task force has been formed for every project and right-of-way functions have been decentralized. Regional offices are now empowered with their own right-of-way division, independent from the Central Office.

We'll explore ten big-ticket projects in Northern Mindanao, a region composed of five provinces — Bukidnon, Camiguin, Lanao del Norte, Misamis Occidental, and Misamis Oriental — and two highly urbanized cities, Cagayan de Oro and Iligan.

Since July 2016, DPWH has completed a total of 2,972 kilometers of roads, 431 bridges, 413 flood mitigation structures, and 9,540 classrooms.

Cagayan De Oro Coastal Road

The 17.80-kilometer Gusa - Igpit Section of the Cagayan De Oro Coastal Road serves as a bypass road starting from Brgy. Gusa in the eastern side all the way to the western side in Brgy. Igpit, Opol in Misamis Oriental, thus connecting six barangays in the city and two barangays in Opol.

The project will reduce travel time from Laguindingan Airport to city proper from one hour to only 20 minutes. It will also decrease travel cost by about 30 percent within the region.

Flood Risk Management Project in Cagayan De Oro River

The Flood Risk Management Project in Cagayan De Oro River, which involves the construction of an 11,928-meter earth dike and a 3,259-meter flood wall, will protect 290 hectares and 18,100 structures.

Marawi Transcentral Road

The reconstruction or rehabilitation of the 18.97-kilometer Marawi Transcentral Road covers the construction of roads severely damaged by the armed conflict in Marawi, including Bacong-Poona-Marantao-Marawi Road, GMA Terminal Access, Marawi-Cadre-New Capitol, Marcos Boulevard, Idarus Road Section, MSU - GMA Road, and Lumidong - Amai Pakpak Avenue.

Panguil Bay Bridge Project

The 3.7-kilometer Panguil Bay Bridge connecting Tangub City in Misamis Occidental and Tubod in Lanao del Norte, is part of the Mega Bridge Masterplan. Once completed in 2023, travel time between Tangub and Tubod will be reduced from 2.5 hours to only 10 minutes. It will also shorten travel time between Ozamiz City in Misamis Occidental and Mukas, Kolambugan in Lanao Del Norte from 2.5 hours (using RORO operations) to only 20 minutes.

CDO - New Western Diversion Road

The 7.88-kilometer CDO New Western Diversion Road is divided into two sections — the Canitoan-CDO Coastal Road Section and the Kauswagan - Bonbon Section. It will reduce travel time from CDO Port to Iligan City by over 50 percent.

Valencia Bypass Road

The 13-kilometer Valencia Bypass Road traverses the barangays of Mailag, Bagontaas, and Lumbo in Bukidnon. It is expected to facilitate the efficient movement of raw materials, from the point of production to the market centers.

Bukidnon - North Cotabato Connector

The 32.07-kilometer Bukidnon - North Cotabato Connector starts in Barangay Puntian in Quezon, Bukidnon and ends in the municipality of Arakan in North Cotabato. The masterplan includes an interconnection structure to three road projects — Davao-Calinan-Bukidnon Road, Digos Cotabato Road, and the Paco - President Roxas - Antipas - Arakan Road.

Malaybalay Bypass Road

The 18.38-kilometer Malaybalay Bypass Road, traversing the barangays of San Jose and Dalwangan in Bukidnon, serves as an alternate route to Sayre Highway.

8

Iligan City Coastal Road

The 5.37-kilometer Iligan City Coastal Road traverses the barangays of Sta. Filomena and Tambacan in Iligan City. It is expected to reduce travel time by at least 50 percent.

9

Iligan - CDO Connector

The 50.57-kilometer Iligan - Cagayan De Oro Connector starts at Barangay Digkilaan in Iligan City and ends in Barangay Bulua in Cagayan De Oro. It serves to address the traffic congestion in BCIR or the Butuan - Cagayan De Oro - Iligan City Road.

10

DA

VAO
REGION

ACCOMPLISHMENTS

2,194
kilometers
of roads

366
bridges

BY THE NUMBERS

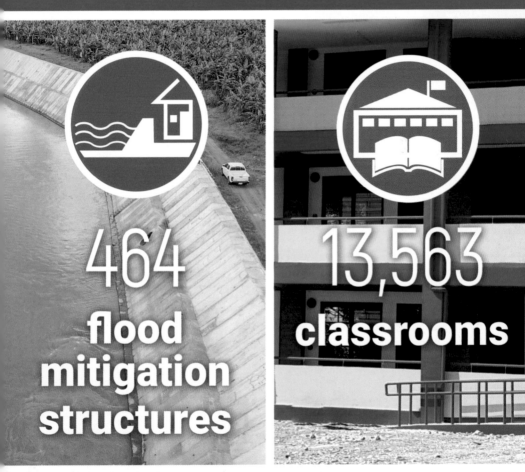

464
flood mitigation structures

13,563
classrooms

Davao City, the Philippines' largest city in terms of land area, was recognized as the second most livable city in the country among the 33 highly urbanized cities in the Philippines. This was among the findings of Dr. John Vianne Murcia, a specialist at the University of Mindanao's Institute of Popular Opinion.

This is impressive if you knew Davao City before the rule of then Mayor Rodrigo Duterte, and subsequently Mayor Sara. It was far from the Davao we know now, the second safest city in Southeast Asia with a Safety Index rate of 72.5 percent and a crime index of only 27.50 percent.

In case you are in doubt, come visit and, I assure you, you only need a week to fall in love with the region.

Explore the Mt. Hamiguitan Range Wildlife Sanctuary, the white beaches of the Island Garden City of Samal, the staircase like boulders of Aliwagwag Falls or the King of Philippine Peaks, Mt. Apo.

Let's explore Davao Region, a region composed of five provinces — Davao Oriental, Davao de Oro, Davao del Norte, Davao del Sur, and Davao Occidental — one highly urbanized city, Davao, and five component cities — Tagum, Digos, Panabo, Island Garden City of Samal and Matti.

According to Build, Build, Build Czar Mark Villar, DPWH has completed a total of 2,194 kilometers of roads, 366 bridges, 464 flood mitigation structures, and 13,563 classrooms in Davao Region.

The Samal Island-Davao City Connector Project

Included in the Mega Bridge Masterplan, the 3.86-kilometer Samal Island-Davao City Connector Project will connect the Island Garden City of Samal to Davao City across the Pakiputan Strait. The main bridge, 1.62 kilometers long, will be designed in a cable-stayed structure with the twin towers and double cable planes.

Davao City Coastal Road

When the 18.5-kilometer Davao City Coastal Road is completed, travel time from Toril to Downtown will be reduced from 45 minutes to only 15 minutes. The project is expected to benefit 7,500 motorists per day.

Tagum City Flyover

The 1.6-kilometer Tagum City Flyover is constructed at the most strategic intersection of Tagum City, catering to the provinces of Davao del Norte, Davao de Oro, and Davao Oriental. It eases the congestion on two national roads – Daang Maharlika or Agusan-Davao Road and Surigao del Sur-Davao Road.

Island Garden City of Samal Circumferential Road

Curious about the Vanishing Island? Drive through the Samal Circumferential Road, which is nearing completion, and witness half of Sanipaan Shoal emerge as a sand bar during low tide and vanish during high tide. You can also rappel at Bito Depression or explore one of 70 caves on the island.

Davao City Diversion Road Extension to Toril, Bangkal-Talomo-Puan Section

When the 1.140-kilometer road project is completed, the new diversion road will decongest Barangay Talomo Road and reduce travel time from Diversion to Toril Road by half, from 30 minutes to only 15 minutes.

Modular Hospital in Davao

To lessen the congestion of Southern Philippines Medical Center, DPWH, in partnership with the Local Government Unit of Davao, built a modular hospital fit to cater symptomatic patients.

Davao City Metropolitan Bike Lane Network

The 43-kilometer bicycle lane network will be completed within the year in Davao. At least 1.56 kilometers has already been installed along Roxas Boulevard; 4.80 kilometers along Davao-Cotabato Road (Magallanes, Governor Generoso Bridge to Matina Crossing, Solariega to Bago Bridge); 1.50 kilometers along Quezon Boulevard; and 1.11 kilometers along Sandawa Road.

Matanao-Padada-Kiblawan Road

The 58.554-kilometer expressway will start at Junction Padada, traverse Colonsabac, Datal Fitak, and end at Columbio, Kiblawan in Davao Del Sur. Four bridges with a total length of 150 meters are also to be constructed to provide better access to farmers planting palay, corn, coconut, banana, copra, and castor beans.

Access Road leading to Lao Integrated Farms-Mt. Apo Trail-Balutakay Waterfalls

Climbing Mt. Apo or heading to Balutakay Waterfalls? Drive through the newly-paved 19.987-kilometer road, which also links Davao-Cotabato Road and Bansalan-Cotabato Road to the local roads of Bansalan.

Construction of revetment along Tagum-Liboganon River

The flood control project is intended to protect low-lying areas along Tagum-Liboganon river through the construction of a revetment structure.

SOC
SAR

CSK
GEN

ACCOMPLISHMENTS

2,125
kilometers
of roads

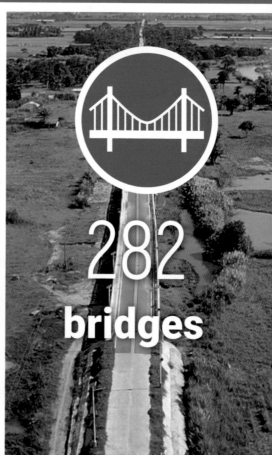

282
bridges

BY THE NUMBERS

342
flood mitigation structures

9,278
classrooms

With Karen Jumarang Tan and Chynna Cuna, two of my closest friends, I watched *The Bucket List* in high school. It was a film starring Jack Nicholson and Morgan Freeman about two terminally ill men on a road trip with a list of things to do before they kick the bucket. After the movie, we decided to write our own. The first thing on my list was to visit every province in the Philippines.

After enrolling at UP Los Baños, I was even more determined. Laguna had a charm that, to this day, I cannot seem to get over. Maybe, I thought, the rest of the Philippines would be as beautiful as Laguna. Rightly so. I couldn't forget the first time I saw Lake Sebu or Lake Holon in South Cotabato. It was a paradise tucked away 1,756 meters above sea level. Fortunately, they are more accessible now.

We'll explore Region 12, more commonly known as Central Mindanao, a region composed of four provinces—South Cotabato, Cotabato, Sultan Kudarat, Sarangani — and one highly urbanized city, General Santos.

According to Build, Build, Build Czar Mark Villar, Department of Public Works and Highways has completed a total of 2,125 kilometers of roads, 282 bridges, 342 flood mitigation structures, and 9,278 classrooms in Region 12.

Datu Paglas - Columbio - Matanao Road

The 23.170-kilometer Datu Paglas - Columbio - Matanao Road in Sultan Kudarat will connect SOCCSKSARGEN (Region 12) and Davao Region (Region 11). It is the shortest route from South Cotabato, Sultan Kudarat, and Bangsamoro Autonomous Region in Muslim Mindanao to Davao City.

Surallah - T'boli - San Jose Road

The 66-kilometer Surallah - T'boli - San Jose Road will connect the neighboring municipalities of T'boli, Surallah, and Lake Sebu to commercial centers, sea ports, and airports of General Santos City. When completed, travel time from Surallah to General Santos will be reduced by 50 percent from two hours to only one hour. It bypasses the municipalities of Banga, Tupi, Polomolok, and Koronadal.

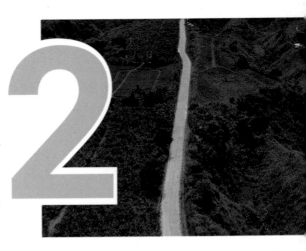

Puntian - Arakan Road

The Puntian-Arakan Road will connect the Central and Northern portion of Mindanao. It starts in Barangay Puntian in Quezon, Bukidnon and ends in the municipality of Arakan in North Cotabato. The masterplan includes an interconnection structure to three road projects — Davao-Calinan-Bukidnon Road, Digos Cotabato Road, and the Paco - President Roxas - Antipas - Arakan Road.

Isulan Bagumbayan - SNA - Lebak -Kalamansig Road Network

The 135-kilometer road network will connect the municipalities of Esperanza, Isulan, Bagumbayan, Senator Ninoy Aquino, Kalamansig, and Lebak in Sultan Kudarat. When completed, it is expected to reduce transportation cost of agricultural and marine products.

Banga - Tupi - Malugon Road

The 102-kilometer Banga - Tupi - Malugon Road will connect the provinces of South Cotabato, Sarangani, Maguindanao, Davao, and Davao del Sur.

5

Koronadal - Lutayan - Columbio - Matanao Road

The 16.514-kilometer Koronadal - Lutayan - Columbio - Matanao Road in Sultan Kudarat will connect Central Mindanao to Davao Del Sur in Davao Region. Motorists from South Cotabato, Sultan Kudarat, and BARMM can take this route to Davao City.

6

Surallah - Lake Sebu - Maitum Road

Heading to Lake Holon or the Seven Falls? Explore the 101-kilometer road network of Surallah - Lake Sebu - Maitum Road, which connects South Cotabato and Sarangani.

7

Sarangani - Davao Del Sur Coastal Road

Heading to Gumasa Beach or Kamlayaman Falls? The upgrading of the 1.5-kilometer Sarangani - Davao Del Sur Coastal Road is almost complete.

8

Pinguiaman Bridge

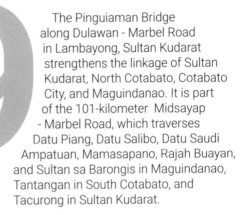

9

The Pinguiaman Bridge along Dulawan - Marbel Road in Lambayong, Sultan Kudarat strengthens the linkage of Sultan Kudarat, North Cotabato, Cotabato City, and Maguindanao. It is part of the 101-kilometer Midsayap - Marbel Road, which traverses Datu Piang, Datu Salibo, Datu Saudi Ampatuan, Mamasapano, Rajah Buayan, and Sultan sa Barongis in Maguindanao, Tantangan in South Cotabato, and Tacurong in Sultan Kudarat.

Cotabato City East Diversion Road

The 13-kilometer Cotabato City East Diversion road will strengthen urban - rural linkages in the provinces of Maguindanao and Lanao del Sur. This will provide an alternate route to decongest traffic along Sinsuat Avenue in the Central Business District of Cotabato City. It will reduce average travel time going to and from Cotabato City proper from 70 minutes to 20 minutes. It starts along the Marbel - Allah - Cotabato Road near Awang Airport in Cotabato City and ends at Cotabato City - Lanao Road.

10

CAR
REGION

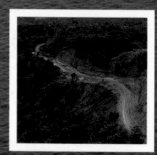

AGA

ACCOMPLISHMENTS

1,435
kilometers of roads

286
bridges

BY THE NUMBERS

298
flood mitigation structures

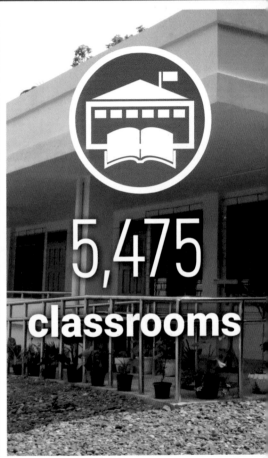

5,475
classrooms

In the second quarter of 2021, the Philippines' Gross Domestic Product (GDP) grew by 11.8 percent, the highest since the fourth quarter of 1988. The biggest contributor to the increase was the construction sector, which was pegged at 25.7 percent. It was followed by manufacturing sector at 22.3 percent and industry and services at 20.8 percent. In other words, the Philippines has ended its recession with the fastest year-on-year growth in 32 years.

In its August 2021 report, International Monetary Fund predicted the recovery to gain momentum with Real GDP Growth expansion of 5.4 percent in 2021 and seven percent in 2022.

IMF agreed that the expansionary fiscal stance struck an appropriate balance between recovery needs and fiscal prudence and that steady structural reforms as well as the continued public infrastructure projects would help rekindle investment and push the Philippines' return to the pre-pandemic rate of 6.5 percent.

Critics have said that the administration of President Rodrigo Duterte should shy away from Build, Build, Build if it were to solve the COVID-19 pandemic. I disagree. The government must not choose between health and economy but rather make mutual compromises that would further health, recovery, job security, and long-term economic potential.

From the onset, the goal of Build, Build, Build has been to create a road network that would not only link Luzon, Visayas, and Mindanao but also tear down invisible walls that have divided us for decades. It means bringing people together from different regions, provinces, cities, and municipalities and rallying them behind the goal of ushering in the Philippines' golden age of infrastructure.

Secretary Mark Villar hoped to create an infrastructure network that would allow Filipinos to dream of a better Philippines.

It is important to remove the roadblocks that hinder us from seeing the beauty of Magpupungko Rock Pools, Hinatuan Enchanted River, Guyam Island, Tinuy-an Falls, Sohoton Cove, Sugba Blue Lagoon, Agusan Marsh Wildlife Sanctuary, Taktak Falls, Lake Bababu, among others.

Since 2016, DPWH has completed 1,435 kilometers of roads, 286 bridges, 298 flood control projects, and 5,475 classrooms in CARAGA.

Agusan del Sur-Bukidnon Connector

The 62-kilometer East West Lateral Road will provide a direct route from Northern Mindanao (Region 10) to CARAGA (Region 13) and connect Agusan del Sur and Bukidnon via the Agusan-Malaybalay Road. The project includes the construction of seven permanent bridges.

Agusan del Sur - Surigao del Sur connector

The 40.73-kilometer East West Lateral Road will traverse Surigao-Davao Coastal Road, Junction Gamut in Surigao del Sur, and Daang Maharlika in Bayugan City, Agusan del Sur. When completed, it will cut travel time from farms to the nearest market by one hour and 20 minutes, reducing the hauling cost of agricultural products. The project will link the provinces of Agusan del Sur, Bukidnon, and Surigao del Sur.

Sampaguita-Makilos Road Project

The indigenous people of CARAGA like the Manobos and Mamanwas will have better access to social services when the 163-kilometer Sampaguita Makilos Project is completed. The project will connect the provinces of Agusan del Sur, Agusan Del Norte, and Bukidnon.

Bukidnon-Agusan Del Norte Connector

The 29-kilometer Bukidnon-Agusan del Norte Connector is now 89.76 percent complete. It is poised to fully open by December 2022. The project is the nearest route to reach Impasug-ong, Bukidnon from Buenavista, Agusan Del Norte. When completed, travel time between the two provinces will be reduced by at least two hours, from six hours to only three to four hours.

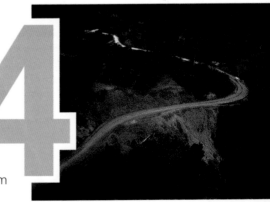

Butuan-Pianing-Tandag Road

The existing national road of Butuan-Pianing-Tandang Road in Agusan Del Sur will be extended and upgraded by 15 kilometers to connect to Surigao-Davao Coastal Road from a 40.40-kilometer new road opening at Surigao del Sur. This is part of the Mindanao Road Development Network, which aims to increase inter-provincial and interregional connectivity in Mindanao.

Cabadbaran-Puting Bato-Lanuza Road Project

The Cabadbaran-Puting Bato-Lanuza Road project involves the opening and concreting of a 73-kilometer road from Junction Daang Maharlika on Surigao-Agusan Road to Junction Surigao-Davao Coastal Road in Lanuza Surigao del Sur. It is now 36.23 percent complete. Two bridges will also be built within the road network.

Nasipit-Buenavista-Masao Port Coastal Road

The 25-kilometer road project will provide a direct route from Nasipit International Port and Masao National Port and decongest the busy Butuan City-Cagayan de Oro-Iligan City Road.

NRJ Rizal-Togbongon-Mat-I-Mabini-Trinidad Road

The 22-kilometer road project will connect eight barangays of Surigao del Norte, namely: Rizal, Togbongon, San Roque, Poctoy, Serna, Mat-I, Mabini, and Anomar — and provide an alternate route to Daang Maharlika.

8

Lake Mainit-Tubay River Basin Flood Control Project

The outlet river from Lake Mainit, the Philippines' fourth largest river, is the 30.8-kilometer Kalinawan-Tubay River. The construction of the two-kilometer flood control structure along the river basin was completed to mitigate the flooding problem in the province.

9

Nasipit-Agusan Del Norte Road

The construction of a 39.81-kilometer access road leading to Nasipit-Agusan Del Norte Industrial Estate Special Economic Zone is now at 92 percent.

10

All roads lead to a better Marawi

Four years ago, the siege in Marawi City, Lanao del Sur, left a trail of death and destruction. What was once a lively and culturally vibrant city was left in utter ruins after five months of battle. There was massive displacement of communities and loss of livelihoods and income.

When the city was finally liberated from terrorist influence, the government did not waste time in coming up with a plan to build back a better Marawi City.

The first time I went there, I was with Secretary Mark Villar. We met a soldier who had shrapnels on his back. He told us that a number of them would have to keep the fragments of the bombs in their bodies so long as they lived. Pro-ISIS militants left roadside bombs and improvised explosive devices (IEDs) everywhere, from doors to windows.

The clearing operations were not easy. IEDs were concealed in houses and roadsides. It was carried and delivered in cars or packages. Sometimes, it was surrounded by enhancements — nails, glass, or metal fragments — designed to increase the amount of shrapnel propelled by the explosion.

We knew the challenges our soldiers faced were life threatening. We saw it first hand, an explosion in a building just a few meters from where our chopper was. Suddenly, the explosion blew out windows and a fire consumed a building.

The armed confrontation in Marawi has displaced majority of the total population of the city, as well as residents in nearby municipalities who were compelled to leave due to severe food shortage. Farmers and fishermen had no access to roads for several months. There were no classes and businesses were closed.

As part of the Task Force, Sec. Mark led a team that would provide a road network infrastructure designed to pave the way for a revitalized economy of Marawi. The rehabilitation and reconstruction of the Marawi Transcentral Roads will improve the flow of traffic, provide people with better access to goods and services, and open opportunities for livelihood and development. More important, it will connect communities and unite peoples, thus, sustaining our peace building efforts.

For this, DPWH has already undertaken two projects — the Program for the Support to Rehabilitation and Reconstruction of Marawi City and Surrounding Areas, and the Marawi Transcentral Road Phase III Under Road Network Development Project in Conflict-Affected Areas in Mindanao.

The first program, financed by a two billion Japanese yen or approximately ₱970 million donation/grant to the Philippine government from the government of Japan through the Japan International Cooperation Agency (JICA), covers the improvement of 18.97 kilometers of Marawi Transcentral Roads.

It consists of three contract packages: Contract Package 1-B (5.45 kilometers), which covers sections of Bacong-Poona-Marantao-Marawi

1st Lieutenant Anna Mae Lamentillo

Road, GMA Terminal Access Road, Marawi-Cadre-New Capitol Road, Marcos Boulevard (Road 19), and Idarus Road (Road 27); and Contract Package 2 (4.11 kilometers), which covers sections of MSU-GMA Road (Road 8) and Lumindong-Amaipakpak Avenue (Road 21), have already been completed on March 15, 2021 and February 6, 2021 respectively. Contract Package 1-A (9.41 kilometers), which covers two sections of Bacong-Iligan-Marawi Road, is set to be completed by September 16, 2021.

Meanwhile, the reconstruction as well as rehabilitation of another 18.78-kilometer road is currently ongoing under the Road Network Development Project in Conflict-Affected Areas in Mindanao. The project amounting to ₱723.26 million is funded by JICA under the official development assistance (ODA) loan financing.

Inspection of Ground Zero in Marawi

It consists of four packages: Package 3-A (4.87 kilometers) covers sections of Sagonsongan-Cabibgab Road (Road 6), 4th Street Road (Road 7), and 1st Street-Mayor Natangcop Indol St. Road; Package 3-B (4.92 kilometers) covers three sections of Saguiaran Road (Roads 9-1, 13, and 14); Package 3-C (4.34 kilometers) covers another two sections of Saguiaran Road (Roads 9-2 and 15) and two sections of Marawi City Road (Roads 25 and 26); and Package 3-D (4.65 kilometers) covers sections of Bangon-Poona-Marantao Road, Bito-Rorogarus Road (Road 11), and Tampilon Road.

Roadworks for these four packages started in the second quarter of 2021. They are expected to be completed by May 2022, well within the term of President Rodrigo Duterte.

Inspection of Marawi Transcentral Road

Laguna Lake Expressway

CHAPTER EIGHT

REFORMS

Reforms in DPWH

Following President Rodrigo Duterte's mandate of increasing transparency and accountability in government, the Department of Public Works and Highway put an end to ghost projects in 2018 as it migrated to a fully automated new monitoring system, the Infra-track App, which would utilize built-in geotagging, satellite technology, and drone monitoring.

When the transition is completed, the Infra-Track App would detect ghost projects real time as the new application plots photos inputted in the system for monitoring in the exact geographic coordinates where it was taken. The system, through geographic identification of photos, videos, and other posts , automatically alerts key DPWH officials when a project is misreported from a different location.

Apart from the Infra-track App, DPWH Secretary Mark Villar has instituted a number of reforms in the department to ensure efficient delivery of infrastructure.

As soon as the system detects a five percent negative slippage, the contractor involved in the project will be given a warning and required to submit a "catch-up program" to eliminate the slippage or delay.

If such slippage furthers to at least ten percent, he will be given a second warning and required to submit a detailed action program on a two-week basis, which commits him to accelerate the work and accomplish specific physical targets, which reduces the slippage over a defined time period. The contractor will be instructed to specify the additional input resources — money, manpower, materials, machines, and management, which he should mobilize for this action program.

At any point that such contractor incurs a delay of at least 15 percent, he will be given a final warning and

SFEX Tunnel Inspection

required to come up with a more detailed program of activities with weekly physical targets, together with the required additional input resources. On-site supervision will be intensified, and evaluation of project performance will be done at least once a week. At the same time, the project manager, district engineer or regional director will also prepare a contingency plan for the termination, or rescission of the contract and/or takeover of the work by administration or contract.

Moreover, all contractors with ongoing DPWH contracts, which have incurred negative slippages of 15 percent or more, have been pre-disqualified from future biddings until after the negative slippage has been reduced to less than 15 percent. No time suspensions are also provided without the prior approval of the secretary or the undersecretary in charge. Negligence or inexcusable failure of the contractor to provide the required equipment, supplies, or materials are also not tolerated.

Moreover, administrative sanctions are now imposed on erring engineers involved in the defective implementation of DPWH projects.

If the Quality Assurance Unit (QAU) reports on any project under the supervision of a DPWH engineer and gives it a rating of 10 or greater based on the values shown, he will receive a warning. Should the defect or deficiency occur again in any of the projects they supervise, the erring engineer will not be allowed to handle or supervise a project for a period of six months to a year. He may also be perpetually disqualified.

One thing is for sure, the Duterte administration is serious about curbing corruption.

Skyway Stage 3 Inspection

Walkable Cities

According to the World Health Organization (WHO), approximately 1.35 million people die each year as a result of road traffic crashes while at least 20 million more people suffer non-fatal injuries, with many incurring a disability as a result. More than half of all road traffic deaths are among vulnerable road users — pedestrians, cyclists, and motorcyclists. Ninety-three percent of the world's fatalities on the roads occur in low- and middle-income countries, even though these countries have approximately 60 percent of the world's vehicles. These injuries, while predictable and preventable, cause at least three percent of their countries' gross domestic product.

The 2030 Agenda for Sustainable Development has set an ambitious target of halving the global number of deaths and injuries from road traffic crashes by 2020. WHO promotes the "Safe System approach," a methodology that accounts for all the road users' vulnerability, including human error. For example the study noted that drivers using mobile phones, whether hands-free or hand-held, are approximately four

Antique Esplanade

times more likely to be involved in a crash than drivers not using a mobile phone. It also advocated for the construction of footpaths, cycling lanes, safe crossing points, and other traffic calming measures.

In the Philippines, it can easily be conceded that development has been mainly to achieve a certain level of scientific efficiency in car mobility. Unfortunately, pedestrians have not been the priority in landscaping most of the urban centers.

In an effort to provide a safer road for cyclists and pedestrians, the Department of Public Works and Highways (DPWH) has opened a separate 5.58-kilometer bicycle lane facility along the stretch of Laguna Lake Highway in Bicutan, Taguig City on February 7, 2019, only three months after the completion of the Laguna Lake Highway.

But what is more interesting is that the vision of incorporating pedestrian infrastructure on public roads is not only happening in Manila, but also in other places in Luzon, Visayas, and Mindanao.

For instance, the Cagayan de Oro (CDO) Coastal Road, a 12.77-kilometer bypass road, which is expected to ease access in the eastern side of Macajalar Bay in CDO, Gingoog in Bukidnon, Misamis Oriental, and Caraga, is also

built with bicycle lanes. The road project, which starts from Brgy. Gusa in the eastern side all the way to the western side in Brgy. Igpit, Opol, in Misamis Oriental, is expected to reduce travel time from the Laguindingan Airport to the city proper to only 20 minutes.

Another project in Mindanao, which would include bicycle lanes would be the Davao City Coastal Road, an 18-kilometer road project, which will span from Jct. Bago Aplaya (south) to Sta. Ana Wharf toward R. Castillo Street.

In the Visayas, pedestrians are also provided the option to bike or walk along the Bacolod Negros Occidental Economic Highway, a 21.8-kilometer road that will serve as an alternate route passing the interior area of Bacolod City leading to Bacolod Silay Airport and other tourist destinations in the area.

The Leyte Tide Embankment project, a 27.3-kilometer flood control project from Brgy. Diit, Tacloban City to Brgy. Ambao, Tanauan, Leyte, built to protect coastal communities from the destructive effects of storm surges, will also include the provision of pedestrian infrastructure.

Bike lanes to the future

When I was in Massachusetts in 2020, the city government of Boston just launched the "Go Boston 2030 Vision Framework", an initiative which hoped to cement Boston's place as America's most walkable city by putting up infrastructure that would improve access into and around the commercial districts for people travelling on foot, by bike or scooter. Ultimately, they intend to increase people walking to work by 50 percent and increase bicycling shares by four-fold within the next ten years.

This has been a trend for many progressive cities around the world. In fact, since 2007, Boston has built more that 144 kilometers of bicycle lanes. In Denmark, they constructed a "cycle superhighway," a "coherent network of cycle highway" spanning over 20 cities and municipalities. In Amsterdam, museum enthusiasts could cycle through the Rijksmuseum, a 19th century museum famous for Rembrandt's *Night Watch*.

In the Philippines, there wasn't much political support or policy or infrastructure that would address the needs of cyclists and pedestrians. It was almost impossible — and to a certain extent unsafe — to walk or cycle alongside national highways.

In 2011, the Asian Development Bank examined walkability and pedestrian facilities in Asian cities. It showed that in Manila, like in Hanoi, a sizeable number of the trips could be made by foot and bicycle because the average distance traveled per trip was low.

Data from the Metro Manila Urban Transport Integration showed that nearly 35 percent of destinations were within a 15-minute walk or bicycle trip, but the majority of short trips were made by paratransit (jeepneys and tricycles) and cars.

Fortunately, the vision for Philippine infrastructure is fast changing.

Laguna Lake Highway Inauguration

Laguna Lake Expressway

Metro Cebu Bike Lane Network

Bicycle lanes in PH will now be mandatory

With the issuance of DPWH Secretary Mark Villar of Department Order 88, all projects that involve new road and bridge construction will include in their design the provision of bicycle facilities, if feasible.

This would mean that projects like the 6.94-kilometer Laguna Lake Expressway, would now be the rule rather than the exemption. Three-meter-wide protected bicycle lanes will soon be a common sight rather than a unique feature of the toll-free expressway connecting Bicutan to Taytay.

Since 2016, DPWH has been working on incorporating pedestrian infrastructure on public roads in Luzon, Visayas, and Mindanao. But the issuance of this new policy hopes to institutionalize the creation of pedestrian infrastructure.

For instance, the Cagayan de Oro (CDO) Coastal Road, Davao City Coastal Road, Leyte Tide Embankment Project, Pasig River Flood Control Project, Tagaytay Bypass Road, Bacolod Economic Highway, Antique Esplanade, Sorsogon Coastal Highway and Boracay Circumferential Road, have been built with bicycle lanes.

Bicycle Facility Classifications

Under DO 88, bicycle facilities will be classified into three classes depending on the prevailing road and traffic conditions: Class I or the Shared Use Bike Path, Class 2 or the Separated Bike Lane, and Class 3, the Shared Roadway.

In Class I, a designated path, completely separated from the roadway, will be identified for the exclusive use of bicycles or shared with pedestrians. In Class 2, a portion of roadway, which is designated for exclusive use of bikes, will be distinguished by a paint strip, curb, or barrier. In Class 3, where limited carriageway width poses a problem, a part of the roadway that has been officially designated and marked as bicycle route may also be used by motor vehicles.

Soon, the Philippines will be a cycling country.

Davao Coastal Expressway

A case for tourism preservation

olit Solis can still remember what Pasig River looked like before it was polluted and pushed to its current state. During the time of President Ramon Magsaysay, it was a vibrant place of transportation and tourism. At ten years old, she would ride the ferry from Paco, Manila, to Malacañang. She remembers lining up to meet the president every Christmas. It was a place where children used to play, until it deteriorated year by year. The transition was gradual. Pasig River did not end up as the garbage-filled dumpsite that it has become in an instant. It was an aggregate of what people thought were minor infractions. Until one day, the people who used it for transportation and the children who used to play in the area, could no longer recognize it. Resources are finite and, while it is easier to take it for granted, we ought to protect the right of the next generation to a healthy ecology.

Before the six-month closure of Boracay, coliform bacteria in Bolabog reached as high as one million most probable number (MPN) per 100 mililiter. Access roads on the island were narrow that cars could not pass through. Pedestrians competed with pedicabs and tricycles for whatever little space was left in the carriageway. There were no sidewalks. Establishments encroached on the shoreline, on the road, leaving some sections with barely any sand. The capacity of the storm drainage infrastructure could only accommodate half of the actual volume of water. The sewerage system was not sufficient to address the volume of waste water on the island. Inland flooding had become a problem.

Six months later, Boracay seems to have turned back time. It was the island that residents knew 20 years ago. Water quality has significantly improved — lower than the acceptable threshold of 100 MPN/100 ml for swimming areas and 200 MPN/100 ml for

areas of non-contact sport. Tourists are now able to enjoy a wider beach front after the imposition of the 30-meter easement from the water's edge.

Critics pointed out that the Boracay beach closure was a drastic and authoritarian move. Such was not the case.

When I visited Arizona as part of the US Department of State's International Visitor Leadership Program (IVLP), I learned that before the National Park Service shifted to a weighted lottery system for the noncommercial river permit system, the waiting list for a river permit in the Grand Canyon rafting was almost 27 years.

It was not an isolated case. For instance, along the border of Utah and Arizona, at the north edge of the Paria Canyon-Vermilion Cliffs Wilderness Area, access to the Wave, a sandstone rock formation located in the Coyote Buttes North Special Management Area, has been limited to only 20 people a day. Spots are either won through the online Paria Canyon permit lottery or secured through a walk-in permit that may be retrieved at the Grand Staircase-Escalante National Monument Visitor Center.

Interestingly, the tightened regulations are not only found in Arizona. In Washington, for instance, before tourists or residents can access the Colchuck Lake or the Little Annapurna, they need to first secure a Core Enchantments Permit, which is also won by lottery. The same is true for the Half Dome in California and Selway River Rafting in Idaho.

Beach closures are not very peculiar either. In Rhode Island, the moment the concentration of Enterocci bacteria in a beach water sample exceeds 60 colony forming units per 100 mililiter, they issue a temporary closure. In 2018 alone, there were at least 40 beach closures in Rhode Island.

Without regulations, there would be no complaints. But if we do not act now, the next generation might never see the beaches and the mountains we have all learned to love.

Manila Bay can be saved

n the United States, the Federal Clean Water Act (CWA) mandates all states to adopt water quality standards that define how much of pollutants can be in the water such that it might meet the minimum threshold for water, fishing, and swimming, and other beneficial uses.

In Minnesota, once the water quality is assessed to be below the prescribed rate, they are automatically included in the Impaired Waters List being managed by the Minnesota Pollution Control Agency. A total maximum daily load (TMDL), which is defined as the "the maximum amount of a pollutant a body of water can receive without violating water quality standards, and an allocation of that amount to the pollutant's sources", is then developed. The TMDL process commences via identification of all sources of pollutants and a scientific determination of how much each source must reduce its contribution in order to meet the standard.

It took almost two decades for Minnesota to clean up First Fulda, a lake in Murray County, which at one point could no longer be used for swimming and recreation.

Cleaning up the Manila Bay, like the Poplar River, is an uphill battle but it can be done with the concerted action of government and the public sector. It is about time, considering that as early as 2008, the Supreme Court already issued a mandamus ordering the national government to clean up Manila Bay, and to put up adequate and appropriate sanitary landfill and solid waste and liquid disposal as well as other alternative garbage disposal systems.

As of February 14, 2019, according to Department of Public Works and Highways Secretary Mark Villar, data-gathering activities relevant to bathymetric or depth

Manila Bay dredging operations

measurement survey and water quality test for both Manila Bay and Navotas River had already been completed. The result will then be the basis of dredging activities, which will be the major mechanism for the removal of the accumulated pollutants. The bathymetric survey is necessary to estimate the amount of material to be removed and specify the areas that must be given focus during the clean-up.

Starting February, an equipment fleet composed of amphibious excavators, dumping scows, dump trucks, debris segregator, street sweepers, and vacuum sewer cleaner will be strategically deployed. DPWH will also procure additional spider excavators and trash skimmer to assist in the rehabilitation efforts.

As of date, three dredging sites have been identified, which include the Navotas River and Estero de Vitas in Tondo, Manila; and the priority 100 meters from the shoreline of Manila Bay spanning approximately 1.5 kilometers from Manila Yacht Club breakwater to the US Embassy.

The clean-up of Manila Bay will not happen overnight. As the old saying goes, it takes more than one cold day for the river to freeze three feet deep. Rome was not built in a day.

The six-month closure of Boracay has proved that it can be done. From registering a coliform bacteria level as high as one million most probable number (MPN) per 100 mililiters, water quality is now down to 19 to 20 MPN/100 ML, according to DENR. This just goes to prove that if you work hard enough at it, you can grind even an iron pestle down to a needle.

Binondo Intramuros Bridge

CHAPTER NINE

DIPLOMACY

Triumph of Duterte diplomacy

President Rodrigo Duterte and Chinese Premier Li Keqiang witnessed the signing of 14 bilateral agreements on November 15, 2017, following the expanded bilateral meeting between the two countries. Included was the exchange of letters on the Binondo-Intramuros and Pantaleon-Estrella Bridge Project, two bridges which would be part of the Metro Manila Logistics Infrastructure Network, Department of Public Works and Highway's traffic decongestion masterplan.

A day after the project's ceremonial launching in Malacañang, DPWH Secretary Mark Villar and Ministry of Commerce Deputy Director General Mr. Zeng Hua signed the implementation agreement on the two bridges, which is expected to benefit 1.3 million passengers daily.

The Binondo-Intramuros Bridge is a ₱4.607 billion steel bow-string arch bridge, spanning 807 meters, with intersecting reclining arches connecting Intramuros (at Solana Street and Riverside Drive) and Binondo (at San Fernando Street); while the Estrella-Pantaleon Bridge is a ₱1.367 billion four-lane bridge, which is expected to increase the road network capacity of Estrella Street in Makati and Barangka Drive in Mandaluyong.

Estrella Pantaleon Bridge Inauguration

World Economic Forum

The project began in 2017. It will be completed in 2021 as part of the Metro Manila Logistics Infrastructure Network, a 12-bridge network crossing Pasig River, Marikina River, and Manggahan Floodway, which aims to effectively decongest major thoroughfares in Metro Manila particularly Epifanio de los Santos Avenue (EDSA).

Apart from this, Department of Finance Secretary Carlos Dominguez III also inked a Memorandum of Understanding (MOU) with China's Vice Commerce Minister and International Trade Representative Fu Ziying to "jointly identify and study" an indicative list consisting of the second basket of key infrastructure cooperation projects for possible Chinese financing.

The Davao City Expressway, a 23.3-kilometer road network, which will improve mobility in Davao City and provide access to Sta. Ana Port, is included among the proposed projects under the second basket.

According to the Department of Finance, China has committed a combined $7.34 billion in soft loans and grants thus far to the Philippines for the implementation of ten big-ticket projects, the construction of two bridges in Metro Manila and two drug rehabilitation facilities in Mindanao, and assistance in the rehabilitation of war-torn Marawi City in Mindanao.

The triumph of the Duterte diplomacy is evident in the strong and robust economic performance of the Philippines, one of the best performing economies in Asia. It is not at all surprising when Socioeconomic Planning Secretary Ernesto Pernia announced the Philippines' impressive Gross Domestic Product (GDP) growth of 6.9 percent in the third quarter of 2021, the second highest in Asia.

Japan-PH Partnership: Subway, bypass, and more

The economic ties between the Philippines and Japan further strengthened in 2018 as Japan fulfilled its investment pledges made during the visit of President Duterte in Tokyo in 2017.

On March 16, 2018, Finance Secretary Carlos Dominguez III and Yoshio Wada, the chief representative of the Japan International Cooperation Agency (JICA), signed the 104.53-billion-yen loan agreement for the construction of the first phase of the Metro Manila Subway Project, a project spanning from Mindanao Avenue in Quezon City to the Food Terminal Inc. (FTI) area in Taguig City, and continuing on to the Ninoy Aquino International Airport (NAIA).

Utilizing cutting-edge Japanese tunneling technology, the Metro Manila Subway Station will involve the construction of a 30-kilometer underground railway with 14 stations.

Data provided by the Department of Finance indicates that the loan agreement for the first tranche carries an interest rate of 0.10

Plaridel Bypass

percent per annum for non-consulting services (which involve civil works, depot, railroad, electromechanical works, power supply) and 0.01 percent per annum for consulting services, payable in 40 years inclusive of a 12-year grace period under the Special Terms for Economic Partnership of JICA.

One day prior to the signing, the Japanese government, through Ambassador Koji Haneda and Mitsubishi Motors Philippines president and CEO Mitsuhiro Oshikiri, also turned over 27 sets of brand new heavy equipment and 26 Mitsubishi utility vehicles to Executive Secretary Salvador C. Medialdea and Public Works and Highways (DPWH) Secretary Mark A. Villar for use in the government's rehabilitation program of Marawi City.

A ceremony in Marawi City also handed over the government seven hydraulic excavators, three bulldozers, three wheel loaders, two motor graders, and 12 dump trucks.

In February 2018, the Philippines and Japan also signed the 9.399-billion-yen loan agreement for the construction of the third phase of the Arterial Road Bypass Project designed to ease traffic congestion in Bulacan and spur economic growth in the province's rural areas.

The Arterial Road Bypass, also known as the Plaridel Bypass, is a 24.61-kilometer arterial road that will link the North Luzon Expressway (NLEX) in Balagtas, Bulacan with the Philippine-Japan Friendship Highway, also called Maharlika Highway, in San Rafael, Bulacan. It will bypass the town proper of Plaridel and the urban areas of Pulilan, Baliuag, and San Rafael (all in Bulacan) along the existing Maharlika Highway.

The loan agreement, which was signed in February, for the construction of the third phase of the Arterial Road Bypass Project provided for interest rates of 1.5 percent per annum for non-consulting services and 0.01 percent per annum for consulting services with a repayment period of 20 years and a ten-year grace period.

President Rodrigo Duterte's state visit to Japan

12 JAPANESE-FUNDED
BUILD, BUILD, BUILD PROJECTS

The Japan International Cooperation Agency (JICA) released "The Project for Study on Improvement of Bridges through Disaster Mitigating Measures for Large-Scale Earthquakes," a study it undertook in collaboration with the Department of Public Works and Highways (DPWH) to prepare a bridge improvement plan that will be highly durable and safe against large-scale earthquakes, including the "Big One," a worst-case scenario of a 7.2-magnitude earthquake from the West Valley Fault, which runs through six cities in Metro Manila and nearby provinces.

Bridges are among the important lifeline infrastructures in times of disasters, such as earthquakes. In line with this, Japan has given its support to help improve the durability and safety of bridges in the country, particularly two major bridges in Metro Manila.

Last year, JICA signed a loan agreement with the Philippine Government to provide a Japanese official development assistance (ODA) loan for the Metro Manila Priority Bridges Seismic Improvement Project, which involves the replacement of the existing Lambingan Bridge in Sta. Ana, Manila, and the Guadalupe Bridge in EDSA, Mandaluyong/Makati City.

Improved seismic performance of Guadalupe and Lambingan Bridges will contribute in the improvement and resilience of the Metro Manila road network in the event of a large-scale earthquake, given that 90 percent of passenger and 50 percent of cargo transportation pass through these arterial roads.

Japan has also committed its support to a number of projects of the Philippine government, including those under Build, Build, Build. Japanese Prime Minister Suga Yoshihide reaffirmed this during his message for the 65th anniversary of Philippines-Japan Friendship in July 2021.

Japan remains the country's top source of ODA, with active grants and loans worth US$11.2 billion, accounting for 36 percent of total foreign aid the country received as of 2020.

Here are the other Build, Build, Build programs funded through loans or grants from Japan, through JICA.

1 Road Upgrading and Preservation Project

This project involves the improvement and maintenance of about 1,088.23 kilometers of arterial national roads across the country, enhancing transportation capability and efficiency, and ensuring sustainability of roads.

2 Arterial Road Bypass Project, Phase III (Plaridel Bypass)

The expansion of the existing 24.61 kilometers alignment from Brgy. Borol, Balagtas along NLEX up to San Rafael in Bulacan reduced average travel time between the two points from 69 minutes to 24 minutes.

3 Davao City Bypass Construction Project

This will improve the transport logistics and mitigate congestions in Davao City and thereby contribute to economic development and sound urban development of the city.

4 Central Luzon Link Expressway Project, Phase I

Once the construction of this 30-kilometer, four-lane expressway is completed, travel time between Tarlac City and Cabanatuan City will be reduced from 70 minutes to 20 minutes.

5 Program to Support the Rehabilitation and Reconstruction of Marawi City and its Surrounding Areas

This involves the reconstruction/ rehabilitation of Marawi Transcentral Road, supporting the development of New Central Business and peace-building efforts.

6 Cebu Mactan Bridge (4th) and Coastal Road Construction Project

The construction of a long-span road bridge connecting Mandaue City of Cebu Main Island and Lapu-Lapu City of Mactan Island and connecting coastal road will improve transport capacity and efficiency.

7 Metro Manila Interchange Construction Project, Phase VI

This includes the construction of interchanges on four major intersections in Quezon City, alleviating serious traffic congestion and enhancing transportation capacity and efficiency around Metro Manila.

8 Flood Risk Management Project for Cagayan de Oro River

This will strengthen the resilience of the communities along the Cagayan de Oro River stretch from the Macajalar Bay to Pelaez Bridge to climate change and other natural hazards by mitigating flood risks in the area.

9 Cavite Industrial Area Flood Management Project

The project area is situated at San Juan River Basin and its adjacent Maalimango Drainage Area in the eastern part of the Province of Cavite. It will mitigate flooding along Cavite Industrial Area covering San Juan River Basin. About 7,000 houses in the area of 556 hectares will be protected from flooding.

10 Road Network Development Project in Conflict-affected Areas in Mindanao (RNDP-CAAM)

This involves the development, construction, and improvement of about 174.58 kilometers of access roads connecting the Bangsamoro Autonomous Region in Muslim Mindanao (BARMM) and other regions in Mindanao. The project will alleviate poverty, suppress and prevent conflict, and promote peace and order in the area.

11 Flood Risk Management Project for Cagayan River, Tagoloan River, and Imus River

This project aims to mitigate the damages caused by flood or inundation in affected communities. For the Cagayan River Sub-Project, there will be construction of revetment structures for the most eroded riverbanks at Alibago, Enrile, and Cataggaman, Tuguegarao City; construction of river dikes, partial excavation of river channel, and drainage channel improvement at Tagoloan River; and construction of two off-site retarding basins along Imus and Bacoor rivers as part of the Imus River Sub-Project.

12 Pasig Marikina River Channel Improvement Project, Phase IV

The project will decrease flood and inundation, reduce flood damages and other ill effects on the population, and mitigate flooding through channel improvement works for Middle Marikina River, including the construction of Manggahan Control Gate Structure and the construction of two floodgates at the joining sections of Cainta and Taytay rivers to Manggahan Floodway.

PH-China signs six bilateral agreements

President Rodrigo Duterte and Chinese President Xi Jinping on April 10, 2018 witnessed the signing of six bilateral agreements following the bilateral meeting held in Hainan, China, including an accord on economic and technical cooperation providing for a $79 million grant for at least four other projects undertaken by the Philippine government in cooperation with China.

The Agreement on Economic and Technical Cooperation, which was signed by Department of Finance Secretary Carlos Dominguez III and Chinese Ministry of Commerce Minister Zhong Shan, involves a 500-million-renminbi grant (approximately $79 million or ₱4.13 billion) to finance the following projects and activities: 1) the Binondo-Intramuros and Estrella-Pantaleon bridges in Metro Manila of the Department of Public Works and Highways (DPWH), 2) the feasibility study for the Davao City Expressway Project of DPWH, 3) the provision of radio and broadcasting equipment to the Presidential Communications Operations Office, and 4) the Philippine-Sino Center for Agricultural Technology-Technical Cooperation Program Phase III of the Department of Agriculture.

The Binondo-Intramuros Bridge is a ₱4.607-billion steel bow-string arch bridge, spanning 807 meters, with intersecting reclining arches connecting Intramuros (at Solana Street and Riverside Drive) and Binondo (at San Fernando Street) while the Estrella-

State visit *of People's Republic of China President Xi Jinping to the Philippines*

Bilateral meeting between the Philippines and People's Republic of China

Pantaleon Bridge is a ₱1.367 billion four-lane bridge, which is expected to increase road network capacity of Estrella Street in Makati and Barangka Drive in Mandaluyong.

Exchange of Letters for the Pre-Feasibility Study of the Proposed 23-kilometer Davao City Expressway Project was also signed by Department of Public Works and Highways Secretary Mark Villar and Chinese Ministry of Commerce Minister Zhong Shan.

When completed, the expressway is expected to decongest traffic in Davao City, ease access to Sta. Ana Port and other suburban areas, and complement proposed high-standard highway projects for Mindanao.

Under the proposed initial plan of DPWH, the Davao City Expressway will be implemented in three phases.

Phase 1 is an elevated viaduct, which has an estimated length of 8.45 kilometers. It starts at the intersection of Leon Garcia Street and Monteverde Street and at junction to Sta. Ana Port. It traverses along Quezon Boulevard, passing through numerous intersections and then turning northwest before reaching the Bolton Bridge up to the upstream of the Davao River until it terminates at the existing Davao City Diversion Road near the Davao River Bridge in Brgy. Ma-a.

Phase 2 is also an elevated viaduct with an estimated length of 8.35 kilometers, which starts at the intersection of Daang Maharlika and Davao City Diversion Road in Brgy. Panacan, traverses the existing alignment of the Davao City Diversion Road, and ends at the Davao River Bridge in Brgy. Ma-a.

Phase 3, on the other hand, which is proposed to start at the end point of Phase 1 and Phase 2, will be a new road opening almost parallel to the existing diversion road and moves to west direction and then southwest direction until it terminates at the Davao City Diversion Road near Catalunan Grande Road.

Build, Build, Build projects funded through PH-Korea partnership

Seventy-one years ago, on September 7, 1950, the Philippine Congress passed Republic Act 573 that authorized the sending of the Philippine Expeditionary Force to Korea (PEFTOK) to help South Korea repel the North Korean aggression.

The PEFTOK was composed of five battalion combat teams with a total number of 7,420 Filipino soldiers who fought alongside South Koreans. Since then, the two nations acknowledged a brotherhood forged in blood. Over the decades, both countries have nourished this relationship.

Today, South Korea, which has successfully transformed from a war-torn country to a highly-developed nation, is an active partner in our economic and development pursuits. The ascent was largely due to the successful implementation of the country's economic and infrastructure program, where government and public enterprises accounted for close to 40 percent of the total domestic investment.

Now, Korea is the fifth largest Official Development Assistance (ODA) partner of the Philippines with loan and grant commitments amounting to $679.65 million as of June 2020. As to ODA grants to our country, it is the ninth largest provider with a total of $47.88 million as of June 2020. It has also committed ODA loans to the Philippines in the amount of $631.77 million through the Korea Export Import Bank- Economic Development Cooperation Fund (KEXIM-EDCF).

The 6th ASEAN Connectivity Forum

Last year, the Philippines and KEXIM have exchanged the signed documents on the $50-million loan agreement for the Philippines-Korea Project Preparation Facility (PKPPF), which will include feasibility studies and other project preparation activities necessary to speed up the implementation of the Build, Build, Build projects. Korea has also expressed interest in the possibility of providing funding support for the 32-kilometer Panay-Guimaras-Negros Bridge Project in Western Visayas.

Let's explore the "Build, Build, Build" projects funded through loan agreements with South Korea.

01 Panguil Bay Bridge Project

The construction of the 3.17-kilometer Panguil Bay Bridge is considered as the biggest infrastructure project in Northern Mindanao not only because it is part of the Mega Bridge Masterplan that aims to link Luzon, Visayas, and Mindanao, but also because of the major economic benefits that the region will reap.

The Panguil Bay Bridge will connect the City of Tangub in Misamis Occidental to the Municipality of Tubod in Lanao del Norte and will lessen travel time to only seven minutes, compared to the 1.5 to 2.5 hours it would take via the 100-kilometer route Tangub-Molave-Tubod Road or via Tangub-Kapatagan-Tubod Road. This is expected to uplift the economic condition and encourage growth of tourism between the provinces of Misamis Occidental and Lanao del Norte.

02 Samar Pacific Coastal Road Project

The construction of an 11.6-kilometer road from Junction Simora to Junction Palapag in the town of Palapag with three bridge components—Simora, Jangtud 1, and Jangtud 2 Bridges—will link the "Pacific towns" of Northern Samar and will complete the Samar Island circumferential road.

Once completed, Taft, Eastern Samar, and the coastal municipalities of Northern Samar will be connected with Catarman, the provincial capital, without having to pass through the island town of Laoang, which is only accessible through small boats.

03 Integrated Disaster Risk Reduction and Climate Change Adaptation (IDRR-CCA) Measures in Low-lying Areas of Pampanga Bay

This project will improve drainage efficiency of the river channel network of Pampanga, particularly the Third River, including the Eastern Branch, Caduang Tete, and Sapang Maragul Rivers. It will reduce flood level and flooding duration in the municipalities of Macabebe, Masantol, Minalin, and Sto. Tomas.

This includes excavation, dredging, and embankment of the river, and construction of three new bridges and five footbridges. Eight sluice gates and 164 fish pond gates will also be built as an additional flood control measure.

Secretary Mark Villar explains that this is part of DPWH target outputs to build disaster-resilient structures in calamity-prone areas.

04 Updating of Master Plan, Feasibility Study, and Detailed Engineering Design of Flood Control for BAPP Rivers

This is under the PKPPF Output 2, the updating of the master plan, feasibility study, and detailed engineering design for the priority four major river basins, namely, Bicol River, Agusan River, Panay River, and Pampanga River (BAPP Rivers).

The updating of the master plan and the feasibility study will determine the required flood control infrastructures in the BAPP Rivers, including the priority flood control projects based on economic, environmental, and social impacts, together with the development of suitable and optimal investment programs. Identified priority projects will then be subjected to detailed engineering design.

A system of collaboration

On September 3, I met 20 people from 14 different countries at the lobby of DC Churchill Hotel, a 112-year-old historic infrastructure, which has come to be a landmark on Connecticut Avenue in Washington, DC. Apart from the 50-year-old elevator, the eight-story place of Beaux-Arts architecture known for its perfect symmetry, arched windows, and flat roof has been renovated to have a modern interior. It was one of the Historic Hotels of America, according to the National Trust for Historic Preservation, a privately funded non-profit organization, whose mandate is to save America's historic places. What particularly caught my attention was the federal government's Historic Tax Credit program, which would encourage private sector investment in the rehabilitation and re-use of historic buildings by allowing participants to claim 20 percent of eligible improvement expenses against their federal tax liability.

According to the US Office of the Comptroller of the Currency, since the Tax Reform Act of 1976, the HTC program has facilitated the rehabilitation of over 42,000 certified historic buildings, and attracting more than $84 billion in new private capital to the historic cores of cities and towns across the whole of United States.

As I walk the streets of Washington and participate

Drone shot of Intramuros, Manila

The author with Kevin Quinn, CEO and administrator of the Maryland Transit Administrator

in the US Department of State's International Visitor Leadership Program, I have come to realize a dynamism that exists in the United States' federal form of government, an interesting mixture of decentralization and collaboration between multi-levels of government, and a critical relationship between the public and private sector in accomplishing what is essentially a public purpose.

While the emphasis at the onset of the narrative seems to be in the differentiation of functions, objectives, and agenda that must be kept centralized and those that must be devolved, the latter part puts premium on a systemic collaboration geared on context and need.

It is interesting how one state is able to address its specific infrastructure needs in a manner that is entirely different from the others.

For example, while Florida may opt for a privately owned, operated, and maintained passenger railway system, as in Brightline, an express intercity high-speed rail system, which connects Miami, Fort Lauderdale, and West Palm Beach, Maryland may choose to establish an independent state agency, as in Maryland Transit Administration in the management of its transit service, which includes local buses, commuter buses, Light Rail Link, Metro Subway Link, Maryland Area Regional Commuter (MARC) Train Service, and a Paratransit (Mobility Link) system.

Counties, a second-level administrative division, also exercise a level of autonomy as seen in the establishment of the 1994 Miami-Dade Expressway Authority, a user-funded, not-for-profit transportation agency created by the Miami-Dade County Commission to regulate toll revenues collected on the expressways.

Decentralization of function has long been perceived as a mode of empowerment and risk management. In the discourse, however, it is important that such is grounded not only in our own history and context, but also in the shared realities among our neighbors in the Indo-Pacific region.

IVLP Indo-Pacific Strategy: Infrastructure Development in the Indo-Pacific Region

IVLP, a gamechanger

For 17 days, I traveled with 20 people from 14 different countries to five different states in America as part of the US Department of State's International Visitors Leadership Program (IVLP). The first time I met them, we were at the lobby of DC Churchill Hotel, a 112-year-old place of Beaux-Arts architecture in Embassy row — which, apart from its 50-year-old elevator, has been renovated to have a modern interior. It was the start of an experience which allowed me to appreciate a value in US culture that espouses unity in diversity, one that exists not only by mere tolerance but by a genuine appreciation of differences.

As I walked the streets of Washington with Khin Khin Kyaw of Burma, Kathleen Mangune, Fetoloia Alama of Samoa, Jintawadee Suksri of Thailand, we were impressed by the conservation efforts. The US Capitol was our first stop and while it was built in 1793, the infrastructure made of sandstone, marble, and iron is still as regal as when the dome of over eight million pounds was constructed. What is even more impressive was the role of private sector investment in the rehabilitation and re-use of historic buildings, incentivized by the federal government's Historic Tax Credit, a program which has attracted more than $84 billion in new private capital and facilitated the rehabilitation of over 42,000 certified historic buildings.

On my second night in Washington, I met Adolfo Arguello Vives and Iris Alon, two classmates from Harvard Kennedy School, at Occidental Grill & Seafood, a dining

Harvard Kennedy School Class Photo

institution, which made it to popular culture for having appeared in the 2014 sequel to *Captain America*. What is more impressive was the restaurant, rumored to have hosted all US presidents, was already over 110 years old. Rather than being the exception, it seems to me that preservation has been the rule.

After a briefing on federalism and meetings with the US Department of State Bureau of East Asian and Pacific Affairs and the Office of the Deputy Mayor for Planning and Economic Development, I grew fond of the interesting mixture of decentralization and collaboration that existed among multi-levels of government and the critical relationship between the public and private sector in accomplishing an essentially mutual priority — with due consideration to the diversity that is innate in US culture and its history.

Washington is a multi-faceted state. In a matter of minutes, you may well be in Pennsylvania Avenue facing the White House, and a couple of kilometers further in Blagden Alley, a neighborhood of small apartments, art murals, and century-old Gothic and Victorian infrastructure filled with hipster bars.

One night, after six meetings, we headed to Colombia Room and there I became acquainted with one of the District of Columbia's historic districts — Blagden. As I marvelled around the area, I saw what seemed to be a

horse stable converted into a coffee shop, a Victorian rowhouse turned into a pub, and a garage renovated to serve American food. Over *guacomole, cerdo,* and *tacos de pescado* at Espita Mescaleria, a restaurant serving Oaxacan cuisine, I sat back to appreciate a juxtaposition before me — one that is able to embrace, reconcile history and progress.

Ultra - We Heal As One Center

CHAPTER TEN

COVID

The need for physical (not social) distancing

On my first night in self-quarantine, one of my classmates, Dr. Melvin Sanicas, a physician and scientist working as medical director, dropped me a personal message on Facebook. "Anna, What happened? Hope it's not serious. Get well soon," he wrote. It was the start of a conversation that I needed to hear. He was after all a digital health expert for the World Health Organization and a fellow of the Royal Society of Tropical Medicine and Hygiene.

And like a tap on the back, he said "Don't worry, this is not going to be like the Black Death."

The Black Death is a pandemic that ravaged Europe between 1347 and 1351 and killed at least 25 million people or about a third of Europe's entire population.

Fortunately, science is way more advanced today. Melvin then told me that when the first cases of AIDS were described in June, 1981, it took over two years to identify the virus (HIV) causing the disease. With COVID-19, the virus SARS-CoV-2 was identified and the genome was available in less than two weeks after the first case was identified in December 31, 2019. Moreover, a test kit to detect the virus became available, the protocol shared with the rest of the world.

81% of the cases are mild

The Novel Coronavirus Pneumonia Emergency Response Epidemiology Team of China CDC (Chinese Center for Disease Control and Prevention) published a paper on their analysis of a total of 72,314 patient records, which included 44,672 confirmed cases. The study reported that the disease causes no symptoms or is mild in 81 percent of the cases, results in severe pneumonia in 14 percent, and is fatal or critical in five percent. In the 60-69 age group, one in 36 died. In the 70-79 age group, one in 12 died. In the 80 and above age group, one in six died.

Citing the report, Dr. Sanicas said severe forms of COVID-19 are usually developed by people who smoked or had pre-existing illnesses (heart disease, diabetes, hypertension, cancer, and chronic respiratory diseases like asthma and COPD).

Handwashing is the best tool

But there was an effective defense against it — hand washing. Dr. Melvin then explained that SARS-COV-2 causing COVID 19 possessed an envelope composed of a fat-like substance that was water insoluble. This type is the most susceptible to environmental disinfectants. In other words, soaps can incapacitate enveloped viruses. The virus can be easily disinfected in just one minute.

Lessons from the flu pandemic

We then discussed the 1918 flu pandemic, the most severe pandemic in recent history, and how the response of Philadelphia and St. Louis resulted in fewer deaths in the latter.

When the first case of the Spanish flu — the H1N1 virus — was first reported in Philadelphia in September 1918, authorities pushed through with a planned Liberty Loan Parade to promote government bonds that were being issued to pay for World War I. In a matter of days, at least 600 had the virus. By the six-month mark, about 16,000 had died and there were more than half a million cases. On the other hand, St. Louis, which cancelled the parade and institutionalized social distancing interventions early on, recorded a far lower death toll of 700 people.

Physical (not social) Distancing

There was a lesson that needed to be learned — "physical (not social) distancing." While there can't be close contact between humans, social connections must still be maintained.

We must come to the table knowing that there is no barangay, city, province, government, or country that can solve the COVID-19 crisis alone. More than ever, human collectivism is key. We have prepared for wars even before they happened. Maybe this time, we ought to work together, collectively and purposively, regardless of race, ethnicity, political affiliation, and religion, in finding a solution to a threat that has shaken our very definition of civilization.

While there is a need for community quarantine, there is no better time to come together than now.

Las Piñas Modular Hospital Inspection

The PH economy will survive COVID-19

The novel coronavirus has disrupted the global economy within just a few weeks. The pandemic has locked down cities, brought travel and tourism to a near standstill, and disrupted life in an unimaginable way. What were considered the most mundane activities in March 2020 are now prohibited and basic human conduct is regulated.

There is a growing economic anxiety over the COVID-19 crisis. However, while the road to resilience will be difficult, statistics shows that the Philippine economy will survive it. If we do it right, Asian Development Bank predicts in its report "Asian Development Outlook 2020" a strong recovery of 6.5 percent in 2021.

Cebu Cordova Link Expressway

The Economist magazine, in its April 2020 issue, also ranked the Philippines sixth out of 66 selected emerging economies in terms of fiscal strength, despite the negative impact of COVID-19. Four measures were used to assess the financial strength of each country — public debt, foreign debt, cost of borrowing, and reserve cover. The Philippines outranked its ASEAN neighbors like Thailand (7th), Vietnam (12th), and Indonesia (16th).

This is not surprising considering the "saving for a rainy day" approach employed by the economic team of President Rodrigo Duterte.

Where are we coming from?

According to Department of Finance Secretary Sonny Dominguez, revenues in 2019 were at 16.1 percent of GDP. This is the highest rate recorded in 22 years. Debt-to-GDP ratio was also at 39.6 percent, the lowest since 1986.

The Philippines also

received a credit rating upgrade to BBB+, the highest the country has ever received.

Moreover, according to the 2019 estimate of the International Monetary Fund, the economy of the Philippines is the world's 27th largest economy by GDP (Purchasing Power Parity). This is one notch higher its ranking in 2018. Under the administration of President Rodrigo Duterte, the Philippines recorded a GDP (PPP) of ₱956 billion in 2018 and ₱1.03 trillion in 2019, joining a trillion dollar club, which included the United States, China, India, Japan, and Germany.

Build Build Build as a socio-economic solution

The Duterte Administration is now pursuing PH Progreso, a phased and adaptive recovery approach founded on a four pillar economic strategy to ensure that the country is able to get back on its positive growth trajectory. One of its five priority measures is to restart and accelerate the Build, Build, Build program, the country's boldest, most ambitious infrastructure program in history.

This is in line with ADB's recommendation of sustained public investment, especially in priority projects under the government's BBB infrastructure development program.

Since it started in June 2016, DPWH Secretary Mark Villar reported 14,670 kilometers of roads, 4507 bridges, 6022 flood mitigation structures, 129,479 classrooms, and 114 evacuation centers have been completed.

The multiplier effect of infrastructure investment is well founded.

In his report "The potential macroeconomic benefits from increasing infrastructure investment," Josh Bivens of the Economic Policy Institute noted that with an output multiplier of 1.5, each $100 billion in infrastructure spending would boost GDP by $150 billion and generate employment for about one million full-time equivalents (FTEs).

Giovanni Ganelli and Juha Tervala also noted in their IMF report "The Welfare Multiplier of Public Infrastructure Investment" that "a dollar spent by the government for investment raises domestic welfare by an equivalent of $0.8 of private consumption."

Based on NEDA estimate, the increase in public infrastructure spending is seen to contribute as much as ₱1.3 trillion to the country's GDP by 2022 by stimulating production of output in different industries, including the construction sector, land transport, electricity, and finance. There is also a positive indirect correlation on trade, food manufacturing, and education.

Clearly, Build, Build, Build is both an infrastructure solution and an effective socio-economic strategy.

The factual narrative of PH's COVID-19 facilities

I n 2017, I attended the Emerging Leaders Program at the Harvard Kennedy School, which was chaired by Dr. Elaine Kamarck and Dr. Christopher Robichaud. In our class on ethics, we discussed the responsibilities of public action via a simulation exercise of an unfolding pandemic.

The question is fairly simple — What decision would you make to save your country from a crisis which you had no prior experience to draw from. We knew from the onset — the state of the country, the infection rate, the public moral, and the likelihood of a country collapse. Every team, which represented a particular sector, knew how to "win" the game. Decisions were time bound and with limited information.

During the de-briefing, I realized that the only way the country would survive the zombie apocalypse was if all sectors decided to set aside their personal interests and collaborate on a unified solution.

The novel coronavirus has disrupted the global economy. The pandemic has locked down cities, brought travel and tourism to a near standstill, and disrupted life in an unimaginable way. But now navigating a pandemic becomes more challenging with the deadly threat of misinformation.

Is there a shortage of isolation facilities? No. The nationwide utilization rate is only at 16.91 percent or 21,362 out of 126,358 beds.

According to Department of Public Works and Highways Secretary Mark Villar, a total of 635 isolation facilities and off site dormitories have been completed, 139 of which are in NCR.

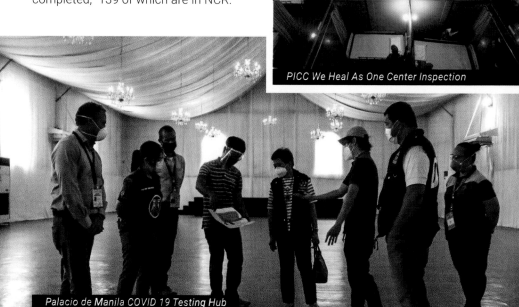

PICC We Heal As One Center Inspection

Palacio de Manila COVID 19 Testing Hub

MOA COVID 19 Testing Hub

Among the facilities already operational are the PICC Forum QF, the Philippine Sports Complex QF, the CCP Complex QF, the Filinvest QF, the Manuel L. Quezon University QF, the Pasay City Sports Complex, the Parañaque City College QF, and the Makati Aqua Sports Arena QF.

In NCR, the utilization rate is now at 75 percent or 4,938 out of 6,576 beds. However, this data does not include the beds, which utilize hotel rooms under Oplan Kalinga.

Modular Hospitals

To augment the country's critical care capacity, DPWH has also constructed modular hospitals.

This week, the Quezon Institute Modular Hospital, which has a total bed capacity of 110 beds, became operational. It is equipped with ICU rooms intended for patients exhibiting moderate to severe symptoms.

Earlier, DPWH also completed two units of modular dormitories with 64-bed capacity for the medical frontliners manning the operation of Quezon Institute.

DPWH also facilitated the creation of extensions for level three hospitals utilizing similar modular fabricated components at Dr. Jose N. Rodriguez Memorial Hospital and the Lung Center of the Philippines.

Five modular hospitals are currently being constructed in the following locations — the National Kidney and Transplant Institute, Quezon Institute, the Lung Center of the Philippines, the Southern Philippine Medical Center, and Dr. Jose Rodriguez Hospital.

CHAPTER ELEVEN

ABOUT THE AUTHOR

Graduation in the time of COVID-19

missed my graduation ceremony in 2020. I am part of the Class of COVID-19, one of 1.2 billion students affected by country-wide or localized closures of educational institutions.

The COVID-19 pandemic has shaken the status quo and disrupted the way we live within just a few weeks. What we once considered to be the most-mundane activities before March 2020 — study sessions, dinner dates, coffee meet-ups — are now prohibited and basic human conduct — walking, driving, and even holding hands — are regulated.

UP Law Graduation photo

Friends have asked me how I felt about not being able to wear the "Sablay." At first, it was frustrating. However, I realized that graduation was not diminished by the absence of celebration or custom. It is momentous for the value it espouses. To me, it was the fulfilment of a promise and an opportunity to aid in rebuilding a country slowed down by the COVID-19 pandemic.

My last conversation with my dad, Manuel Lamentillo, before he died was about law school.

Before leaving for Boston, I went to visit my parents. My dad told me, "I'm proud of you. But I hope Harvard is not an excuse not to finish law at UP. Babalik ka di ba?" I laughed.

My dad persisted, "Di ka pa sumasagot. Tawa lang ng tawa."

I continued laughing and asked him "Gusto mo ba?" He said "Oo."

It was at that point when I said, "Don't worry, Pa. Tatapusin ko ang law school."

He knew I was having a hard time balancing work and school. There were many times I wanted to quit, take a break. Often, UP Law has a way of making you feel inadequate, ill prepared, and in need of improvement. Over time, I got used to the feeling and maybe, in admitting that I was inferior, I worked harder to survive.

Just about two years ago, I remember having dinner with two of my mentors at UP Law — Atty. Gaby Concepcion and Atty. Charlie Yu. When we were about to leave, I told them I was planning to file a leave of absence. My exhaustion was getting the best of me. I couldn't forget what they told me — "We won't stop you but you should know that if you do take a leave of absence, you will never be a lawyer."

I knew they were right. This wasn't the first time I thought about it. In fact, to be honest, I thought about giving up on my first month at law school. Every day was a struggle. But if there is one lesson UP law taught me, it was to show up for class, regardless of circumstances or how prepared I was.

That night, I went home to visit my mom, Nora, only to find out that she had converted our patio into a library. She thought I only had one more year in law school. I laughed and told her, "Delayed *akech*. Wag masyado magexpect."

In a span of six years, from when I started at UP Law in 2014, I held four different jobs in four different organizations: the United Nations Development Program, the Food and Agriculture Organization of the United Nations, the Office of Congressman Mark Villar, and now, the Department of Public Works and Highways.

I can still remember how difficult it was to give up my job at the United Nations so I could pursue law school.

Since our classes would end at 9 p.m., the only option was to take the last flight to Cebu at 11 a.m. and a connecting 4 a.m. flight to Tacloban. There were many days I'd sleep at the airport. I read my cases in moving cars, and at airport terminals hoping to finish the coverage for my 6 p.m. class.

UP Law follows the Socratic Method. The professor has a deck of class cards with each student's name on one card. He shuffles it, picks a card, and calls a name. This was our routine every evening for the last six years (even when there were power interruptions).

Admittedly, there were many days I fell short. But I couldn't give up my job without putting up a fight. It was beautiful to be a part of an initiative bigger than myself.

I can never forget the first time I saw Tacloban. Thousands of cadavers lay in debris, the streets smelled of death and decay, and in several barangays, not a single house survived. Students who were just studying for their exams woke up the next day with nothing but their shirts. One had to choose between saving his girlfriend and her one-year-old niece.

Despite the devastation, however, residents affected by Typhoon Yolanda were already rebuilding only a few weeks after the storm. One of them told me, "Isa ka adlaw, tatlo nalang kami. Waay na ang akung duha ka anak. Masubo pero kailangan mag-ubra. Wala man kami sarigan. (One day, there were only three members of my family left. Two of my children died. I'm sad but I have to work. We couldn't depend on anyone else)".

Work at United Nations taught me survival, resilience, and fighting— even and most especially, in the most unfortunate of circumstances.

One day, while camping out at Starbucks to study for my exams, I met an old acquaintance, then Las Piñas Representative Mark Villar, wearing a UN hoodie, a pair of shorts, and flip flops. The banter ended with an impromptu initial interview and a question — "Wala kang balak bumalik sa politika (Don't you have any plans of returning to

*Author with **HKS Professor Matt Andrews***

politics)?" I joked — "Kung kukunin niyo ako, Boss".

On February 14, Sec Mark formally offered me a job and by April 1, I was hired. What started as a decision primarily based on instinct as Batasang Pambansa was only 15 minutes away from UP Law turned out to be one of the most fulfilling jobs I ever had.

I have lived in Metro Manila all my life, and I'm part of a generation that has accepted (and complained about) traffic as a way of life. To be a part of Build, Build, Build, President Rodrigo Duterte's infrastructure program, which aims to connect 81 provinces, 146 cities, and 1,489 municipalities across the country, is an opportunity I will always be thankful for.

Friends are often surprised as to how I survived UP Law while maintaining a full-time job. It would have been impossible without the support of Sec. Mark who understood the value of education and pushed me to be a better version of myself. He would often remind us — to think outside the box, to speak up, and to take accountability for our actions.

Some of my classmates were asked to choose between their job and law school. It never happened to me. In fact, when meetings would go past 4 p.m., I'd often receive a message: "Do you have class? Go ahead". At the end of the semester, when I returned to work after a leave for my final examination, Sec. Mark would ask, "Pasado naman?" On every occasion, I would just laugh.

But now finally, after six years, four jobs, 14,670 kilometers of roads, 4507 bridges, 6,022 flood mitigation structures, 129,479 classrooms, and 114 evacuation centers, I'm finally graduating with a Juris Doctor Degree.

To mom, dad, and April, we finally made it.

Economic briefing with Department of Finance

Author awarded the Veritas Medal by the Harvard Kennedy School Alumni Association at the Bureaucrat's Ball

Jamil Mahuad and the Peru-Ecuador peace treaty

t was a Wednesday afternoon and our professor, Nobel Peace Prize nominee Jamil Mahuad, asked us to sit as his cabinet members and navigated through the crisis of Ecuador in the year 1998, when he was elected president. For eight hours, we learned from the man himself how he handled the Ecuador-Peru border dispute, a conflict described by former United States President Bill Clinton as "the last and longest running source of armed conflict in the Western Hemisphere."

When I went to Harvard Kennedy School this month, I never imagined our class would have the opportunity to ask a president of his decisions and more surprisingly, walk in his shoes. Prof. Mahuad is many things to different people, but at that moment, he was neither his lawyer nor propagandist to us. He was a professor who taught the peace process, world politics, and negotiation the best way he could, a simulation of a period from which he gained the most realizations.

The situation was this — Four days before his assumption of office, he was informed by his military that a Peruvian invasion right after his inauguration was imminent. At that time, troops from Ecuador and Peru had already occupied what was previously conceded to be a "demilitarized zone." This was happening at a time when oil prices hovered at one of their lowest levels in a 40-year period. It was important for Ecuador as oil accounted for about half of its exports as well as of the government's revenue. This problem was even exacerbated by the Asian Financial Crisis and the El Niño phenomenon, which caused extensive damage to vital infrastructure and agriculture.

And so he asked the class, "Given all the information, what would you have prioritized?" The majority said — peace.

Ecuador and Peru had a long-standing border dispute, which dated back at least five decades. Its "roots can even be traced to the 1532 precolonial Indian war for the control of the Inca Empire between Quiteño Atahualpa (now

Author with her professor, Jamil Mahuad

Emerging Leaders Program - Harvard Kennedy School

Ecuador) and Cusqueno Huascar (now Peru)." Over the course of time, several armed conflicts had erupted, the most recent of which was just in 1995, three years prior his assumption of office.

"An international war would have escalated our already critical situation into a desperate one. How could Ecuador face an international war with the economy already in shambles. I needed a definitive peace accord with Peru?" he told us.

In pursuing peace, Pres. Mahuad knew there must be a widespread belief among the majority that the war could be resolved. It was important that the project was not just a government issue. The citizens of both Peru and Ecuador must own the issue. It must be a "people's project."

The negotiation process is a gradual undertaking that requires equal regard for both process and substance. The small steps were as critical as the big ones. At the onset, no one might have foreseen that the unexpected meeting between Pres. Mahuad and Peruvian President Alberto Fujimori in Asuncion del Paraguay just four days after the former assumed office would eventually lead to the historic signing of the peace accord that would lay down the boundary points along a 50-mile border strip, ending a decades-long territorial dispute.

I will never forget the last eight hours we spent navigating each decision point from the time the peace treaty was being negotiated to the point of his eventual ouster, not because it provided a better framework for analysis but rather because I saw a man who took risks for a country he deeply cared about.

My father taught me waiting for 21 years was worth it

For 21 years, Manuel wanted to marry Elnora but it wasn't until he was 47 years old that they were finally able to walk down the aisle.

Manuel and Elnora first met in 1964. To him, it was love at first sight. At 79, he could still recall how she looked and the clothes she was wearing when they first met, the same day he decided she was the woman he was going to marry. My dad would often tell us that it only took him a little over ten minutes to fall in love with my mom.

However, the circumstances were not easy. His friends often joked that the romance seemed impossible – "The Great Wall of China was too difficult to climb." They would remind him that they were born 18 years apart and that she was of Chinese descent. But Manuel could not be stopped. None of these could douse his resolve to win the heart of the woman he loved.

Distance, age, and even culture were insignificant. He only needed to hear that she loved him too. Everything after that did not matter. It was surmountable.

Several months into the relationship, Manuel proposed marriage. He did not want to wait any longer. After all, he had already been waiting for 21 years. The

Author's childhood photos

fact that none of my mother's family knew she even had a boyfriend did not intimidate him. Getting their approval was work he was willing to take.

After 32 years, their life had been far from perfect, if you believe in fairy tales. My dad was no prince charming, and my mom was no damsel in distress.

They would quarrel over the simplest things, from crispy lechon to maintenance medicines, making us realize that love was not always mushy and sweet.

But what struck me the most about this seemingly odd couple was the way they would reconcile day after day, without any need for apologies. (We'd know there was a big fight when he brought green mangoes home. Dad knew it was a better peace offering than red roses or tulips.)

While we were growing up, they would often remind us that love was never meant to be easy. There will be moments when you will have to learn to live far from each other, when you have to fight over who switches the light off, when you don't just see eye to eye, and when you have to endure the sight of the other suffering in a hospital.

Love is choosing someone every day, even when you are disenchanted and disappointed, even when the rest of the world offers brief, short-lived, and uncomplicated romances, even when the easier option is to simply let go.

Manuel and Elnora Lamentillo

When Manuel and Elnora married 32 years ago, no one thought they would stay together. But they did. My mom stood by my dad's side whenever he was in the hospital, even when he could no longer feed himself, or remember most parts of his life.

They would have celebrated their 33rd anniversary in November but my dad passed away. But even with Alzheimer's, his last words were true – "I love you, Ma."

My mom told me not to believe in Cinderella

Most of my friends are a bit surprised when I order sinigang, tinola, or KBL for breakfast. To me, it was routinary. We grew up with sabaw on the table. But now that I'm old enough to know, I thought about all the years my mom, Nora Yu Lamentillo, had to wake up extra early just to cook.

It took me a while to know, she never ate a single piece of the chicken tinola she frequently prepared. She never told us about it. She'd simply cook it like it was the most natural thing to do.

When her friends surprised her with a feast, the starring dish was Kadyos, Baboy, Langka, or KBL. I guess they assumed it was her favorite considering the amount of time she'd usually spend cooking it or sourcing the ingredients she could use. What they didn't know was that it was my dad's favorite as well as mine. My mom would be happy with paksiw.

Every breakfast, when we were much younger, mom would remind us we could be anything we wanted to be. There was nothing that was beyond our reach.

Cinderella, Snow White, or Red Riding Hood wasn't our role models. We were taught from a very young age that girls need not be saved, that they could be heroes, protagonists of their own stories. Girls are not inferior to men, not in this generation or the ones before it.

1st Lieutenant Anna **Mae** Lamentillo

Elnora Lamentillo

In our toddler days, we were made to wear a petticoat (almost) every day (even for Jolly Spaghetti.) My mom would also comb our hair 100 strokes a night. But when we were mature enough to decide, she allowed us to choose our own identity and style. It didn't matter if people perceived it as a bit odd or eccentric or aggressive. Identity was an important aspect of growing up and she respected it.

Back in high school, I told my mom I was called to the principal's office for initiating a signature campaign to be a senior muse. Instead of scolding me, she said, "Karapatan mo yan, anak!"

In the family, we were not expected to subscribe to traditional gender roles. Whether or not we wanted to cook, or dance the ballet, or play the piano, it was our decision. We need not play the part of a princess or a damsel in distress.

Elnora Lamentillo

My mom often reminded us that it was important that we are able to write our own stories, that our potentials be realized, and that we were confident enough to tackle the boulder ahead of us.

After all, a turtle travels only when it sticks its neck out. But she cautions: Success is not final, and not possible without hard work.

Author with her mother

What I learned after my boat sank

In 2012, a few months before my graduation, I decided to visit the indigenous people of Tagbanua in Sitio Calauit. They had no electricity, no cellphone signal, and no access to basic education. On our way to Palawan, at about 10 p.m., our boat capsized. There were 12 people. Only three knew how to swim. There was only one life vest, a plastic container more commonly used as a water dispenser. For almost an hour, we clung to a bamboo pole in the middle of the sea to survive. At first, we tried to save everything we could. We clung to our bags but when we realized we were too heavy for the 'katig' to keep afloat, we untied them and let them loose.

What I learned that evening changed me. I was always told that youth was never a guarantee of opportunity or time, that chances were in fact illusory. But it was never real until that moment of danger. In that instant, nothing was ever "too fast", "too drastic", or "too risky." True enough — in those difficult minutes — I only thought of three things: the people I loved, the things I'd always wanted to do, and the words I never said.

A few hours after the incident, we were given several options. The first one was to leave for Manila the morning after, and the second was to proceed still with the immersion. We chose the latter and after four days in the community, we witnessed how the people of Tagbanua, strengthened by challenges of ownership, rose to rebuild their life through the spirit of "gulpi-mano" or bayanihan.

Classrooms with no nails

The National Commission on Indigenous Peoples declared Calauit Island as an ancestral domain in March 2010. The Tagbanuas have been fighting for the land for

over 36 years. The first school, which offered an elementary diploma, had about 200 elementary students. When they graduate, they would usually leave for Coron, a town two hours away, to study high school or college.

In the afternoon, a few hours before the sunset, men would gather to improve the community's infrastructure while women would meet to take out weeds in the banana plantation. They used materials readily available in the community. Instead of nails, the group made use of various kinds of knots.

Meals are always served fresh

The people of Tagbanua are heavily dependent on sea for food and livelihood. They taught us that survival and sustainability would only be possible when the body of water was protected. To preserve their natural environment, they would regularly conduct reforestation of mangroves and alternately plant seeds during low tide.

Here, water is the most valuable commodity. They are stored in drums and used sparingly. Bathing is limited to a pail of water.

And for several days, what seemed "essential" did not matter.

With no access to electricity, Wifi or TV, meals are always served fresh, girls play bahay-bahayan under the leaves of the palm trees and boys are not afraid to enjoy flowers. In this part of town, with no cellphone signal, everyone knows the middle name of everyone in the village, separation and annulments are rare, and tasks are done by the entire community.

Sitio Calauit was indeed a home well taken care of.

CHAPTER TWELVE

EPILOGUE

Happy to be back in public service

It has been my dream to see the Philippines achieve its full potential. When I was with the Department of Public Works and Highways (DPWH) and the "Build, Build, Build" team during the Duterte administration, every road, bridge or similar project we completed was important for me because it meant more opportunities for Filipinos, better development for our country, and greater connectivity within and among our communities.

Today, I am happy to be back in public service and to continue working on the goal of connecting our communities and every Filipino, but this time on a different platform — through digital connectivity. It is high time that we fast track the improvement of our digital infrastructure. The world is evolving at a high speed and we must keep up.

I am grateful to President Ferdinand "Bongbong" Marcos, Jr. and to Department of Information and Communications Technology (DICT) Secretary Ivan John Uy for their trust in me. It is my privilege to be of service to our nation once again.

The President has made it clear that he wants to ensure universal connectivity so that no citizen is left behind. The DICT's top agenda is to deploy digital connectivity across our various islands. We will prioritize providing and improving internet connectivity in far-flung areas and in Geographically Isolated and Disadvantaged Areas (GIDAs).

Since the inception of the "Free Wi-Fi For All" project, a total of 4,469 live sites were established as of June 2022. This covers 75 provinces and Metro Manila, and 584 localities. Out of the 4,469 Free Wi-Fi sites, 36 sites are at the GIDAs. The target for 2023 is an increase of 4,972 Free Wi-Fi sites in public places.

Time for digital infrastructure

The National Broadband Program (NBP) is the blueprint for the deployment of broadband connectivity across the nation. Part of this is the National Fiber Backbone Phase 1 Project, which is already 73.56 percent completed as of June 30, 2022 and is scheduled to be finished by May 2023.

In 2020, the Bases Conversion and Development Authority (BCDA) and the DICT have completed the construction of the International Cable Landing Stations in Baler, Aurora and San Fernando, La Union and the 250-km fiber conduit which will carry the two Tbps optical spectrum to DICT's points of presence and BCDA's ecozones. The BCDA handed over the keys of landing and repeater stations to DICT last November 2021.

Meanwhile, 1,000 government offices/agencies in 13 provinces, in 13 different regions, are now connected through the GovNet project, of which 981 are online and 86 additional offices/agencies will be activated by the 3rd-4th Quarter of 2022. In 2023, three Govnet sites will be established with 234 agencies to be connected.

Among other targets of the Department next year in terms of building digital infrastructure include the establishment and activation of National Fiber Backbone Phase 3; the establishment of Digital Infrastructure Center; and the establishment of Inter-island Network Connectivity (IRU Domestic Submarine Cable) that would provide inter-island network connection in Southern Luzon, Bicol, Visayas, and Mindanao.

Advancing digitalization

In a bid to accelerate digital connectivity and improve digitalization efforts of the government, the DICT is welcoming new technology to reach GIDAs, areas of the country where laying fiber cables or establishing cell towers prove to be challenging.

Author with President Ferdinand R. Marcos, Jr.

For instance, through SpaceX's satellite internet constellation, Starlink, which boasts speeds of up to 200 Mbps and latency as low as 20ms for residential use, we can provide connectivity in unserved and underserved areas.

Moreover, we will continue to collaborate with fellow governments to advance our digitalization efforts through exchange of knowledge, technical expertise, and best practices.

Official photo as DICT Assistant Secretary

During the recent state visit to Singapore of President Marcos, the Philippines' DICT and Singapore's Ministry of Communications and Information, signed a memorandum of understanding (MOU) on digital cooperation, including on digital connectivity, particularly in interoperable systems and frameworks that enable electronic documentation; cybersecurity, such as organizing training courses and technical programs through the ASEAN-Singapore Cybersecurity Centre of Excellence (ASCCE) to develop and enhance skills related to cybersecurity; and digital government/e-governance, such as in the areas of digital government strategy, digital government services, and digital identity.

The MOU also covers exchange of knowledge, technical expertise, and best practices on measures relating to scam calls and scam short message services; on personal data protection; and in emerging technologies such as artificial intelligence, 5G, cloud computing, Internet of Things, big data, analytics and robotics; among others.

There will also be cooperation and exchange of knowledge to boost the digital innovation ecosystem, including connecting business owners with potential solution providers; exploring cooperation on digital capability and capacity building programs; and exchange of knowledge and best practices on digital infrastructure.

Aside from these programs, projects, and cooperation initiatives, we will continue to explore opportunities and partnerships that will help us in our goal of ensuring universal connectivity. The task may be daunting, but we will face the challenges head on because we can no longer afford to be left behind.

100 Mbps minimum speed for the most remote areas

According to the United Nations, about 3.4 billion people living in rural areas worldwide can have better quality of life through improved access and internet connectivity.

In the UN's 2021 World Social Report "Reconsidering Rural Development," digital technologies can help bridge the rural-urban divide if rural populations are provided with access to digital finance, precision tools for better crop yields, and jobs that can be done remotely.

According to UN Secretary-General António Guterres, many jobs that are considered to be urban can be performed in rural areas as well if there is high-quality internet connectivity and flexible working arrangements.

Here in the Philippines, President Ferdinand "Bongbong" Marcos, Jr. has tasked the Department of Information and Communications Technology (DICT) to bridge the digital divide and provide more opportunities for Filipinos to create wealth through participation in the digital economy.

In line with this, the DICT under the leadership of Secretary Ivan John Uy is prioritizing the deployment of digital connectivity and building of vital infrastructure to reach the underserved and unserved areas of the country.

DICT Secretary Ivan John E. Uy and SpaceX Executive Rebecca Hunter

For instance, the National Broadband Program aims to close the digital divide and elevate the Filipinos' living standard by deploying broadband connectivity across the country through fiber optic cables and wireless technologies.

The construction of the International Cable Landing Stations in Baler, Aurora and in San Fernando, La Union; and the 250-km fiber conduit, which will carry the 2Tbps optical spectrum to DICT's points of presence and Bases Conversion and Development Authority's (BCDA) ecozones, was completed in 2020 and the keys of the landing and repeater stations have been handed over to DICT.

For the free Wi-Fi in public places, the target of DICT is to have a total of 5,951 free Wi-Fi sites in public places, which will now cover all 81 provinces including Metro Manila and 863 municipalities and cities, by the end of 2022. For 2023, additional 3,273 sites in public places will be established, spanning 81 provinces including Metro Manila and 1,034 municipalities and cities.

In order to reach remote areas that cannot be serviced by telcos, the DICT is tapping new technology like satellite connectivity, which is ideal for areas where internet connectivity is unreliable or completely unavailable.

Starlink, a satellite internet constellation operated by Elon Musk's SpaceX, is expected to roll out in the country before the end of the year. The company aims to have as many as 42,000 satellites to be able to deliver high-speed, low-cost internet to remote regions across the globe.

Starlink can provide 100 Mbps internet speed for the most remote areas. Through this, internet connectivity can reach Filipinos in remote areas and they can have access to education, health services, and online banking, among other digital needs.

These technologies help developing countries like the Philippines bridge not only the digital divide but also the urban-rural divide. They provide new opportunities to transform rural economies.

Author with Starlink's Chad Gibbs

Starlink dish

Build Better More

The improvement and upgrade of the country's digital infrastructure has been a top concern of President Bongbong Marcos even during the campaign. He has placed this as a top priority of his administration.

The importance of digital connectivity cannot be overemphasized. It was a crucial instrument of healing, surviving, recovery and rebuilding amid the global health crisis.

While the pandemic caused the great pivot to digital transformation, it also further emphasized the need to immediately address the Philippines' inadequate information and communications technology (ICT) infrastructure, which has widened the digital divide.

President Marcos will "Build Better More" by continuing his predecessor's "Build, Build, Build" infrastructure program, incorporating a strong digital infrastructure program to ensure that Filipinos will have access to affordable and reliable internet.

In fact, the United Nations said that about 3.4 billion people living in rural areas worldwide can have better quality of life through improved access and internet connectivity.

According to UN Secretary-General António Guterres, "The experience of the pandemic has shown that where high-quality Internet connectivity is coupled with flexible working arrangements, many jobs that were traditionally considered to be urban can be performed in rural areas too."

Oath taking of DICT Secretary Ivan Uy

Bridging the digital divide is thus building better more. In this aspect, the Department of Information and Communications Technology (DICT) takes the lead. The Department is now led by Secretary Ivan Uy, who previously headed the then Commission on Information and Communications Technology (CICT). His expertise in technology law and comprehensive experience in information technology project management are vital assets in the government's goal of achieving digital inclusion.

The DICT's Connect, Harness, Innovate and Protect (CHIP) Implementation Plan lays out the strategies that would allow the country to accelerate national digital transformation.

Among the DICT's projects is the development of another internet cable landing station (ICLS) to enhance the country's international connectivity. Under the Luzon Bypass Infrastructure (LBI) project, a Landing Party Agreement (LPA) was signed among the DICT, the Bases Conversion and Development Authority (BCDA), and Edge Network Services Ltd. (Edge) for the construction of two cable landing stations (CLS) — in Baler, Aurora and in Poro Point in La Union — linked by a 240-kilometer fiber corridor with repeater stations spaced 50 kilometers apart.

Upon completion, the BCDA will turn over the facilities to the DICT, which will run and maintain the facility for the next 25 years (extendable for another 25 years). Edge will be the first party to utilize the LBI, but it will compensate the Philippine government with two terabytes per second (Tbps) of cable capacity. While Edge is the first to use the infrastructure, the DICT intends to expand the existing government owned CLS to other submarine cable providers from the private sector.

This ICLS will serve as the gateway for the National Fiber Backbone (NFB), which will link to middle-mile networks and terminate to last-mile components and digital endpoints.

The DICT will develop a demand-responsive, neutral fiber backbone for the country by utilizing the National Grid Corporation of the Philippines' (NGCP) electrical transmission system. Other than this, the Department will also create regional rings of fiber to provide connectivity to provinces, cities, and municipalities.

Meanwhile, the Provincial Broadband will connect the national government agencies (NGAs), local government units (LGUs), Free Wi-Fi sites, and government data centers to the NFB to establish the government domestic network. This enables the LGUs and NGAs to form part of the broadband infrastructure network. This will connect the provinces and their nearby cities and municipalities to the NFB either through wired or wireless connection. This will allow remote communities within provinces to access digital opportunities through improved connectivity services.

These projects are crucial in building digital infrastructure that will not only connect communities including those in far-flung areas, but would also provide citizens with better quality of life through the delivery of speedy and efficient government services to the people.

Empowering IP Youth through Digital Literacy

50 Mbps connectivity for SPMC's Telemedicine Program

PHOTOGRAPH CREDITS

Sofa in the drainage
Flood Risk Management Project for Tagoloan River *(Department of Public Works and Highways)*
Iloilo Esplanade *(Department of Public Works and Highways)*
Cagayan River Flood Control Project *(Department of Public Works and Highways)*

Connecting Luzon, Visayas, Mindanao via land travel
Cebu Cordova Link Expressway *(Ken Jover)*

Final Inspection of Cebu Cordova Link Expressway *(Cebu Cordova Link Expressway Corporation)*
[L to R: Metro Pacific Tollways Corporation Chief Communication Officer Romulo Quimbo, PCOO Secretary Martin Andanar, DPWH Secretary Mark Villar and officials of Cebu Cordova Link Expressway Corporation]

Bataan Cavite Interlink Bridge *(Department of Public Works and Highways)*
Panguil Bay Bridge *(Department of Public Works and Highways)*

Chapter Two: Profile
Daang Katutubo *(Ken Jover)*

Who is Rodrigo Duterte?
Portrait of President Rodrigo Duterte *(Presidential Photographers Division)*
President Duterte visits Marawi *(Presidential Photographers Division)*

Candon City Bypass Inauguration *(Presidential Photographers Division)*
[L to R: Sen Bong Go, President Rodrigo Duterte, and DPWH Secretary Mark Villar]

The Other Side of Mark Villar
Portrait of Mark Villar *(One Mega Group)*

Inspection of Cebu Cordova Link Expressway *(Cebu Cordova Link Expressway Corporation)*
[L to R: DPWH Secretary Mark Villar, Cebu Cordova Link Expressway Corporation (CCLEC) President and General Manager Allan Alfon, COWI-DCCD Project Manager Robert Uthwatt, Cebu Link Joint Venture Project Director Daniel Muñoz, and CCLEC Vice President and Project Manager Herbert Laboy]

NLEX Connector Inspection *(Metro Pacific Tollways Corporation)*
Inauguration of Mella Hotel *(Presidential Photographers Division)*
[L to R: DPWH Secretary Mark Villar, Department of Justice Undersecretary Emmeline Aglipay Villar, Emma Therese Villar, and President Rodrigo Duterte]

Art Tugade: Man of Action
(Portrait and photos provided by Department of Transportation)

Executive Secretary Salvador Medialdea: Big Task for the Little President
(Portrait and photos provided by the Office of the Executive Secretary)

BGC - Ortigas Center Link Project Inauguration
[L to R: MMDA Chairman Benjamin Abalos, Taguig Representative Lani Cayetano, Executive Secretary Salvador Medialdea, DPWH Secretary Mark Villar, DPWH Undersecretary Emil Sadain, Makati Mayor Abigail Binay, Department of Transportation Secretary Arthur Tugade, Makati Representative Luis Campos, BCDA President Vince Dizon, and Pasig City Mayor Vico Sotto]

Estrella - Pantaleon Bridge Inauguration
[L to R: Sen Bong Go, President Rodrigo Duterte, Chinese Ambassador to the Philippines Huang Xilian, DPWH Secretary Mark Villar, and Executive Secretary Salvador Medialdea]

Skyway Stage 3 Inauguration
[L to R: President Rodrigo Duterte, Executive Secretary Salvador Medialdea, House Speaker Lord Allan Velasco, DPWH Secretary Mark Villar and San Miguel Corporation President Ramon Ang]

What's on Vince Dizon's To Do List
Portrait *(Bases Conversion and Development Authority)*
Clark International Airport New Passenger Terminal Building Inspection *(Bases Conversion and Development Authority)*
2019 Labor Day Tribute at the New Clark City Aquatics Center *(Bases Conversion and Development Authority)*
Clark International Airport New Passenger Terminal Building *(photo courtesy of LIPAD Corp.)*

Philippines' Gatekeeper: Sec. Sonny Dominguez
(Portrait by Department of Finance)
State Visit to China *(Presidential Photographers Division)*
Cabinet officials pose after successful state visit in China *(Presidential Photographers Division)*

The many hats of Ben Diokno
(Portrait and photos by Bangko Sentral ng Pilipinas)

Oath Taking Photo *(Presidential Photographers Division)*
[L to R: President Rodrigo Duterte and BSP Governor Ben Diokno]

Ulat ng BSP sa Bayan *(Bangko Sentral ng Pilipinas)*

Bong Go: The Rise of the Probinsiyano
(Portrait and Photos provided by Office of Senator Bong Go)

Cavite Laguna Expressway Inauguration
[L to R: Metro Pacific Tollways Corporation President Rodrigo Franco, Department of Transportation Secretary Art Tugade, DPWH Secretary Mark Villar, Senator Bong Go, and Executive Secretary Salvador Medialdea]

Chapter Three: The Philippines
Tarlac Pangasinan La Union Expressway *(Hans Melvin Ang)*

The Philippines is no longer Asia's 'Sick Man'
NLEX Connector *(Dmitri Valencia)*
Cavite Laguna Expressway *(Dmitri Valencia)*

A counter-narrative of Philippines
Panguil Bay Bridge *(Department of Public Works and Highways)*

Team Philippines
The Philippines Investment Forum *(Euromoney Conference)*
[L to R: Australia Philippine Business Council Chairman Jose Leviste Jr., BDO Capital and Investment Corporation President Eduardo Francisco, Anna Mae Yu Lamentillo, Euromoney Institutional Investor Asia Bureau Chief Matthew Thomas, Macquarie Infrastructure and Real Assets Managing Director Michael Rodriguez, and Sun Life Financial Philippines Chief Investment Officer Michael Enriquez]

Bacolod Economic Highway *(Department of Public Works and Highways)*
Davao City Coastal Road Project *(Department of Public Works and Highways)*

To Dream the Impossible Dream: Connecting NLEX to SLEX in 30 minutes
Skyway Stage 3 *(Dimtri Valencia)*

Solving the ₱3.5 billion problem in Metro Manila
Inspection of Skyway Stage 3 *(Ali Vicoy)*
[L to R: Anna Mae Yu Lamentillo and DPWH Secretary Mark Villar]

9 new bridges across Pasig River
BGC Ortigas Link Bridge *(Ken Jover)*

Right-of-way reforms critical in Skyway Stage 3 completion
Inspection of NLEX Connector Project *(Ali Vicoy)*
[L to R: Anna Mae Yu Lamentillo, North Luzon Expressway (NLEX) Chief Operating Officer Raul Ignacio, DPWH Public-Private Partnership Service Director Alex Bote, NLEX Vice President for Tollway Development and Engineering Nemesio Castillo, and DPWH Secretary Mark Villar]

Reimagining the Smokey Mountain Alignment
Inspection of NLEX Harbor Link Project *(Ali Vicoy)*
[L to R: Anna Mae Yu Lamentillo, NLEX Vice President for Tollway Development and Engineering Nemesio Castillo, and DPWH Public-Private Partnership Service Director Alex Bote]

The truth about two Build, Build, Build projects
NLEX Connector Project *(Hans Melvin Ang)*

Chapter Five: Luzon
Daang Kalikasan *(Ken Jover)*

Reimagining Luzon
Tarlac Pangasinan La Union *(Hans Melvin Ang)*
Central Luzon Link Expressway *(Hans Melvin Ang)*

Luzon Spine Expressway Network
Infographics *(Christian John Santos)*

Build Build Build: From 385 km to 1,101 km of High Standard Highways in Luzon
South Luzon Expressway Toll Road 4 *(Hans Melvin Ang)*
Cavite Laguna Expressway *(Dimitri Valencia)*

10 Build, Build, Build Projects in Ilocos Region
(Photos provided by Department of Public Works and Highways Region 1)

10 Build, Build, Build Projects in Cordillera Administrative Region
(Photos provided by DPWH CAR)

10 Build, Build, Build Projects in Cagayan Valley
(Photos provided by DPWH Region 2)

10 Build, Build, Build Projects in Central Luzon
(Photos provided by DPWH Region 3)

10 Build, Build, Build Projects in Calabarzon
(Photos provided by DPWH Region 4A)

10 Build, Build, Build Projects in Mimaropa
(Photos provided by DPWH Region 4B)

All roads lead to a better Marawi
Inspection of Marawi City *(DPWH)*
[L to R: DPWH Undersecretary Rafael Yabut, District Engineer Mikunug Macabantog, Anna Mae Yu Lamentillo, DPWH Secretary Mark Villar, Regional Director Virgilio Eduarte, and District Engineer Khalil Sultan]

Inspection of Ground Zero in Marawi *(DPWH)*
[L to R: DPWH Secretary Mark Villar, Regional Director Rey Peter Gille, and District Engineer Khalil Sultan]

Chapter Eight: Reforms
Laguna Lake Expressway *(Ken Jover)*

Reforms in DPWH
Subic Freeport Expressway Inspection *(DPWH)*
[L to R: NLEX officials and Anna Mae Yu Lamentillo]

Skyway Stage 3 Inspection *(Ali Vicoy)*
[L to R: San Miguel Corporation Technical Operations Head Norberto Conti, DPWH Secretary Mark Villar, and Anna Mae Yu Lamentillo]

Walkable Cities
Antique Esplanade *(DPWH Region 6)*

Bike lanes to the future
Laguna Lake Inauguration *(Ali Vicoy of Manila Bulletin)*
[L to R: Anna Mae Yu Lamentillo, DPWH Regional Director Ador Canlas, and DPWH Secretary Mark Villar]

Laguna Lake Expressway *(Ken Jover)*
Metro Cebu Bike Lane Network *(Ken Jover)*
Davao Coastal Expressway *(DPWH Region 11)*

A case for tourism preservation
Amphibious excavators deployed for Manila Bay clean up

Manila Bay can be saved
Start of dredging operations in Manila Bay coastline

Chapter Nine: Diplomacy
Binondo Intramuros Bridge *(Ken Jover)*

Triumph of Duterte Diplomacy
Estrella Pantaleon Bridge Inspection *(Presidential Photographers Division)*
[L to R: Sen Bong Go, President Rodrigo Duterte, Mark Villar and Chinese Ambassador to Philippines Huang Xilian]

Cabinet members pose with President Rodrigo Duterte at the World Economic Forum *(Presidential Photographers Division)*
[L to R: Sen Bong Go, DPWH Secretary Mark Villar, DTI Secretary Mon Lopez, President Rodrigo Duterte, Speaker Alan Peter Caytetano, PCOO Secretary Martin Andanar]

Japan - PH Partnership: Subway, bypass and more
Plaridel Bypass *(DPWH)*

President Rodrigo Duterte's State Visit to Japan *(Presidential Photographers Division)*

12 Japanese-funded Build, Build, Build Projects
(Photos provided by DPWH Unified Project Management Office)

Build, Build, Build: PH-China signs six bilateral agreements
(Photos provided by Presidential Photographers Division)

State visit of People's Republic of China President Xi Jinping to the Philippines
[L to R: DPWH Secretary Mark Villar, People's Republic of China President Xi Jinping, and President Rodrigo Duterte]

Bilateral meeting between the Philippines and People's Republic of China
[L to R: DPWH Secretary Mark Villar and Chinese Ministry of Commerce Minister Zhong Shan]

Build, Build, Build projects funded through PH-Korea Partnership
Author speaks at The 6th ASEAN Connectivity Forum at Seoul, Korea by ASEAN-Korea Centre
[L to R: Ministry of Public Works and Transport Director General Pich Chhieng (Cambodia), Ministry of Transport Technical Expert Otto Ardianto (Indonesia), Ministry of Public Works and Transport Director General Sengdarith Kattignasack (Lao PDR), Ministry of Transport and Communications Aung Ye Tun (Myanmar), Public-Private Partnership Center Division Chief Ria Dooc (Philippines), Land Transport Authority Director Goh Kok Hwa (Singapore), Ministry of Planning and Investment Officer Pham Viet Tuan (Vietnam), Public-Private Partner Division Chief Nguyen Hong Van (Ho Chi Minh City), and Anna Mae Yu Lamentillo]

Panguil Bay Bridge *(DPWH)*
Integrated Disaster Risk Reduction and Climate Change Adaptation (IDRR- CCA) Measures in Low-lying Areas of Pampanga Bay *(DPWH)*

A system of collaboration
Intramuros *(Ken Jover)*
The author with Kevin Quinn, CEO and Administrator of the Maryland Transit Administrator
IVLP Class - Infrastructure Development in the Indo-Pacific Region

IVLP, a gamechanger
(Photos provided by Yu - Lamentillo family archives)

Chapter Ten: COVID-19
Ultra We Heal As One Center *(Anna Mae Yu Lamentillo)*

The need for physical (not social) distancing
Inspection of the Las Pinas Modular Hospital
[L to R: Anna Mae Yu Lamentillo, Las Piñas Representative Camille Villar, and DPWH Secretary Mark Villar)

The PH economy will survive COVID-19
Cebu Cordova Link Expressway *(Ken Jover)*
Portrait of author of Oly Ruiz, Alike

The factual narrative of PH's COVID-19 facilities
Palacio de Manila COVID 19 Testing Hub Inspection
[L to R: National Task Force for Covid-19 Officials, Anna Mae Yu Lamentillo, Department of Health Director Paz Corrales, and National Action Plan Against COVID-19 Deputy Chief Implementer Vince Dizon]

PICC We Heal As One Center Inspection
[L to R: DPWH Regional Director Ador Canlas and Anna Mae Yu Lamentillo]

Chapter Eleven: About the Author
Portrait of Author *(Oly Ruiz, Alike)*

Graduation in the time of COVID - 19
(Photos taken from Yu - Lamentillo family archives)

Economic briefing with Department of Finance
[L to R: Department of Finance Assistant Secretary Antonio Lambino and Anna Mae Yu Lamentillo]

Author awarded the Veritas Medal by the Harvard Kennedy School Alumni Association at the Bureaucrat's Ball
[L to R: Rafael Alunan III, Anna Mae Yu Lamentillo, and Anthony Abad]

Jamil Mahuad and the Peru-Ecuador peace treaty
(Photos taken from Yu - Lamentillo family archives)

My father taught me waiting for 21 years was worth it
(Photos taken from Yu - Lamentillo family archives)

My mom told me not to believe in Cinderella
(Photos taken from Yu - Lamentillo family archives)
Portrait of author *(JB De Leon)*

What I learned after my boat sank
(Photos taken by author during an immersion trip in Sitio Calauit)

Chapter Twelve: Epilogue

Happy to be back in public service
Author with President Ferdinand R. Marcos, Jr. *(Office of the Undersecretary for Strategic Communications)*

Author's official photo as Assistant Secretary of the Department of Information and Communications Technology *(DICT)*

100 Mbps minimum speed for the most remote areas
DICT Secretary Ivan John E. Uy and SpaceX Executive Rebecca Hunter shed light on satellite connectivity *(DICT-Information and Strategic Communications Division)*

Author with Chad Gibbs, Head of Starlink Business *(Anna Mae Yu Lamentillo)*

Starlink dish *(Starlink official website)*

Build better more
President Ferdinand R. Marcos Jr. and Department of Information and Communications Technology Secretary Ivan John E. Uy *(Office of the Undersecretary for Strategic Communications)*

Empowering IP Youth through Digital Literacy *(DICT Region 3)*

50 Mbps connectivity for Southern Philippines Medical Center's Telemedicine Program *(DICT Region 11)*

Endpage
(Graphics by Sean Lorenzo)

Let the last five years be remembered as a collective movement of the Filipino people who wanted change and acted on it. We may have set our sights too high — but our country and the men who stood behind it deserve nothing less.

www.nightowl.ph